Louise L. Stevenson is a faculty member in the American Studies Program and the Department of History at Franklin and Marshall College.

D0948393

Scholarly Means to Evangelical Ends

New Studies in American Intellectual and Cultural History
Thomas Bender, Consulting Editor

Scholarly Means to Evangelical Ends

The New Haven Scholars and the Transformation of Higher Learning in America, 1830–1890

Louise L. Stevenson

The Johns Hopkins University Press

Baltimore and London

This book has brought to publication with the generous assistance of Franklin and Marshall College.

The Johns Hopkins University Press,
701 West 40th Street,
Baltimore, Maryland 21211
The Johns Hopkins Press Ltd, London

The paper in this book is acid-free and meets the guidelines for permanence and durability of the Committee on Production Guidelines for Book Longevity of the Council on Library Resources.

Library of Congress Cataloging-in-Publication Data
Stevenson, Louise L.
  Scholarly means to evangelical ends.

  (New studies in American intellectual and cultural history
  Bibliography: p.
  Includes index.
  1. Learning and scholarship—United States—History—19th century. 2. Education, Higher—United States—History—19th century. 3. Yale University—History—19th century. I. Title. II. Series.
AZ505.S74   001.2'0973   85-27502
ISBN 0-8018-2695-0

For my teachers,
but especially for Annette Kar Baxter

Contents

Acknowledgments   ix

1 Introduction   1

2 The New Haven Milieu   14

3 New Haven Scholarship   30

4 The College, the Scholar, and the Liberal Man   50

5 Science: Observing a Fact, Knowing the Divine   67

6 History: From Fact to Providence   87

7 Political Science: The State as Means to Self-development   102

8 From Whole Man to Whole Society   118

9 Connections   138

Appendixes   149
Notes   169
Bibliography   199
Index   217

Acknowledgments

T his book has many beginnings. Certainly some of them
lie in the classes of talented teachers with whom I was
fortunate enough to study. To these teachers, who offered
so many invaluable lessons from high school through graduate
school, I wish to dedicate this book.

An especial dedication belongs to the late Annette Kar Baxter.
At Barnard College, I was lucky enough to meet her and smart
enough to choose American Studies as my major and her as my
adviser. She guided me through those turbulent years—term paper research in the library was inevitably interrupted by a bomb
scare; class discussion ended with debate about the futility of reforming The System. And of greatest importance, she opened the
prospect of history as the study of cultural life.

First as a professor and then as a friend, Annette perplexed me.
To a naive undergraduate in the late sixties, it seemed as though
a certain disregard for conventional wardrobe and personal neat-
ness were prerequisites for a critical stance toward the America
that was bringing us the Vietnam War. With her well-coiffed hair,
elegant clothes, and flashy diamond, Professor Baxter was a puzzle.
Ferociously committed to learning and cognizant that learning needs
a community for its nurture, she always took the stance of a critic.
After her death, trying to recover a part of Annette that still lived,
I read her 1958 biography *Henry Miller: Expatriate*. It provided
the elusive key to understanding her. Her attention to Miller the
man and his adherence to conventions of polite and considerate

behavior in his private life and correspondence brought to light her own enduring commitment to a humane America and to the usefulness of an expatriate stance. From it she could offer criticism and perform constructive actions that she believed would bring about her desired America. An advocate of American Studies, she expatriated herself from departments of history and literature. And as advocate of women's studies, she enlarged and specified her expatriatism to gain critical perspective on the male-centered concerns that she perceived in academic departments. From the late seventies until her death, she went beyond advocacy of women's studies to argue for the woman's college against the male university, in this case Barnard versus Columbia. In a 1978 *New York Times* op-ed piece, she wrote that women's college made it possible for students "to value ideas that society discredits but increasingly needs."

Annette Baxter was an inspiration as friend, teacher, and scholar. Her lessons lie behind the concerns of this book, and her friendship, from college years through the first years of college professing, was vital to its creation.

There are two other scholars whose teaching and encouragement have been above value. David Hall was a demanding dissertation director, but his vast knowledge of intellectual life and his generous sharing of it make this a richer book. Aileen Kraditor has always taken time from her own research and writing to help me explore the inevitable questions that confront researchers and to push me toward a higher degree of clarity in thinking and writing. I thank both for their assistance and encouragement. Any errors of commission or omission remain my own.

Since entering the community of Franklin and Marshall College three years ago, I have incurred many debts. Professor of Religious Studies Robert Mickey gave the entire manuscript a careful reading; his acute comments led to refinements in language and terms. The staff of Academic Computing, especially John Wiley, introduced the wonders and horrors of word processing. Their timely assistance often rescued portions of the text from consignment to oblivion. Linda Danner helped enter the manuscript onto a word processor. The staff of the Shadek-Fackenthal Library were helpful beyond call, and I especially wish to thank the staffs of the circulation desk, the interlibrary loan service, and the reference department. I am most grateful also to Peggy M. Bender, who cheerfully, accurately, and promptly typed and duplicated materials and generally made the publication process less onerous, and to students Candace Lynn Bell and Holly Righter, who assisted checking bibliography, facts, and references. Though I am sure that the tensions between the demands of teaching and scholarship expressed by Noah Porter in chapter 3 are timeless, the consideration and encouragement of colleagues in the history department and American Studies program have reduced their severity. The Franklin and Marshall College committee on grants generously provided funds to subsidize manuscript preparation and publication costs, and I thank them for this tangible and much needed support.

In the larger community of scholars, I especially wish to thank Donald Bellomy for his generosity, though he assures me that he acted only as William Graham Sumner would have wanted him to—in enlightened self-interest. He provided a copy of his scrupulously thorough dissertation on William Graham Sumner and offered chapters of his in-progress biography of Sumner as they became available. James McLachlan suggested improvements for chapter 3 as it was developing. As editor of The Johns Hopkins University Press Series, New Studies in Intellectual and Cultural History, Thomas Bender has been most helpful in moving this project from promising manuscript to finished book. His enthusiasm for the project was often a vital tonic.

The Beinecke Rare Book and Manuscript Library, Edinburgh University Library, Miss Porter's School, Princeton University Library, and Yale University Library granted permission to quote from manuscripts in their possession. The Putnam County Historical Society gave permission to reproduce John Ferguson Weir's *The Gun Foundry*.

Last but not least, my husband Philip Zimmerman offered encouragement when I doubted and bore, almost without complaint, the many burdens of a scholar's spouse. No New Haven scholar could have been as fortunate. This book is as much his as mine.

Scholarly Means to Evangelical Ends

1
Introduction

*And it might be suggested that if history is approached in this
way—not as a question of origins but as a question of transitions,
not as the subject of 'causes' but as the subject of 'mediations'—
historical interpretations would become less whig and change would
seem less cataclysmic. History would lose some of the paradoxes which
are at least implied in the statement: 'Capitalism is the social
counterpart of Calvinist Theology'; and the world of the historian
would become much more like the world as it appears in life.*

Herbert Butterfield,
The Whig Interpretation of History

In antebellum America, voices from many quarters—Harvard
professors and Unitarian ministers, transcendentalist lecturers
and ministers, Yale professors and Congregationalist ministers,
New and Old School Presbyterians, Southern publicists and politicians—formed a chorus critical of American life.[1] Yet, the strong
influence of religious heritage, regional loyalty, and vocation caused
these educated elites to produce distinct, often dissonant tunes.
From the 1840s through the 1880s, one important voice in the
chorus came from a group of professors who taught at Yale College. They addressed an audience of educated men, often college
professors or students, who shared their liberal Congregationalist
faith and beliefs.

These Yale professors will be referred to as the New Haven
scholars because of their place in religious history as successors to
Nathaniel William Taylor and his New Haven theology and because of their place in the history of American education and
intellectual life as one of the groups of college professors responsible for introducing scholarly methods and the idea of scholarship
as a vocation to nineteenth-century America. As religious men,
the New Haven scholars wanted to infuse the past, the present,
and the natural world with religious meaning—to show that all
parts of the visible world revealed what they called divine truth.
As scholars they were committed to using the most advanced
learning of their age, which for them meant German historical and
philological methods. These men were James Dwight Dana, min-

eralogist and geologist; George Park Fisher, historian of American and church history; James Hadley, professor of Greek; James Mason Hoppin, art historian; Noah Porter, moral philosopher and psychologist; Edward Elbridge Salisbury, Sanskrit and Arabic scholar; William Dwight Whitney, philologist and Sanskrit scholar; and Theodore Dwight Woolsey, political scientist.

Each of these men enjoyed a national and even international reputation. Dana corresponded with Charles Darwin and edited the *American Journal of Arts and Sciences*. Substantially revised, his *Manual of Mineralogy*, first published in 1849, reached its nineteenth edition in 1977. Fisher helped found the American Society of Church History, and he was president of the American Historical Association in 1898. His Lowell Lectures of 1871 were published as *The Reformation* (1873) and reprinted for the last time in 1920. Salisbury founded the American Oriental Society (1842) and edited its journal. Woolsey served on various committees of the American Social Science Association. The third edition of his *Introduction to the Study of International Law,* first edition 1860, was reprinted in 1908. Whitney, the preeminent scholar by modern standards, was elected in 1881 to the Prussian Order of Merit in Science to fill the vacancy caused by the death of Thomas Carlyle. Harvard University Press was still publishing his *Sanskrit Grammar* (1889) in 1984. With James Hadley, who wrote the history of the English language for the 1864 edition of Webster's *American Dictionary of the English Language,* Whitney founded the American Philological Society. Porter earned his scholarly reputation as author of *The Human Intellect* (1868), the first textbook to introduce the modern term *psychology* into American academic discourse, and as editor-in-chief of Webster's *American Dictionary of the English Language* (1864) and the first edition of *Webster's International Dictionary of the English Language* (1890). The University of Edinburgh recognized Porter's accomplishments by awarding him an honorary degree after his retirement from the presidency of Yale College. (See appendixes 1 and 3.)

The New Haven scholars have much to tell us about the whole of nineteenth-century American intellectual life, for it is more than the story of the mainstream to the twentieth century. Rather, there were both mainstream and flourishing backwaters in the nineteenth century. The New Haven scholars occupied one of these backwaters, but they had no notion that they did not belong to the mainstream. They saw themselves as members of an evangelical world; we see their evangelicalism as the basis for provincialism.

We know what they could not: that their theistic framework for scholarly thought and vocation would not survive into an age that reduced religious authority to the role of arbiter for the private conscience. But in the antebellum decades the New Haven group were young men who fashioned careers and adopted ways of knowing that they thought would rule the future. They broke from a ministerial past in revolt from its dogma and debates. Then they adopted and adapted German historical and philological methods, thought of themselves as cosmopolitans (even though we may see them as provincials), and fended off the criticism of more conservative Congregational ministers, who preached doctrinally, read the Bible literally, and remained uninfluenced by the new currents of thought originating in Germany.

Whatever their academic specialties, the New Haven scholars taught the same lessons about the relation between God and the world. Readers of Dana's *Mineralogy* found a text that accurately described and classified minerals and an introduction that asked them to share Dana's awe of God's creations. Fisher's history of the Reformation built to a conclusion that affirmed the promise of Christianity to uplift people and to ennoble all of their works. The thoroughly secular modern scholar tends to see these affirmations of God and the Christian millennium as unscholarly accretions; the New Haven scholars saw them as integral to *true* scholarship.

They used the adjective *true* and the noun *truth* to signify a universal, divine unity, or order. Truth, as historian George Park Fisher explicates it, expressed "a common bond . . . between thoughts and things, mind and the world."[2] Leonard Bacon, a close friend of the scholars and minister of the First Church (Congregational) in New Haven, said that it was the "very spirit of true science that finds truth in facts,—God's truth in God's facts."[3] When scholars discovered truth, they showed that scholarly activity had a common purpose, and they informed human history, the natural world, and contemporary culture with a single theistic value system. Truth made commitment and practice serve evangelical ends.

The concept of truth belonged to a larger complex of ideas, *organicism*, which the New Haven group shared with other American and English Victorian elites. Organicism implies wholeness, a condition created by biological growth, historical development, or nurture. Mechanical devices, imposed systems, or radical changes interfered with these processes and created an "inorganic" society, individual, or institution.[4] When organicists adopted this Romantic concept, they rejected the mechanistic Enlightenment world view and the abstract social theories of French rationalism. The New Haven scholars, however, did not reject God as well; trained scholars such as they could find divine meaning in nature, history, and art. Wholeness implied a historical progression toward perfect human freedom. Unnatural restraints on human freedom belonged to the past; in the future people and human society would reach a state of wholeness and realize their ultimate dependence on God.

Walter Houghton's *The Victorian Frame of Mind* influenced a generation of historians to identify doubt as a dominant characteristic of Victorian intellectual life.[5] Unlike Houghton's Victorians, the New Haven group never doubted their faith or became intellectual ostriches like Bishop Wilberforce. They remained optimistic that Americans would see truth. Their careers were attempts to manifest this truth and to persuade others that Christians could be well-educated and engaged with crucial issues of the times and still believe in God. Profound faith and evangelical vision gave hope, while research confirmed that history was providential, that evolution furthered God's order, and that human creations could express divine meaning. The New Haven scholars shared their vision with an audience of ministers, publicists, college professors, and an educated reading public. For these evangelical scholars, the college had replaced the church; books and articles, itinerant preachers; and intellectual conviction gained from study, the emotional experience of the revival.

On many levels the New Haven scholars mediated between alternatives of their age. In the realm of thought New Haven philosophy and science mediated between the realism of Scottish philosophy and German idealism; New Haven history between Romantic Bancroft and positivist Guizot. The New Haven concept of scholarly vocation struck a middle way between the concept of the minister who preached from his pulpit and that of the secular scholar who taught from a college lectern. The scholars saw education as *culture,* or the development of the intellectual and aesthetic potential of students. They considered culture an alternative to antinomian and Arminian concepts of individual reformation. Although college education supposedly effected a total change in the nature of men, this process was disciplined and slow in comparison with the cataclysm of a revival. Neither a do-gooder nor an ascetic, the good man participated in his world. His example and values worked to change men in the world around him.

Historians of American higher education presently split the nineteenth century into two periods: the first the age of the old-time college and the second, starting in the 1870s, the age of the modern university. A transitional generation between Enlightenment teachers of the old-time college and research-oriented professors of the modern university, the New Haven scholars combined elements of Enlightenment and Romantic thought and anticipated definitions of scholarship and knowledge that took hold in the last years of the nineteenth century. In the antebellum period, the scholars rejected both old-time college of mental discipline and religious revival as effective means for turning individuals into agents of the millennium. Continuing the concerns of their Federalist forebears, this mid-century generation emphasized that true human freedom was possible only when institutions restrained the bad aspects of human nature and developed the good. But as men of the Romantic age, the New Haven scholars recast their fathers' belief. They saw the college as an institution organically related to the life of its students and the nation. This view strongly resembles their close friend Horace Bushnell's idea of the family as an institution of Christian nurture promoting individual and ultimately national regeneration.[6] Appreciation of the New Haven scholars as a distinctive generation of educators influenced by Romanticism modifies the way historians divide the nineteenth century. Instead of two periods, there are three: the college of mental discipline belongs to the portion of the Enlightenment that Henry May identifies as *didactic*; the New Haven scholars' Yale, to the Romantically influenced mid-nineteenth century; and the university, to the modern, scientific age.

As Romantics who saw institutions promoting individualism, Bushnell and the New Haven scholars stand apart from the line of cultural critics that runs from Ralph Waldo Emerson through Van Wyck Brooks. George Fredrickson characterizes this type of intellectual as the nonseceder.[7] These men found careers in established institutions and propounded theories that elaborated on the value of institutions to society. They saw man as a social being whose fullest freedom was to be found within society.

The New Haven scholars spoke for Whiggery—a dominant strain in nineteenth-century social, political, and cultural thought. Whiggery stood for the triumph of the cosmopolitan and national over the provincial and local, of rational order over irrational spontaneity, of school-based learning over traditional folkways and cus-

tom, and of self-control over self-expression. Whigs believed that
every person had the potential to become moral or good if family,
school, and community nurtured the seed of goodness in his moral
nature. Richard Jensen identifies Whigs as the party of modernizers
who promoted some aspects of the nascent middle-class economy
and society while restraining others. The Whig program for desirable social and moral change was three-pronged. Whigs opposed
institutions that they perceived as inhibiting or preventing moral
development, such as the Catholic church and southern slavery;
they identified and sought to eliminate evils, such as intemperance
and overdevotedness to material luxury, that tempted free individuals from the goal of self-development; and they founded and
supported institutions, such as Bushnell's and Beecher's ideal family, Horace Mann's common school, and the New Haven scholars'
Yale, that promised to encourage the growth of an ideal individual,
one who embodied and supported Whig values and beliefs.[8]

Daniel Walker Howe's study of Harvard moralists and D. H.
Meyer's and Wilson Smith's studies of northern moral philosophers show the extent to which antebellum northern colleges were
outposts of Whiggery. Currently scholars are discovering the debt
that early twentieth-century social science owes to Whiggery. For
example, Daniel Walker Howe notes connections between Bushnell's thought and ideas of late-nineteenth-century sociologists; and
Hoeveler traces the assumptions of E. A. Ross and John R. Commons back to Whig thought.[9] Both Hoeveler and Howe assume
rather than prove this connection, since they have no proof of the
actual link between the moral philosophy of the old-time college
and the social science of the modern university. The New Haven
scholars' thought illustrates this transition. At mid-century Yale,
moral philosophy dissolved into their courses in history, political
science, and mental philosophy. Also, their Whiggish conceptions
permeated their courses in Latin, Greek, literature, and art history.
Thus Whiggish beliefs did not vanish from American colleges with
the appearance of the social-science disciplines. At mid-century
Yale, the realm of knowledge, even though divided into disciplines, formed an intellectually coherent whole. As A. O. J. Cockshut writes, "A large part of mid- and late-Victorian intellectual
history consists in the careful transplanting by reverent hands of
this precious enthusiasm, grown in the Evangelical hothouse, into
different intellectual soils."[10]

To make the college and their vocation into effective means for
propagating Whiggish beliefs, the New Haven scholars reformed

the old-time college of mental discipline by combining *new* ideas of scholarliness and scholarly vocation with *inherited* religious faith. The insights of sociologist Peter L. Berger help explain why. According to Berger, the modernizing process increased the number of choices that people could make. These ranged from the mundane choice of food or a job to the religious choices of whether to become, say, either Episcopalian or Unitarian or whether to believe in a god at all. Modernization also includes development of particular value systems. In the nineteenth century these were the cult of domesticity and the work ethic, on the popular level, and the rise of science for intellectuals and academics. Thus, discrete, specialized value systems replaced the universal system of values that religion once had furnished. Modern society is secular; religion is one value system among many and usually rules areas of private concern only.[11]

For instance, scientists assume that their knowledge of nature and social systems can neither confirm nor deny any ultimate reality. They belong to many organizations in which overt expression of a specific religious creed would cause dissension. As a member of the Veterans of Foreign Wars, a scientist might hear a religious invocation at the start of a meeting, but he would never hear a statement of innate human depravity. The possibility that a scientist might belong to the VFW shows that modern society has opportunities for individuals to belong to organizations that tap different, though sometimes interrelated, loyalties. To paraphrase Berger, modern society has lost the traditional, religious canopy of meaning that furnished symbols for the meaningful integration of society.[12]

The New Haven scholars perceived the nineteenth century as a time of decline from the social cohesion and unity provided by shared beliefs. Noah Porter believed that religious principle previously had regulated both the "external conduct" and the "inner springs of action." New Englanders were then a "tribe" who celebrated their unity and common dependence on God when they attended church. Town institutions all helped to perpetuate social cohesion and common faith; family, church, and school were "nurseries of order and decorum." George Park Fisher described the minister in a seventeenth-century New England town as a sort of omnicompetent professional. The townspeople consulted him on matters of public policy, and his sermons planted seeds for intellectual growth.[13]

The mid-nineteenth century, however, was a time when choices multiplied.[14] During the antebellum years, educated, moderately well-to-do people confronted choices unknown to eighteenth-century grandparents. Agricultural towns became commercial cities, and factories began to replace artisan shops. In the unsupervised social space between home and work, men could choose what to do with their time. By the 1850s, invention of the steam printing press and new methods of book distribution made inexpensive books widely available. These books were new in form and content as well as in price. Readers still could buy sermons and religious tracts, but they could also buy novels and stories by foreign authors, newspaper reporters supplementing their salaries, and Hawthorne's bane, "scribbling women." Art forms also became more diverse. They now included photographic or chromolithographic reproductions of Renaissance masterpieces, western landscapes by Thomas Moran, or sentimental pictures, such as *Whittier's Barefooted Boy,* by Eastman Johnson. In architecture and design, too, consumers could select from various revival styles—Gothic, Italianate, Greek, Egyptian, and Roman. New magazines like *Godey's Ladies Book* and *Graham's Monthly* helped consumers make their choices.

Men had a much wider array of careers to choose from, and the word *career* acquired its modern meaning, "life-long occupation." Members of older professions, such as the ministry, became more self-conscious, ceased to think of themselves as engaged in a calling, and transferred their loyalty from a local institution, such as a town church, to a profession, which often had a national organization. Scholars, architects, editors, and teachers began to think of themselves as professionals, to form organizations, and to develop codes of behavior. The new professional organizations and the new magazines were only several among the many voices that tried to influence choice. Their messages often conflicted, because they stemmed from the material needs of an increasingly complex, industrial society. To the ears of the New Haven scholars, these messages produced worldly din, not Godly harmony. The ordered life of the tribe was no more.

In this world of choice, the New Haven scholars had a dual role: they participated in the modernizing process insofar as they adopted scholarship and scholarly vocation as means, but they used these means to resurrect a world infused with religious meaning.[15] Their replacement canopy of meaning was artificial and learned, the fruit of their scholarship. Whereas the premodern community had unconsciously held aloft a canopy of meaning, the New Haven canopy was a sea of umbrellas held aloft by students and readers.

The New Haven scholars saw these men as members of a national elite based in communities across the nation. Their moral example would draw other men toward moral improvement and transform them into agents of the millennium.

Scholarship gave the New Haven scholars the opportunity to rebuild religious belief on historically and scientifically credible bases. But scholarship also had the potential to further the process of secularization, for it involved the assumption of a secular role in a secular institution. Consequently, the scholars were helping to reduce the authority of the minister and to increase the authority of the academic. To speak authoritatively as an academic, each scholar had to become an expert in one field of knowledge. Specialization created a tension between means and ends. Although each scholar wanted to witness universal truth, he had to perceive it through the ever-narrowing window of an academic discipline.

By the early twentieth century, the New Haven system of seeing the world had died. A younger generation of scholars—William Graham Sumner, William James, Daniel Coit Gilman, Frederick Jackson Turner—were not concerned with showing how a system of religiously based values could inform all areas of human activity. Although the New Haven scholars did not stop the flood tide of modernization, they did help to make the practice of modern scholarship a criterion for cultural authority. At Yale, for instance, scholarly training became a prerequisite for a faculty position. It may even be argued that the New Haveners' religious belief served to advance scholarship by making this new form of authority credible to the vast majority of God-fearing Victorians. It may also be true that the individual reared in a religiously earnest home found in New Haven lessons the means to reconcile traditional beliefs with the demands of his adult roles as wage earner, husband, and citizen.

Early twentieth-century cultural critics disowned the philosophic tradition to which the New Haven scholars belonged. George Santayana labeled nineteenth-century idealism "genteel." Expanding on Santayana's criticism, Brooks and then H. L. Mencken attributed what was narrow and bigoted in American life to this "Puritanism." They criticized the older generation's search for truth and accused them of ignoring what was real and vital. The younger critics perceived a Puritan tradition that, abetted by Victorian sentimentalism, had perpetuated a reign of "mush."[16] Similar to the intellectuals whom they had disowned, the younger men searched for wholeness and authentic meaning, but their thoroughly secular viewpoint blinded them to the fact that idealists like the New Haven scholars had not been complacent cultural apologists. For example, like Brooks, the scholars thought that at some time in the eighteenth century the Puritan tradition had split between the extremes of Jonathan Edwards and Benjamin Franklin.[17] They thought, however, that New Haven ideas of scholarship and religion would enable them to teach Americans how to moderate their overemphasis on either practicality and materialism or emotion and sentiment.

Until recently, historians have taken early twentieth-century intellectuals at their word and emphasized the discontinuities between the nineteenth and early twentieth centuries. For example, although Morton White offers valuable analysis in his *Social Thought in America,* he emphasizes revolt and ignores that his "formalists" had contemporaries who both criticized their thought and taught that man could control his destiny. Another example is Laurence Veysey, who, in *The Emergence of the American University,* describes the university as taking shape around one of three ideals: practical education, research, and liberal culture. He says that the ideal of liberal culture emerged from the previous conception of the college as a school of discipline as defined in the Yale Report of 1828. Veysey uses Porter and James McCosh of Princeton as spokesmen for this earlier form of education and does not appreciate that Porter and his colleagues, the New Haven scholars, introduced the ideal of education as culture and practiced the new German scholarly methods.[18]

Recent interest in Victorian America, evangelical religion, and the Scottish philosophy of common sense is encouraging reassessment of nineteenth-century intellectual life. Historians now stress the continuities between nineteenth-century evangelical Whig and twentieth-century Progressive America. Hoeveler's and Howe's work on social-science thought are two examples; Robert M. Crunden's biographical analysis of Progressives is another. Historians also stress the positive contributions of evangelicalism and Victorianism to change. For example, Hoeveler presents a sympathetic biography of James McCosh that describes his evangelical faith as a force behind his reform of Princeton. Theodore Dwight Bozeman and Herbert Hovenkamp see ways in which the empirical drive of the Scottish philosophy fed the development of pre-Darwinian science. James McLachlan and Burton Bledstein ask us to see Porter and other college presidents as reformers—men who educated their students to be the creators of a better world.[19]

In the area of religious thought, late-nineteenth-century Protestant modernists Newman Smyth and Theodore Thornton Munger were the successors of the New Haven scholars. In the early
twentieth century, *modernism* meant at the most widely accepted
level, William R. Hutchison writes, "the conscious, intended adaptation of religious ideas to modern culture." Stopping there,
popular writers tended to explain modernism functionally, as "the
direct opposite and negation of biblical literalism." Theologians
and scholars went further, revealing that modernists believed "that
God is immanent in human cultural development and revealed
through it" and "that human society is moving toward realization
(even though it may never attain the reality) of the Kingdom of
God." Searching for the source of these modernist beliefs, most
historians turn to liberal Unitarians and Horace Bushnell. At times,
historians make the Hartford minister seem to be the one antebellum Protestant south of Boston who contributed anything to
the development of late-nineteenth-century Protestant thought.[20]
The unearthing of the New Haven scholars reveals that religious
modernism had broader and deeper roots. New Haven thought
laid the groundwork for modernism in three ways. Breaking from
the line of Puritan doctrinal argument carried on by Nathaniel
William Taylor, the New Haven scholars discovered a new, Romantic way to understand religion. They redefined sanctity to mean
human self-development, an essential precondition for the millennium. And they believed that the trained scholar could find evidence of human development in history, since successive civilizations
allowed their citizens to realize ever higher degrees of self-development. Modernists' appreciation of idealism, history as process,
and culture as evidence of the divine rested on the early spadework
of the New Haven scholars, who used scholarly means for evangelical ends.

The following chapters try to uncover this pattern in Victorian
intellectual life. New Haven gave the scholars a religious heritage
and social milieu that both fed their religious faith and supported
their scholarly commitment. In the 1830s and 1840s the scholars
were young men disturbed by denominational squabbling that they
thought weakened the evangelical efficacy of the church. Ministers
preoccupied themselves with doctrinal matters and overlooked
what the New Haven scholars called the new infidelity. It was not
preached from pulpits; rather it was found in historical, scientific,
and political writings of the day, and its theories stemmed from
the errors of religious rationalism and transcendentalism (chapter

2). These concerns impelled these young men to search for a career, and they found it through their definition of scholarship and scholarly vocation (chapter 3). New Haven theories of knowing and history showed how the mundane fact testified to divine truth. It was "scientific," in New Haven terms, to observe the facts of this world and then to make an analogy between them and an all-embracing divine world of meaning (chapter 5). New Haven historiography also taught that ideas had developed through time. The scholar could analyze the idea of, say, representative democracy and discover what it said about its own time and providential history (chapter 6). The concepts of development, culture, and wholeness also gave the New Haven scholars tools with which to devise theories in the areas of political science, social criticism, and art criticism (chapters 7 and 8). To guarantee the success of New Haven ideas, the scholars conceived the college as an institution that would produce whole men, future members of an educated elite who could detect and reject the wrong ideas found in contemporary thought (chapter 4).

Richard Hofstadter's description of nineteenth-century historians provides a foil for my analysis. Hofstadter writes that pre-Progressive scholars had a "New England" point of view and that "post–Civil War nationalist conceptions" influenced them. Their scholarship "embodied the ideas of the possessing classes about industrial and financial issues, manifested the complacency of white Anglo-Saxon Protestants about social and ethnic issues, and, on constitutional issues, underwrote the requirements of property and of national centralization as opposed to states' rights or regional self-assertion."[21] Here, Hofstadter sees historical thought emerging from the interests of an economic system and a region and neglects other cultural factors that create interest. Indeed, the New Haven scholars would have liked the entire United States to be recreated in the image of their ideal New England, and they wanted to perpetuate an economic system based on private ownership and entrepreneurship. But New Haven scholarship also grew from a ministerial tradition and looked forward to an evangelical future. To serve these "interests," the scholars adopted the most sophisticated means that the nineteenth-century intellectual world offered. They sought to understand how their world was moving toward this future and to guarantee that the evangelical host would contain educated leaders.

During several years of thinking about the New Haven scholars, I slowly became aware of another sense in which Hofstadter conceived of interests too narrowly. For New Haven thought was thoroughly male. That is, the scholars saw men as the central actors in history, developed an educational system designed to nurture men who could play this role in desirable ways, conceived of politics as an arena in which men could influence public life, and wrote for an audience of educated men. Because nineteenth-century college and intellectual life was male at every level of thought and projected action, I retain the sex-specific language of the New Haven group. To suggest that they used the word *men* as a generic term for all human beings is a gross distortion. They meant that men were and are the leading characters in history and the proper subject for study by other men.

If the New Haven group had concerned themselves with women and the home, then we might suspect a defensive posture—that the scholars were responding to what some contemporary historians call "the feminization of American culture." But the New Haven men had surprisingly little to say on the subject of women and their social role. Most of the time they concerned themselves with how men should act and think; they left thinking about women to women. Their model man, nevertheless, would have been a most suitable marriage partner for the ideal wife of the cult of true womanhood.[22]

The Victorian world of the New Haven scholars is difficult to enter. As contemporary Americans, we believe more easily in the extremes of irrational passion and rational self-interest. We readily believe both the religious ascetic who says he is praying for divine revelation and the entrepreneur who dedicates himself to accumulating as much wealth as possible. We are more skeptical of people who, combining faith and reason, attempt a middle way. And we refuse to believe anyone who claims that individualism and community are not contradictory ideals, that individual success and its rewards enhance his and everyone else's chances for spiritual freedom. The New Haven scholars did not share this modern skepticism. Though departing from the way of their Puritan forefathers and thinking about religion in terms discovered in the Romantic mid-nineteenth century, the New Haven group retained the Puritan belief in the congruence of individual and national destiny. In all good faith, they thought that they had solved the dilemma of how a righteous man can live in society.[23]

2
The New Haven Milieu

In the First Church of New Haven, on the twentieth of October, 1846, Theodore Dwight Woolsey, professor of Greek language and literature at Yale College, received the charge of ordination to the ministry from Noah Porter, Sr., a member of the Yale Corporation and pastor of the Congregational church in Farmington, Connecticut. Speaking for the other ministers of the Yale Corporation, who were then acting as an ordination council, Porter told Woolsey, "We do not make you a minister, that you may be President of the college, but that as President of the College you may do the work which belongs to a minister of Christ." Four hours later the professors of the college reconvened with the ministers, now acting in their capacity as members of the Yale Corporation, to inaugurate Woolsey as president.[1]

In an age when colleges chose their presidents from their own alumni, Woolsey was both a typical college president and a typical president of Yale. Like all previous presidents, he had graduated from the college and then studied theology. Further, Woolsey's uncle was Timothy Dwight, the former Yale president who had successfully combated deism and infidelity at the college during the 1790s. To this extent Woolsey's inauguration was a continuation, but it was also a departure. After graduating from college, Woolsey had also studied law, and then after completing his theological studies he had not been ordained. Instead he had continued his formal education with the study of Sanskrit and German at French and German universities. Woolsey was the first Yale president to have pursued postgraduate study in a secular field. (See appendix 1.) That this study at French and German universities did not disqualify Woolsey from the presidency was remarkable, for Nathaniel William Taylor, spokesman for the New Haven theology, was then the central figure in the Yale Theological Department. He and his followers perceived Germany as a synonym for infidelity and as the home of a "wild and mystical" metaphysics.[2]

Woolsey's selection shows that these ministers probably agreed with Woolsey's identification of himself and the institution that he now headed as progressively conservative—"conservative of great principles, and of a system which long reflection and experience have approved; and enterprising in carrying forward that system towards its perfection as fast as its means and powers will allow."[3]

Woolsey conserved the Taylorites' evangelical hopes but sought new means to make them real. False notions of piety and the good man plagued American society in the 1840s, he told the ministers in his inaugural address. On the one hand, a Calvinist asceticism solely interested in self-perfection promoted an unhealthy cultivation of the inward self; on the other hand, an Arminian commitment to works fostered a spiritually debilitating emphasis on action. Colleges, Woolsey explained, should offer an education based on the new ideal of *culture*. Then they would create good men who were "useful in the highest sense of that word, in order that they may themselves be and may make others truly good."[4]

Twenty-five years later, Noah Porter, Jr., was inaugurated as Yale president. At his inauguration, ministers from the churches of the many different Protestant denominations in New Haven marched with members of the legal and medical professions. Guests from other colleges attended, too, and President James McCosh of Princeton greeted Porter on their behalf. In the ceremony, Woolsey passed the symbols of office to Porter and expressed his hope that "the spirit of true science" would "more and more" become "the spirit of Yale College." Responding to this charge, Porter confirmed that the college should be an institution of culture that nurtured its students to true goodness. But for Porter the college did more. It provided a home for the scholar and ensured that the nation would develop intellectually as well as materially.[5]

A wide gulf of change seems to separate the inaugurals of Woolsey and Porter. In 1846 the president of the college appeared as a minister, whereas in 1871 he appeared as a leader of secular and religious professionals and as a colleague of college presidents. While Woolsey refuted false theories of virtue, Porter used his address to rebut theorists who said that the college should not be a Christian institution and that scholarly investigation would disprove Christian truth.

Underneath the differences in the two inaugural ceremonies and speeches, nonetheless, lies unity. Porter and Woolsey shared an evangelical religious faith and a commitment to scholarship as a means that would hasten the millennium. This faith and commitment distinguish Porter and Woolsey from earlier and later generations of professors at Yale. The previous generation included professors like Jeremiah Day, who wrote the famous Yale Report of 1828, and preachers like Nathaniel William Taylor. These men shared Porter and Woolsey's evangelical hopes but not their commitment to scholarship. The next generation included professors in the college like Porter's former students social scientist William Graham Sumner (Yale, 1863) and historian Franklin Bowditch Dexter (Yale, 1861) and professors in the Divinity School like church historian Williston Walker, a German-trained doctor of philosophy. These men shared Porter and Woolsey's scholarly practice, but they did not see scholarship as a means to evangelical ends.

Both Woolsey and Porter defined the college as an institution of culture, and scholarship as the pursuit of truth. The scholar discovered truth as he examined the objective facts of natural science, history, literature, political theory, and art history. Then he showed that these facts stood before an all-embracing divine wholeness. Culture implied a process of self-development toward independence and completeness. The cultured man was well-rounded and had developed character, whereas the religious bigot, the genius, and the political partisan were one-sided.

For the authors of the Yale Report, mental discipline was the purpose of a college education. Although Day, the author of the report, used the word *culture* in his explanation of the purpose of a college education, he used it to refer to the development of the mind, not of the whole person. "The two great points to be gained in intellectual culture," he said, "are the *discipline* and the *furniture* of the mind; expanding its powers, and storing it with knowledge." The concept of the college as an institution that would discipline the mind had two corollaries. First, college teachers were supposed to discipline students—their minds inside the classroom and their behavior outside. Second, lessons of mental discipline taught students the intellectual arguments on which their faith rested. Religious revivals supposedly complemented the lessons of the classroom and won students' hearts.[6]

The assumption that the college would teach lessons of truth and produce cultured students seemed secure until 1879. Then Porter learned that Yale professor William Graham Sumner was using Herbert Spencer's *The Study of Sociology* as a classroom text. Sumner thought that a professor should be able to choose the best available text without interference from the college president. For Porter the issue was truth as the end of knowledge and purpose of college study. If Spencer had discussed the facts of this world in his *Sociology,* then a properly trained scholar could have related the facts to a theistic framework. But as Porter explained to Sumner, Spencer had done more. He had attacked "every Theistic Philosophy of society and of history," sarcastically and coolly arguing "that material elements and laws are the only forces and laws which any scientific man can recognize."[7] Porter thought that Spencer had denounced his ideal of truth and even his ability to discover it. Spencer had suggested not only that Porter could not know truth but, what is more serious, that his theistic theories made it impossible for him to know anything at all.

When Woolsey spoke of the college as an institution of culture in his inaugural discourse, only one man in his audience surely knew what he was talking about. Edward Elbridge Salisbury had studied in Germany, as Woolsey had, where he had learned the new methods of philology from professors who believed that their lessons would encourage the growth of culture in their students. In the next two decades, Woolsey brought to Yale young professors who also knew what he meant by culture and who practiced the new philological techniques in their analysis of texts, art objects, and historical documents. These men—Noah Porter, James Hadley, James Dwight Dana, William Dwight Whitney, George Park Fisher, and James Mason Hoppin—were the New Haven scholars.

To explore their shared commitment and common scholarly practice is to enter a particular time in American educational and intellectual history. The college was in flux as the modern disciplines of history, the social sciences, and the liberal arts were emerging from the old curriculum and its senior course in moral philosophy. Lines between disciplines were imprecise; literature, history, and political science all appeared as moral sciences. The New Haven scholars had no idea that future generations would

separate these disciplines between the liberal arts and the social
sciences or that distinct methods of inquiry would come into being
for each discipline. All the New Haven scholars were empiricists
who used facts to explain the development of man, civilization,
and the world. Further, each scholar had a Romantic and evangelical faith that his trained way of knowing could explain one
aspect of divine truth.

For the New Haven men, the community of discourse and
inquiry that they shared was of paramount importance. It existed
alongside membership in the academic and professional organizations then forming. From the perspective of today, these nascent
professional organizations seem to have been centrifugal forces
pulling the New Haven scholars from their shared center of evangelical understanding toward a future of specialized academic disciplines with distinct methods of inquiry. But from the perspective
of the New Haven scholars, academic organizations such as the
American Oriental Society seemed to be new means for spreading
their learning.[8]

The New Haven scholars' use of culture and truth as concepts
that bridged the gap between the demands of evangelical faith and
career gives them their identity as a unique nineteenth-century
generation. These new means of thinking and vocation allowed
the scholars to step beyond the difficulties that their elders, the
ministers and professors of Taylor and Day's generation, had encountered. To the younger men, Taylor's New Haven theology
and Day's college of mental discipline seemed counterproductive,
furthering sectarian discord and skepticism. The New Haven scholars
hoped to produce unity and certainty by arguing for the historical
validity of a Christianity that resided in any one of several churches
and in theological traditions other than strict Calvinism.

In the 1820s Taylor had reformed Calvinist theology in hopes
of stopping Congregationalists from deserting their inherited faith
for the more intellectually satisfying rationalism of Unitarianism
or the more emotionally satisfying ritual of Episcopalianism. Taylor
drew on Scottish philosophers Dugald Stewart and Thomas Reid
to argue that the human mind had a direct and immediate perception of the real world. Thus, that institutions such as church,
government, school, and family nurtured individuals to the point
where they made a choice for God should impress itself on people's
minds. Realizing that God intended this purpose, people would
become convinced of divine beneficence and make their choices

for God. This outcome was merely probable, for people retained "power to the contrary."[9]

Instead of winning Christians, Taylor's New Haven theology caused dissension among Congregationalists and Presbyterians. Many thought that Taylor had embraced the Arminian heresy by emphasizing nurture and minimizing the original sin of human nature. At Princeton, Archibald Alexander and his student Charles Hodge reaffirmed predestination. Controversies between these Old School Presbyterians and New School ministers such as Taylor resulted in the end to the United Front for the Settlement of the West and produced the charged climate in which Lyman Beecher, one of Taylor's allies, was tried for heresy. Within Connecticut Congregationalism, Bennet Tyler founded the anti-Taylor Hartford Seminary. Even Noah Porter, Sr., a Yale College graduate and member of the Yale Corporation, so distrusted Taylorism that he advised his son to attend the Andover Theological Seminary.[10]

If Taylor's system had worked, then the college should have been an institution of Christian nurture developing in all students an awareness of God's moral government and a recognition that they should own divine truth. In fact, this was not happening. The college of Jeremiah Day might have disciplined students' minds, but its studies did not give students religious conviction. As a complement to the curriculum, college revivals intensified the piety of some students and won others to Congregationalism, but these revival experiences further persuaded students, such as the young New Haven scholars, that the college of mental discipline could not develop Christian faith. Further, the religious feeling of a revival made New Haven theology a subject of controversy and encouraged some students to question whether a religion that provoked such division was a true religion at all.[11]

This tension between learning and faith had been present since the 1740s. Then, for example, New Light student John Cleaveland had to choose between piety and his studies. Choosing piety, he was dismissed from the college. In the 1790s the threat of deism and the rationalism of French philosophy caused Timothy Dwight to reevaluate revivals. He found them useful for stemming the popularity of these two heresies and encouraged faculty-supervised revivals. For Dwight and then his successor Day, revivals became necessary complements to college studies. But the religious enthusiasm of the revival movement during the antebellum period made this combination unstable once again.[12]

In the 1830s and 1840s the Taylorites' New Haven theology created a new source of tension between intellectual life and faith through its insistence on the absolute truth of the Bible. It presented readers with all moral truth and an accurate account of natural history. Given the assumptions of the Scottish philosophy, readers could not fail to see the truth of these facts. Thus, while the Taylorites emphasized the slow growth of faith, they also presumed that pious individuals automatically would see the Bible as literally true. They further believed that investigations in natural science would continue to confirm the Biblical account of Creation. By the 1840s, however, natural scientists were discovering fossils and geological formations that contradicted or at least qualified Genesis. Instead of modifying their philosophy so that religious faith became independent of the literal truth of the Bible, the Taylorites responded with hostility to natural scientists and their discoveries.[13]

James Hadley, a New Haven scholar, recounted in his diary an incident that illustrates the Taylorites' position on natural science. One Sunday in 1850, the eminent Harvard scientist Louis Agassiz accompanied his equally renowned friend Yale scientist Benjamin Silliman to the First Church in New Haven to hear Leonard Bacon preach. Bacon was Taylor's successor in the pulpit of the First Church, but he was also a friend and collaborator of the New Haven scholars. To impress Agassiz, Silliman, and the other members of the American Association for the Advancement of Science who were then meeting in New Haven, Bacon argued for the authority of natural science and called for the modification of Scriptural interpretation "to answer the demands of science."[14]

Bacon's twitting of the Taylorites was as rebellious as any act by the New Haven scholars and their supporters. Among these men there was no Emerson, no "Divinity School Address," no "Nature," and no Brook Farm. The New Haven impulse was to reform existing institutions and ways of knowing. Like Emerson's, their concern was wholeness and development of the individual. And like Emerson, the New Haven men received inspiration from Coleridge and German idealistic philosophy. But while Emerson turned to the study of nature, the New Haveners turned to the promise of German methods in history, philosophy, and philology. They used this new learning to discover a historical Christianity that all denominations could share. This education was different in content and purpose from the education that had prepared the Taylorites. That generation of ministers had studied British and

American theologians in the reformed tradition. From the point of view of New Haven church historian George Park Fisher, the study of doctrine was a suitable preparation for reforming a theological system and pointing out the errors of rival sects and denominations, but it was not an education that would promote evangelical unity.[15]

From the perspective of the New Haven scholars, Woolsey's progress from college through the study of law, theology, and then philology in Germany was a search for new means to address the old problem of the relationship of piety to religion and the new problems of the 1840s. Through the new means of culture, scholarship, and truth, Woolsey hoped to serve evangelical ends.

In the 1890s, looking back on the lives of the New Haven scholars, Timothy Dwight the younger found that "the individual scholar and teacher in this home of learning is not alone by himself— moving forward under the power of his own personal inspiration, and dependent wholly on the force within."[16] The community to which Dwight referred was Yale, but in a larger sense it was New Haven. In the city, ties of kinship, religious faith, and social background bound the scholars to not only the older generation of Yale faculty but also a larger community of Congregationalists and Yale graduates. The scholars lived within walking distance of the college and each other's homes. The families on whom they paid calls or with whom they attended entertainments such as a Shakespeare reading by Fanny Kemble usually sent their sons to Yale and were Congregationalists. The few who were Presbyterians or Episcopalians shared the scholars' evangelical hopes and did not permit doctrinal issues to intrude and divide. In these families evangelicalism and its concerns were usual topics of conversation. Adults were familiar with scholarly developments because they were well-read and because ties of kinship created interest. Not limited to their own age group, old and young mixed easily with one another. Informal social life consisted of calls on neighbors and friends on every day but Sunday, which was devoted to worship and family activities. That houses had no door knockers or bells suggests that families expected their friends to call and had no fear of intruders. Until mid-century, when women began to buy fashionable dresses in New York City, one black silk dress adorned with a simple brooch was adequate "for all festive occasions," such as suppers and receptions. When James Hadley was courting his future wife Anna Twining, the daughter of a Yale graduate and New Haven lawyer, the couple spent evenings in the Twining parlor reading and sharing their ideas on history, theology, and philosophy. Anna was the daughter of Woolsey's close friend and Yale classmate Alexander Twining. Woolsey himself married the sister of his colleague Salisbury, and Salisbury married the daughter of Woolsey's predecessor, Jeremiah Day. Three other New Haven scholars married the daughters of their Yale professors: Porter married Taylor's; Dana, Silliman's; and Thacher, Day's. Even death was an occasion for affirming the community that the New Haven group shared. At Mary Taylor Porter's funeral, James Dwight Dana, George Park Fisher, and Timothy Dwight were among the pallbearers. Their presence suggested both the husbands' bonds of shared purpose as New Haven scholars and their wives' bonds of friendship.[17] (See appendix 1.)

The scholars' social origins were similar to those of their New Haven friends. The reference books that give biographies of these men say that a significant number belonged to "old Connecticut" or "old New England" families. These descriptive phrases signify middle- or upper-class origins and suggest membership in a single social world. At one extreme were Woolsey and Salisbury, whose fathers had accumulated wealth as successful merchants, and at the other were Porter and Hadley, who relied on their salaries, the first being the son of a minister and the second the son of a college professor. With few exceptions, these New Haven friends grew up in the first third of the nineteenth century in thoroughly Protestant New England cities or towns where a family was known by an entire community and not merely by a circle of friends and business associates. (See appendixes 1 and 2.)

Institutions also united the New Haven scholars and the gentry of the city. For instance, both scholars and gentry belonged to a discussion group called The Club. An interest in current events probably caused Woolsey and his friend and college roommate Leonard Bacon to found The Club, an association that brought together men of like background, ideas, and religious faith. While in college, Bacon and Woolsey were members of the Brothers-in-Unity, a literary society, and they founded the *Talebearer,* a satiric newsletter in verse read at meetings. Later, as a New Haven minister and a Yale professor, respectively, Bacon and Woolsey had no forum where they could share ideas. The Club, founded in 1838, brought them together again. It also allowed Bacon and

other members who were New Haven ministers, doctors, or law-
yers to learn how academics applied their learning to current events.[18]

Over the years, friendship, an active interest in Yale, and a desire
to keep abreast of recent scholarly developments continued to
define who entered The Club. It grew from the original six members to an active membership of about thirty. As the number of
members grew, the percentage who were ministers decreased and
the percentage who were Yale professors increased. While the
number of New Haven Congregational churches stayed at three,
by 1879 the Yale faculty had tripled in number to fifty-six professors in all schools. About one-third of these belonged to The
Club. Most of the professors who were members taught in the
college or the Theological Department, but some also taught in
the Law School, the Sheffield Scientific School, and the new School
of Fine Arts. Increasingly, The Club became a forum for the
exchange of ideas among academics in different disciplines. John
Ferguson Weir, painter and first director of the Yale School of
Fine Arts, noted these changes. Remembering The Club of the
1870s, Weir observed that "specialism" in scholarship had not yet
arrived. Still, "the older men seemed broader in their sympathies
and interests than the younger professors."[19]

By the 1870s Club members who had brought the new scholarship from Germany in the 1840s and 1850s were the older
generation. Then hostility to the new science of John Stuart Mill
and Herbert Spencer began to distinguish members who were
Yale professors. As this new generation came to dominate The
Club, members became more reticent about their religious faith.
They no longer mentioned their religious values when discussing
current events; ministers and Divinity School professors were the
sole speakers on religious topics.[20]

Club meetings were occasions when members could restate and
reaffirm their common values and belief through reading of a paper
and participating in the ceremony of a meeting. Club members
always met the second and fourth Wednesdays of each month at
the home of a member. No matter who held the meeting, the
menu was the same, the dress formal, and certain taboos, such as
prohibited smoking, prevailed. The agenda for each meeting was
as unchanging as the values that informed each paper. First there
was dinner, at which the wife of the host was often in attendance,
and then, after she had retired, the paper and discussion followed.
Although the paper read at each meeting could lie in any one of
a variety of fields, ranging from political parties to hymnology,

each paper told how a liberal evangelical Protestant should view the topic.[21]

Even with so much similarity of thought, background, and social experience, personality and taste created inevitable differences in professional and private behavior. Most often these differences were superficial. While Presbyterian Charles Scribner published most of the scholars' books, Whitney sometimes placed books with his friend Henry Holt, who was also William Graham Sumner's publisher. Some of these Yale professors were reserved in their dealings with students; others were open and friendly. Some taught with great vigor, supplementing recitations with brief lectures; others taught with great empathy for students who responded hesitantly to questions. Porter was an enthusiastic walker; Hadley was limited by lameness. Some cared little for ministerial councils; others saw ministers as natural supporters for the college. All believed in simplicity of taste, but its expression took different forms in each scholar's home. While Porter decorated his study with busts or engraved portraits of Kant, Coleridge, and Sir William Hamilton, Fisher purchased a pair of stone lions from Augustus St. Gaudens to flank his front stoop. Often differences were more fundamental. Remarks in letters suggest that Noah Porter and George Park Fisher were not mutual admirers, for Porter had opposed Fisher's employment at Yale on the grounds that he was a superficial scholar and "not a first rate man." Nevertheless, no evidence, published or private, suggests that this disagreement divided the New Haven scholars; larger commitments apparently prevailed and encouraged unity.[22]

The city of New Haven provided the scholars with an associational life that connected them to a national world of scholarship. The city was the home of the Connecticut Association of Arts and Sciences, which held regular meetings and attracted an audience of learned men from the region. Silliman's *Journal* and New Haven connections with the American Association for the Advancement of Science gave the scholars access to a network of scientists that included Agassiz and Asa Gray at Harvard and Joseph Henry at Princeton.

Among themselves the scholars formed discussion groups. Edward Elbridge Salisbury founded the Oriental Society and developed it into a national organization with its own publication, the *Journal of the American Oriental Society*. In the early 1850s some of the scholars formed a discussion group in philology. After William Dwight Whitney returned from his studies at German universities, he became its leader and developed it into the American Philological Association (1869). At meetings of the Oriental Society and the philology group, members either read papers on a topic that they had researched or reported on recent writings. Sometimes these papers were published in the *Journal of the American Oriental Society* or in the *Transactions of the American Philological Association*. These scholarly societies probably owed as much to the literary societies that the New Haven scholars had belonged to as Yale students as to the model of the German graduate seminar.[23]

The New Haven scholars' accomplishments in their individual fields won them audiences beyond New Haven. Woolsey delivered a Phi Beta Kappa address at Harvard and published in the journal of the American Social Science Association. Fisher became president of the American Historical Association. In his presidential address to that organization he proposed that a historian should be a moral judge, while in an address to ministers of the International Congregational Council he defended the value of historical studies for Biblical scholars. Timothy Dwight the younger, Woolsey, and James Hadley used their skills as philologists and Greek scholars on the American Committee for the Revision of the English Bible. Whitney defined *philology* for the *Encyclopaedia Britannica* and wrote or edited many grammars and texts for Ginn and Company. Charles Scribner, a Presbyterian and graduate of Princeton, published New Haven texts and collections of the scholars' sermons. Charles Merriam, a Congregationalist, chose Porter to edit the 1864 edition of Webster's *American Dictionary of the English Language* and the first edition of *Webster's International Dictionary of the English Language* (1890). Porter persuaded Merriam to hire him by telling the publisher that since Webster had first prepared his dictionary, "comparative philology has come into existence as a science" and made his etymologies "notorious." Under Porter's direction the dictionary became an outlet for New Haven scholarship and an American showcase for the new philological scholarship. He hired a German trained in the new science to prepare etymologies and called on his Yale colleagues to supply and edit definitions. The New Haven scholar James Hadley wrote a history of the English language that appeared as the preface to both editions.[24]

The New Haven scholars also formed a subset within the world of Congregationalist benevolent, reform, and journalistic activity. This world included the Society for the Promotion of Collegiate and Theological Education at the West, later the American Education Society, and the weekly newspaper the *Independent*. Friendships usually strengthened working alliances with Congregationalist ministers and journalists. Following one such friendship pattern allows us to see how this world worked. Leonard Bacon became a close friend of Joseph Parrish Thompson (Yale, 1838) when Thompson was pastor of the New Haven Chapel Street Church. Thompson joined The Club and served as an editor of the *New Englander,* a journal managed by the New Haven scholars and Bacon. In 1845 Thompson left New Haven and became pastor of the Broadway Tabernacle Church in New York City. With Bacon and Richard S. Storrs, a Congregationalist minister involved in antislavery, he edited the New York–based *Independent,* a Congregationalist, free-soil paper with the largest circulation of any northern weekly newspaper. For the New Haven men, the presence in New York of Charles Scribner's firm, Thompson at the Broadway Tabernacle Church, and the *Independent* made the city a center for evangelical association and publishing activity. Theirs was not the genteel New York of the Gilded Age which had its social headquarters at the Century Club and published political and literary articles in E. L. Godkin's *Nation* and Richard Watson Gilder's *Century Magazine.*

When Bacon died in 1881, the *Independent* carried a series of memorial articles. One by Noah Porter recalled the so-called great college (Yale) revival of 1831. As a young minister in New Haven, Bacon had evidently been caught up in the revival with Porter, then a college senior, and his friend Horace Bushnell, a Yale graduate (1827) and then a tutor. During the previous year Porter had read Coleridge's *The Aids to Reflection* and had discovered that people could share religious faith even when the language of their doctrines differed. In the 1840s Porter and Bushnell served on the editorial board of the *New Englander* with Thompson and Bacon. Porter reviewed Bushnell's *Christian Nurture* (1847) favorably for the journal, and the editorial board stood by Bushnell despite the furor caused in more conservative Congregationalist circles by his *God in Christ* (1849) and *Nature and the Supernatural* (1858). Further, Bushnell, Thompson, Woolsey, and Porter all shared similar opinions on political theory. Woolsey taught this theory in his Yale classes, it underlay Thompson's and Bushnell's sermons, and it was the subject of articles by all these men for the *Independent* and the *New Englander.*[25]

In these journals and in the associational life of New Haven, the scholars found support and an audience who respected their religious faith and scholarly commitment. When the New Haven men wrote as scholars, they presumed an audience who shared their religious faith and did not require its bracketing. And when writing for religious readers, they presumed an audience who hoped that college-based learning would enhance understanding of religion. In fact, in the mid-nineteenth century publishing, institutional, and social world of the New Haven scholars, they rarely encountered tension between the scholarly and religious aspects of their identity, for scholarship permitted the expression of religious belief, and religious belief called upon the findings of scholarship.

Outside New Haven and the associations and journals that carried their beliefs, a member of the New Haven group was likely to find that his scholarship and religious commitment were not so compatible. When James Dwight Dana, the natural scientist, made a lecture tour through New England and New York, he read a lecture to a small audience in Utica, his hometown. Describing the evening, Dana explained that he "had the parlors hung with the legs and and bones of the various wild beasts of which the lecture treats. All passed off satisfactorily, they say." But the audience included a minister who rejected the new Biblical criticism and remained an uncompromising literalist. Dana delighted in the absurdities that resulted from this man's reading of the Bible. The minister "was quite sure that there was no death in the world until the sin of Adam. The tigers could not have given loose to their flesh-eating propensities until the fall."[26] Thus, Dana spoke for university-based knowledge and contended against the provincial parish minister who held to the lessons of his youth.

Evangelical faith split American college professors into supporters and opponents of the New Haven group. Professors at evangelically inspired colleges throughout New England and the Midwest, such as Grinnell and Illinois, often were Yale graduates and contributors to the *New Englander*. But the New Haven men found little comity with professors at either Harvard or Princeton. In the 1820s and 1830s Taylor's revision of Calvinism, emphasis on human ability, and stress on institutions as aids to conversion seemed to constitute heresy in the opinion of Princeton theologians Archibald Alexander and Charles Hodge, who were reaffirming predestination and literal interpretation of the Bible. At

Harvard the antebellum professors, whom Daniel Walker Howe refers to as the Harvard moralists, agreed with the New Haven scholars that education should be moral and that society was organic and God-given, but the issue of the relationship of religion to art, literature, and education divided the two groups. The New Haven men thought that the issue of spiritual regeneration had become extraneous to the Unitarians' definition of culture. From a New Haven perspective, the Cambridge group had made culture into the equivalent of virtue by elevating it from the status of a means to that of an end. They seemed to ignore the regeneration of the soul and to confuse good manners with true virtue. Nevertheless, beneath the public irenics often lay friendship. Theodore Parker, for instance, thanked Noah Porter for the "unusual fairness of your treatment of me." And after a visit to Boston, Porter reported to his New Haven friends that Parker had told him that Thacher and Salisbury were "well thought of in Germany."[27]

In the late 1860s the New Haven scholars, Harvard moralists, and Princetonians recognized the threat to all theistic belief posed by the psychology and social science of Herbert Spencer and John Stuart Mill. Harvard moralists and New Haven scholars joined forces when they contributed to an anthology, the *Boston Lectures*, addressed to the question of *Christianity and Scepticism* (1870–72). Relations with Princeton improved with the arrival of James McCosh as president in 1868. A great admirer of McCosh, Porter praised his inaugural address as "conservative yet progressive" and said that he would have dedicated his recently published *Human Intellect* to him "as a kind of sheaf from the learned profession in America" if his professor in Berlin, Adolf Trendelenburg, had not had prior claim. McCosh attempted to revive the previously moribund *Princeton Review* by making it more of an outlet for evangelical scholarship and less of an exclusive platform for Old School Presbyterians. Soliciting articles that were timely and written "to defend truth and not engage in mere speculation," he wrote Porter and Fisher, who supplied pieces critical of positivistic social science and psychology.[28]

While the 1870s brought unity among previously contentious theistic scholars, in New Haven the increasing specialization of academic disciplines divided scholars and multiplied associations. For instance, in the 1850s Porter had belonged to Whitney and Hadley's philological discussion group, but in 1869 he did not join the national philology association. By the 1890s academic discussion groups had multiplied until they existed in the fields of classics, philosophy, Semitic languages, comparative religion, modern languages, English, political science, mathematics, physics, and engineering. These groups did not belong to the intellectual life of the city but were extensions of the graduate courses at Yale and were composed solely of its faculty and students.[29] The days of the 1850s, when Greek scholar and philologist James Hadley contributed to meetings of philologists and Orientalists and attended meetings of the American Association for the Advancement of Science, were gone. New Haven scholarship and the community of discourse that it represented disappeared when scholars no longer had as their purpose the search for and affirmation of divine truth.

Some of the lessons of New Haven scholarship lived on. The scholars taught men who became college presidents in the last third of the nineteenth century including Daniel Coit Gilman (Johns Hopkins), Andrew Dickson White (Cornell), Franklin Carter (Amherst), and Arthur Twining Hadley (Yale). Another student, William Torrey Harris, founded the *Journal of Speculative Philosophy* (1867), became U.S. commissioner of education (1889–1906), and succeeded Porter as editor of *Webster's International Dictionary*. All these men rejected their teachers' synthesis of religion and scholarship. But rejection of that synthesis did not mean the repudiation of all New Haven lessons. For instance, when Daniel Coit Gilman became president of The Johns Hopkins University, he joined no church in Baltimore and did not include a chapel in his building plans. Gilman wished the university to stand above religious debate and thought a president should favor no one system of religious truth. Nevertheless, Gilman retained his membership in the New Haven church to which he had belonged when he had lived in that city and had been Yale librarian. When Gilman went to Baltimore, he left his public allegiance to a church in New Haven with his former Yale teachers, while he took their lessons about the meaning of scholarship and his private religious faith with him.[30]

When the New Haven scholars were young men in the 1830s and 1840s, they could not foresee that their student Gilman would have to make this choice. In those earlier decades New Haven scholarship promised that the college could be a means to the millennium and that a career would combine religious faith and scholarly practice.

3
New Haven Scholarship

*The existence of a community of men, more or less educated
themselves, supposes and demands another class of men whose culture
is wider and more profound, both special and general, whose
sharpened wit, ample generalizations, responsive sympathy, and
prying scrutiny are at hand to examine and to judge, to help and to
hinder the aspirants after elementary knowledge, and to diffuse
truth of every sort among those who are capable of understanding
their words. In other words, for the very reason that knowledge is
more thorough, more varied and widely diffused, it follows that we
need and must produce a class of men who deserve to be called
scholars by eminence. . . .*

Noah Porter, "The Ideal Scholar," 1887

When the New Haven scholars were young men in the
1820s and 1830s, they found no vocation ready-made
for their intellectual talents and religious beliefs. The
ministry and college teaching had become unappealing, and the
profession of scholarship did not yet exist. These conditions meant
that Woolsey, Porter, and Salisbury had to search for their vocations
without having the advantage of role models or even knowledge
of what it was that they wanted to become. The younger philologist
Whitney and natural scientist Dana were more fortunate. Whitney
could follow the example of the older scholars, and Dana could
take advantage of the established course of professional training
that existed for scientists. It included working as an apprentice for
a known scientist, in this case Benjamin Silliman of Yale College,
and then joining an expedition to some little-known part of the
globe, in this case the United States Exploring Expedition to the
South Pacific, led by Captain Charles Wilkes.[1]

Even by the 1840s no American had any idea of what it meant
to be a scholar in the modern sense that German university professors were establishing. Bostonians Joseph Cogswell, George
Bancroft, George Ticknor, and Edward Everett had returned from
study at German universities without having become scholars. They
might consult and interpret primary sources, but they neither practiced nor applied the principles of German classical philology.
Further, they did not pursue careers that in any way resembled
those of their German professors. Scholarship for them was an

accomplishment of a learned man or a device for the literary artist.[2]

The faculty of Yale College contained no role models either. The scholars' teachers were the authors of the Yale Report, who had written that college education should discipline the mental faculties through the study of mathematics and Greek and Latin grammar. They saw themselves as *in loco parentis* and thought that a college teacher should supervise students' lives. Further, they looked to the revival as the primary means of strengthening college men in their Christian faith. College presidents or faculty members often led prayer groups to encourage these awakenings.[3]

For the evangelically committed and intellectually serious college graduate of the antebellum decades, the ministry often did not appeal as a career. Attacks from within and without threatened the foundation and organization of New England Protestantism and made the ministry seem to be a profession that divided Christians instead of uniting them. The attacks from within included quarrels between Old and New School Presbyterians that resulted in heresy trials like that of Lyman Beecher and the end of the United Front for the Settlement of the West. Within Connecticut, Bennet Tyler objected to Nathaniel W. Taylor's revision of Congregationalist theology and founded the Hartford Theological Seminary. The attacks from without included geological discoveries and advances in Biblical criticism, which seemed to undermine the literal truth of the Bible, then a foundation for faith and belief. Taylor and the authors of the Yale Report greeted these intellectual developments with hostility and disbelief. They insisted that the facts of natural science would continue to confirm the Biblical account of Creation, they rejected Biblical criticism, and they denounced Germany as the home of infidelity.[4]

The New Haven scholars did not retreat from these challenges to their traditional faith. They searched for a new understanding of its sources and a new pulpit from which they could teach Christian lessons.

Two events during Noah Porter's college years impelled him on his search for a vocation: he read Samuel Taylor Coleridge's *Aids to Reflection* (1829) and he participated in the college revival of 1831. The book came into great demand in New Haven soon after publication of the American edition by James Marsh, president of the University of Vermont. Like other young men in Andover and Cambridge, Porter and his New Haven friends Horace Bushnell and William Augustus Larned bought a copy and circulated it among themselves in hopes of discovering a new way to understand religion and its expression. For practical and intellectual reasons, their New England religious heritage appeared inadequate. The New Haven theology was dividing Protestants, and the Taylorites defined religion only in terms of rational understanding. Their theology was yet another modification of the Scottish philosophy and retained the Lockean psychological principle that the facts of this world impress their meaning upon the mind. Taylor and his followers "in effect perpetuat[ed]," historian Philip Gura finds, "the barren line of theological argument developed by those who first interpreted Edwards's system of divinity."[5] In *Aids to Reflection,* Porter and Bushnell glimpsed a horizon beyond the Scottish philosophers, and under its inspiration they began to think critically about the words they used to describe religious experience.

As Porter later wrote, Coleridge drew attention to the fact that the study of words and of the mental acts that they designated was a prerequisite for "any rational knowledge of the central and absolute ground of all being." This understanding of language as symbolic helped Porter discover that "the same faith may be held under different formulas of expression." Applied to theological questions of the late 1820s and 1830s, this meant that sectarian debates among Presbyterians, Congregationalists, and Unitarians obscured the underlying essentials of true religion. Porter also found a vision of career based on what he described as "the high view of man," that he "was capable of science and faith." To a young man worried that he had to choose between emotional and rational piety, that is, between revivals and the sterile discourse of the New Haven theology, Coleridge brought solace, for he had made "the piety of the Christian subservient to the highest accomplishment of the student."[6]

The college revival of 1831 drew Porter into a circle of students from the college and the Theological Department who met and prayed at the home of Chauncey Goodrich, professor of homiletics. These prayer meetings gave Porter a forum in which to express his religious feelings and contrasted with the college church that he was required to attend. There he heard the preaching of Elizur T. Fitch. Instead of addressing the religious needs and doubts of young men, Fitch preached a cycle of sermons that expounded the tenets of Congregationalism. Holding to the Scottish philosophy, Fitch believed that if he explained religious doctrines clearly, the young men in his congregation could not fail to see the truth. The revival strengthened Porter's conviction that he had to do something so that college men could have religious faith and an understanding of its basis. Porter hoped for a "renovation of religious culture in our schools of learning" so that preaching would be adapted "to [the students'] hearts and feelings."[7]

After college, Porter balked at the prospect of attending any theological school, for he expected that it would teach merely one system of doctrine. He wanted instead to go to Vermont and study with President Marsh for six months or a year. His father frowned on this plan and urged his son to "pray *much, much, much*" (emphasis in original). The father counseled that he would not want any friend of his to form his "character and modes of thinking and feeling" after the model of Coleridge and advised attendance at Andover Theological Seminary. Father and son must have compromised, for the younger Porter entered the Yale Theological Department and continued to read on his own the works of British Romantics and translations of German philosophy.[8]

After assuming a pastorate, Porter started to publish articles in the *Quarterly Christian Spectator* and *Bibliotheca Sacra,* journals published in New Haven and Andover, respectively. He praised Burke and Wordsworth but accused the transcendentalists of pantheism and Theodore Parker of propounding "a frigid and soulless neology." Yet Porter still felt dissatisfied. Though he "like[d] to preach, and could hardly live without preaching," he objected to "the details involved in the care of a congregation and the oppression that brood[s] over me in the care of souls." There were other ways, he wrote his friend Woolsey, "in which I can influence men, in which I can be learned to a better account."[9]

Porter discovered how he could "be learned to a better account" by redefining *scholar* to include a statement of scholarly method and a vision of vocation. His definition was new, for in the 1840s *scholar* meant either "student" or "man of learning." In baccalaureate addresses college speakers often called graduating seniors scholars. When George William Curtis spoke on "The Duty of the American Scholar" (1856), he was summoning young men to participate in political life. An adult scholar was a man with suf-

ficient wealth and leisure to pursue advanced studies or one whose
vocation required it. In this sense a learned minister or statesman
was *scholarly*.[10]

In rethinking the meaning of *scholar* Porter was not alone. Another young man, Ralph Waldo Emerson, also had read the Scottish philosophers as a college student and had received inspiration
from Coleridge. His 1837 Harvard Phi Beta Kappa address, "The
American Scholar," departed from the custom of giving advice to
the senior class on their careers. Instead, Emerson made a personal
statement in which *scholar* connoted a vocation. Emerson's scholar
qualified for his vocation by studying life. His career was "to cheer,
to raise, and to guide men by showing them facts amidst appear-
ances." The scholar found truth "in the secrets of his own mind"
which revealed "the secrets of all minds." Although no bookish
recluse, Emerson's scholar disdained what was popular as "the
vulgar prosperity that retrogrades ever to barbarism." Truth had
its price. The scholar had to accept that he stood like a prophet
bearing a cross made of solitary endeavor and endure the pain
arising from "the state of virtual hostility in which he seems to
stand to society, and especially to educated society."[11]

Porter, too, scorned the merely bookish man and compared him
to a "learned pig." But he did not carry Emerson's disdain for
"bibliomaniacs" to the extreme of embracing intuition and re-
nouncing schooling as vital training for the scholar. Prerequisites
of scholarship were "the discipline and knowledge that is gained
by a training in the schools, and a close and long contact with
books." The scholar had an exact knowledge of facts and the ability
to use them "scientifically." Scientific method was a crucial ingre-
dient of scholarliness and meant the arrangement of facts under
principles generally accepted as forming the theoretical base of a
discipline. Measuring Scottish philosophers Stewart and Reid, authors of his college texts, by this standard, Porter found that they
wrote in an indistinct, inaccurate, and loose manner.[12]

Method thus set the scholar apart from the learned man much
as it separates historians from antiquarians today. Porter's scholar
was not like the divine, who relied on "private and peculiar inspiration." The scholar found truth through the observation of
facts and their arrangement into an argument that he set forth in
an unbiased and candid spirit. Emerson and Porter both took
authority from those who claimed religious sanction and gave the
scholar power to find truth.[13] Emerson's scholar found truth through
intuition; Porter's, through mastery of facts and conscious suspen-

sion of prejudices. Emerson seceded from traditional institutions and brought his message to audiences through lyceums. Porter remained loyal to the college but rethought its relationship to American society. He saw that scholarship could provide a means of reaching and persuading an educated reading public.

In 1847 Porter left his pastorate to fill the newly endowed chair of mental and moral philosophy at Yale College. He hoped that this position would give him the opportunity to pursue his scholarly studies and to write an adequate textbook. But now he felt torn between being a teacher and being scholarly just as before he had felt torn between his minister's duties and his studies. He complained to Woolsey repeatedly, pointing out that his eighteen-hundred-dollar salary was so low that to support his family, he had to tutor, write for the press, and take in boarders. He foresaw that the "whole work of scientific study is still to be done." Although he had read the classics and Hegel, he felt "sixteen years too late in the field by means of age" and in need of "facility in German and German philosophy."[14]

Study at the University of Berlin during the academic year of 1853–54 gave Porter his opportunity. Instead of fearing Germany as the Taylorites had, he was drawn to it as the home of an evangelical, humanistic scholarship. Historian Rudolf Pfeiffer describes this scholarship as a powerful movement started by art historian Winckelmann and continued by classical and linguistic philologists such as F. A. Wolf (1759–1824), Boeckh (1785–1871), Bopp (1791–1867), and Bekker (1785–1871) and historian Barthold Georg Niebuhr (1776–1831). Porter learned the lessons of this humanistic scholarship directly from philosopher Adolf Trendelenburg, who built upon the lessons of these earlier German scholars.[15]

In New Haven, reading, study, and friends had brought this movement to Porter's attention. Josiah Willard Gibbs, Porter's teacher in the theology department, was interested in the new methods of Biblical criticism, and Woolsey had been introduced to this learning while studying with both Boeckh and Bopp in the late 1820s. Niebuhr's history and his *Life* were read by the New Haven men. About 1850 Gibbs, Woolsey, and Salisbury, as well as the younger Porter, Whitney, and Hadley started a philology club to discuss the new learning, and they read the *British Quarterly Review* and the *London Quarterly Review,* which regularly contained articles on new developments in philological matters.[16] (See appendix 5.)

Table 1 The New Haven Scholars Study Abroad

Name	Dates	University	Subjects and Professors
Woolsey	1827–30	Paris Leipzig Bonn Berlin	Arabic (Garcin de Tassy) Greek (Godfrid Hermann) (Welker) Philology (Boeckh); Sanskrit (Bopp)
Salisbury	1836–40 1842–43	Paris Berlin Bonn Paris	Sanskrit (Garcin de Tassy and de Sacy) Sanskrit (Bopp) Sanskrit (Freytag) Sanskrit (Lasser)
Hoppin	1845–46	Berlin	Church history (Neander)
Whitney	1850–53	Berlin Tübingen	Egyptology (Lepsius); Sanskrit (Bopp) (Rudolph Roth)
Fisher	1852–54	Halle	Hebrew grammar and Jewish history (Hupfeld); history of rationalism (Tholuck); homiletics and practical ethics (Müller); Oriental languages (Roediger)
Porter	1853–54	Berlin	Geography (Ritter); Hegelian logic and metaphysics (Werder); history of moral philosophy (Helfrisch); history of philosophy (Trendelenburg); theological morality (Twisten)
Dwight	1856–56	Berlin	Church history (Neander)

Sources: Dictionary of American Biography, 1932 ed.; George Park Fisher, "Diary, 1852–1854," Yale Divinity School Library, Yale University, New Haven, Conn.; King, *Woolsey*, 25; Noah Porter to Theodore Dwight Woolsey, 12 December 1853, Woolsey Family Papers.

A changed, enthusiastic Porter wrote Woolsey from Berlin. Porter now saw how he could use German philosophy to show men of different sects that they shared the same religious faith; he wanted "to lay the philosophy of Schleiermacher and its basis before the American public and have it understood." It would show that the theological positions of Edwards Amasa Park of Andover Theological Seminary, Charles Hodge of Princeton, and Horace Bushnell were only superficially different, that in fact these men "would find themselves close bedfellows."[17]

After returning to his teaching duties at Yale, Porter recommended study at a German university to aspiring scholars. He told them not to fear that German philosophy would tempt them from their faith. The Germans were "teachers of the world" who were inspiring the current "Renaissance of the English mind." Hegel was passé; current philosophers' "sobriety of judgment" was replacing the previous generation's "fantastic theorizing." Among the Germans were those whom he called "true believers" because he perceived that their intellects were free from any "narrowing bondage to bigotry." These German thinkers could furnish the weapons that Christian scholars needed to encounter the "foes of a true science of a believing faith." The Germans could teach American students how to become scholars. Merely reading their books taught ideas but not scholarliness; for that, their example was essential.[18]

Porter could not fulfill his scholarly ambition for fourteen years after his return from Germany. He was convinced that he must write a textbook, but the drudgery of teaching robbed him of the necessary time even as it persuaded him that a textbook was needed. It frustrated him

> to be dragged up before breakfast to hear recitations, out of textbooks, which excite only disgust at their deficiencies—and yet to be unable in consequence of the sleepiness of my audience and myself to do anything, which is satisfactory, in supplying their defects; to be unable to prepare textbooks to my mind, because the best of my time and the best of my energies must be given . . . to earn the means of living; that to feel for all this time I must neglect the studies appropriate to my profession.[19]

Besides, Porter needed the royalties to support two unmarried daughters and a semi-invalid wife. Publication of *The Human Intellect* in 1868, a text designed for the use of both college students and more advanced scholars, must have eased his anxiety. In 1871 he published an abridged version *Elements of Intellectual Science* for classroom use and in 1885, a companion volume *Elements of Moral Science*. These books were standard college texts until the beginning of the twentieth century. By then William James's *Principles of Psychology* (1890) had superseded Porter's psychology.[20] (See appendix 3.)

Fisher, Whitney, and Woolsey meanwhile were traveling paths similar to Porter's. Fisher and Woolsey were converted in college revivals, and all three men studied in Germany. In the 1860s their paths converged when each man held a professorship at Yale and published a major text. Porter's *Human Intellect*, Woolsey's *Introduction to the Study of International Law* (1860), Whitney's *Language and the Study of Language* (1867), and Fisher's *Essays on the Supernatural Origin of Christianity* (1865) all introduced their American readers to new fields of study, new methods of analysis, and a new style of argument. The scholarship that Porter, Fisher, Whitney, and Woolsey were introducing was New Haven scholarship—a particular nineteenth-century hybrid of the conventions of German academic scholarship grafted to the stalk of Scottish philosophy. The New Haven group took care to explain their method and style, which they knew were unfamiliar to their readers. Porter defined scholarly method as the presentation of findings and conclusions "in the forms of exact observation, precise definition, fixed terminology, classified arrangement, and rational explanation."[21] This definition had four corollaries.

First, scholars belonged to recognizable disciplines that were defined by their subject matter and certain guiding principles and methods. Whitney's subtitle, *Twelve Lectures on the Principles of Linguistic Science,* indicated that his book *Language and the Study of Language* was an extended definition of a discipline. Porter's *Human Intellect* described psychology as "the science of the human soul." Fisher started his texts and history courses with the explanation that history was "the biography of society," a formulation that he attributed to Thomas Arnold and Barthold Niebuhr.[22]

Second, the scholar belonged to a community of scholars and built upon its work. Salisbury called for the specialist who alone "can do the critical investigation of languages," and he promised to attract others to the cause of research. Dana explained that the scientist should "advanc[e] by his researches the sciences to which he is devoted." The scholar was expected to cite in footnotes and bibliographies the works of other members of his scholarly community and to follow its rules of discourse. George Park Fisher helped to enforce these rules in his role as historical consultant to the publishing firm of Charles Scribner's Sons. Fisher recommended that a competent historian know the German works in his field. Although a historical work might predict the millennium, it should betray no sectarian sympathy.[23]

Third, the scholar consulted the facts. It is easy for contemporary readers to recognize as modern Fisher's description of historical facts. To find them, he said, the historian must study manuscripts as well as the architecture, art, literature, statutes, and official documents of an era. Psychologist Porter's facts, however, are more difficult to appreciate as modern; that is, they did not result from laboratory research or direct observation of behavior. Porter's facts were those that "the soul" could discover "concerning itself." Like his teacher Trendelenburg, Porter thought that the psychologist found facts through the etymologically correct understanding of the language of everyday life. Porter's psychology thus was modern to the extent that it was based on facts and departed from the practice of previous mental philosophers such as Francis Wayland, who merely refined the theories of the Scottish philosophy.[24]

Fourth, scholarly argument followed certain rules of style. Fisher recommended that the historian write in a warm and candid manner, differentiating among facts, hypotheses, and inferences in other historians' arguments. Whereas the nonscholar, Whitney found, "surrounded and dimmed" his argument with "a halo of fancy," the scholarly argument had "sharply cut outlines and distinct lineaments." It was "the analytic rather than the synthetic, the inquiring rather than the dogmatic." The scholar always strived "above all things, after clearness." He proceeded "always from that which is well-known or obvious to that which is more recondite and obscure, establishing the principles by induction from facts which lie within the cognizance of every well-educated person."[25]

Further, the New Haven scholars assumed that their writing and teaching positively affected social change. Induction from facts revealed principles that the educated person, as Whitney said, could not fail to grasp. Thus, he and his colleagues assumed that their scholarship would influence properly educated men. That educated men have right ideas was vital for the moral development of society, for social change, the scholars believed, proceeded from men with right ideas, whose influence improved other men. This theory emphasized the role of agencies of cultural transmission— schools, colleges, churches, and printed materials. It minimized, on the one hand, the influence of political and economic institutions, which merely structured society, and, on the other hand, the effects of religious revivals, which merely awakened or intensified religious feeling.[26] When explaining social change, Porter and the New Haven scholars simply ignored the role of women and the family. The scholars assumed that the welfare of society depended upon right ideas, religious in essence, and that educated men played a vital role in society as initiators of ideas, both good and bad, that ordinary people accepted. It followed that irreligion, or wrong thinking, was more dangerous among educated than among common men. The latter were more susceptible to religious truth; they could read the Bible and "feel" its truth. For educated men to accept religion and avoid skepticism, they had to understand the principles and methods upon which statements of truth were based. With this accomplished, right ideas would flow through society. "The principles and conclusions of the few who think," Porter suggested, "affect the opinions, the feelings, and the interests of the many who act."[27] Assuming a deferential society where ideas were forces of change, the New Haven scholars wanted to make sure that a male elite disseminated right ideas.

This theory of social change implied that scholarly texts had a social purpose and a specific audience. Through the printed word, the scholar could guide the thinking of educated men. For example, Woolsey saw readers of his *International Law* as "young men of liberal culture, in preparation for any profession or employment, who need the enlarging influence of a study like this; who in a republic like ours are in a degree responsible for the measures of government." The New Haven scholars applied their theory of social change in the relatively unspecialized world of nineteenth-century publishing. Until the last third of the century, only natural scientists and Orientalists had journals in which to publish specialized studies. Thus, it was the norm for books to be designed for both well-educated and scholarly readers. Porter said, for instance, that his *Human Intellect* was "a text book for colleges and higher schools" *and* "for advanced students of psychology and speculative philosophy."[28] In a dual-purpose text such as his *Human Intellect,* footnotes or paragraphs in small type segregated information of exclusively scholarly interest. Single-purpose texts were usually intended for well-educated readers and introduced them to scholarly developments or applied the specialized knowledge of the scholar to questions of current interest. For example, Whitney's two books on philology introduced his readers to that subject, a new frontier of knowledge in the mid-nineteenth century. Fisher wrote a series of articles for the *North American Review* in which he attempted to dispel the popular notion that Christianity was a "Puritanical" force and to create a fair-minded view based on recent scholarship. Porter, the most widely published among the scholars, wrote on education, reading, and popular philosophers in the *American Biblical Repository,* the *British Quarterly Review,* the *Atlantic Monthly, Hearth and Home, Hours at Home, Christian Union,* the *International Review,* the *Nation,* the *North American Review,* the *Princeton Review,* and *Round Table.*[29]

The New Haven men's theological training and religious heritage may explain why they wrote so readily for both scholarly and educated audiences. As theological students, Woolsey, Porter, Fisher, and Hoppin studied homiletics and learned the principles of an effective sermon. They eschewed the doctrinal expositions of their former teachers and called for a preaching style that appealed to both spiritual and worldly needs of congregations. The preacher should give, Hoppin advised, "a practical application to what he preaches, directing it to the conscience and heart of his hearers." All sermons followed a formula. The preacher presented a passage from Scripture, then an exegesis of its meaning, and finally its import for his congregation's lives. The same pattern can be found in New Haven texts and more popular articles. Where the minister had one pulpit from which to preach to all, the New Haven authors had two in their scholarly and popular publications, each with its appropriate style and tone. The exegesis was the scholarly book or journal article, which emphasized information; the practical application was the article in the *New Englander* or the *North American Review,* which applied the information in morally didactic lessons. That educated men would see the truth in these lessons and then carry out the New Haven reform agenda was assumed.[30]

The income from publishing in popular journals was a necessary supplement to the low Yale salaries, which we have heard Porter bewail and which encouraged Harvard to try to lure Whitney to Cambridge in 1869. Nevertheless, the need to eke out Yale salaries insufficiently explains why the New Haven men chose to write for a popular audience; even the independently wealthy Woolsey wrote articles and books for an educated male audience. Whereas some of the scholars needed extra income, all believed that an educated elite played a crucial role in bringing about desirable social change. While only some New Haven men needed to supplement their salary, all were popularizers by choice.[31]

The *New Englander,* a journal published in New Haven and edited by the New Haven scholars and their supporters from 1843 to 1892, shows how the group defined and addressed this reading public. In the early years the journal's editors were clergymen and Yale professors. From 1848 on, Yale professors increasingly dominated the editorial board, and the *New Englander*'s close relationship with Yale became more explicit. In 1885 it became the *New Englander and Yale Review,* and each issue carried a section called "University Topics."[32]

Despite these changes, the purpose of the journal remained the same throughout its forty-nine years of publication. The editors tried to make the *New Englander* a popular journal, that is, a journal for all educated men. *Popular* meant appealing to "intelligent Christian men" "in every profession and position" who were the leaders of their communities. An editor advised a potential contributor to see himself as either a "wise man" giving advice to "the selectmen of a town" or a commissioner advising "the people of a district."[33]

The content of a popular journal informed "Christian citizens" on all the subjects that concerned them. The editors said that they would not conduct doctrinal debates, which would have split evangelical unity, or print any articles of interest exclusively to ministers and theological students, which would have bored the layman. *New Englander* articles would have a religious but nonsectarian point of view. The journal also did not appeal to a single interest, such as antislavery, or to men in a single role, such as fathers. The six to eight articles in each issue reviewed current books in the fields of politics, economics, current literature, and scholarly developments.[34]

The *New Englander* gave the scholars an opportunity to address subjects outside their disciplines and to apply New Haven ideas to current events. Fisher applied historical criticism in his review of Harriet Beecher Stowe's *Dred,* and he presented a historically based theory of rights to argue that freedmen should not receive the vote. Porter used his understanding of the implications of positivistic social science to reveal that a materialistic ethical system motivated the characters of popular novels.[35] The *New Englander* also gave Woolsey, Fisher, and Hoppin, whose disciplines did not have journals, an outlet for their work. It published Woolsey's essays on international law, Fisher's essays on Biblical history, and Hoppin's art criticism. Philologist Whitney, for example, whose discipline had a journal, published his comparison of Confucian and Christian ethics in the *New Englander* but placed his discussion of the accent in Sanskrit in the *Transactions of the American Philological Association.*[36]

In sum, the *New Englander* was a how-to manual for educated male Congregationalists, who learned how they could be godly while participating fully in American life. The review introduced ideas from the cosmopolitan world of German, English, and French universities and assured its pious readers that this world contained believers and that advances in learning were not exclusively atheistic. An editors' note in 1857 suggested that "Christian readers" should "rise above the habits of a national or provincial theology, and . . . become freely and fearlessly acquainted with the modes of thought that prevail among devout and learned men in other lands and of other languages." Other articles analyzed new works by authors such as Americans Emerson and Theodore Parker and British authors Thomas Carlyle, John Stuart Mill, Matthew Arnold, and Herbert Spencer. Reviewers showed what readers could learn from these thinkers but cautioned when assumptions and hypotheses differed from New Haven ideas.[37] Following New Haven ideas, readers could perceive the world in Christian terms. A sort of postgraduate course, the *New Englander* continued the lessons that the New Haven group offered at Yale College. Thus, comparison of the *New Englander* with its predecessor and its successor can illustrate significant differences between the Yale College of the New Haven scholars, the Yale of the 1828 Yale Report, and Yale as a modern university.

The predecessor to the *New Englander* was the *Quarterly Christian Spectator* (1819–38), which Nathaniel William Taylor and his supporters owned and edited. From this platform they propounded their system of evangelical Congregationalism, the New Haven theology, which stressed human ability to attain individual salvation. The Taylorites also used their journal to respond to charges of more theologically conservative Presbyterians and Congregationalists who accused the Taylorites of heresy. The Taylorites tried to explain why their theology should commend itself to educated men, especially those who were deserting their inherited Congregationalism for Unitarianism or Episcopalianism. Coverage of current events in the *Quarterly Christian Spectator* comprised accounts of missionary activities, revivals, and the lives of pious Christians—all news of interest to evangelicals. Reports of cultural events appeared infrequently; reviewers warned readers against the theater and the novel, recommending instead the poetry and essays of English authors such as Dryden and Pope.[38]

As the middle generation, *New Englander* editors were more secular than their predecessors. Instead of warning readers about new cultural and literary developments, they put those developments under a religious canopy of meaning. The *New Englander* was filled with reviews of current books in science, politics, and scholarly affairs. These reviews connected readers with a network of European and American scholars based in colleges and universities, whereas the *Quarterly Christian Spectator* belonged to the transatlantic evangelical connection.

The successors of the New Haven scholars, the editors of the *Yale Review* (1892–1911), said that their journal promoted "the advancement of sound learning" and spoke for "no party" and "no school." The editors promised to "present the results of scientific and scholarly investigation and political science." The first issue contained articles on the current economic and political issues—

the remonetization of silver, the Standard Oil Trust, German tariff policy, price regulation, the relationship between ethics and political science, trade unions, and a historical study of a New England town.[39]

The three generations of editors shared certain characteristics that make the differences between their journals even more striking. All three generations were Congregationalists and, with few exceptions, Yale graduates. Thus, the editors of the *Christian Spectator* were among the teachers of the *New Englander* editors, just as the *New Englander* editors taught the *Yale Review* editors. The second and third generations, however, gave Congregationalism specifically and religion in general a successively less visible place in their journals. The *Christian Spectator* drew upon religion for its subject matter and test of truth. The *Yale Review* replaced religious truth with conclusions from "scholarly and scientific" investigation. The scope of the journals changed too—from comprehension of all the affairs of Christian gentlemen to inclusion of only those issues that interested men in their role as public citizens. *Yale Review* editors thought that social-science articles could produce a consensus among educated men; *New Englander* editors assumed that New Haven scholarship could produce the same result; and the Taylorites hoped to win all educated men to New Haven theology. *Yale Review* editors continued their predecessors' purpose of influencing the educated few but dismissed religious faith as irrelevant to this purpose and excluded the religious values that the New Haven scholars thought were the essence of practicality.

The different ways in which the editors treated the issue of Puritanism illustrate this successive bracketing of religious belief and faith. For the Taylorites, Puritanism was a matter for theological debate on questions of human will and ability. At one extreme, when Taylor modified doctrine to allow for ability, the theologically more conservative Bennet Tyler took exception and started a rival seminary to counter the influence of Taylor's Yale. At the other extreme, Unitarians found the New Haven theology insufficiently liberal. Charges and countercharges between Boston and New Haven engendered bitter feelings. On his deathbed, a principal of the *Christian Spectator* regretted these polemical exchanges and said "that sometimes an unwise course had been pursued toward the Unitarians, that they were in error and did not see some truths so clearly as we might desire, yet great allowances were to be made for their prepossessions and education." Writers for the *New Englander* avoided factionalizing doctrinal questions altogether and sought unity among Protestants by considering Puritanism as a historical problem. Fisher, for instance, denied the charge of Catholic historians that the Reformation had given rise to the excesses of the French Revolution and argued instead that it contained seeds for democratic achievements. This stance permitted the New Haven group to share a sense of purpose with other ministers and college professors who had been influenced by German idealism and historical approaches to Biblical criticism. Philip Schaff, of the German Reformed seminary at Mercersburg, for instance, wrote a *New Englander* editor that his journal was "liberal" and would have influence on the salvation of the country, unlike Boston publications such as the *Recorder* and *Observatory,* which still propounded "Puritanism." Writers for the *Yale Review* avoided religious polemics altogether and treated New England religion as a subject for historical consideration. In the first volume, Williston Walker, a German-trained doctor of philosophy who taught at the Hartford Theological Seminary and later succeeded Fisher as American church historian at Yale Divinity School, discussed why Massachusetts had no Saybrook Platform and reviewed Charles Francis Adams's study of Quincy, Massachusetts.[40] From the *Christian Spectator* to the *Yale Review,* scholarship provided a new basis for unity among educated men.

These three generations of Yale professors and editors rejected certain of their teachers' lessons while retaining and developing others. The New Haven scholars abandoned their teachers' ministerial stance. They adopted the conventions of scholarship and used German idealism to modify the Scottish philosophy in order to bring about the same evangelical future that their teachers had hoped for. The *Yale Review* editors laid aside these evangelical hopes while carrying forward *their* teachers' respect for scholarship and the findings of empirical research. Each generation assumed that it had an audience among educated elites, but each generation adopted a progressively less religious and more secular strategy for reaching that elite.[41] The New Haven scholar stood between Nathaniel William Taylor and his theology and the social scientist of the *Yale Review*.

The Progressive idea that scholars could serve their society through application of research to social and political problems, an idea embodied in the career of political scientist Charles Merriam, had one of its origins in the way that the New Haven scholars thought about their profession and its usefulness.[42] The scholars did not choose vocational role models from among the professors who had taught them in Germany. Instead they chose Thomas Arnold and Barthold Georg Niebuhr, men known for their evangelical faith, contributions to scholarship, and public activism. Niebuhr's history of Rome introduced the critical evaluation of sources as a historical method, and Arnold's *History of the Later Roman Commonwealth* (1838–42) brought this method into English historiography. Arnold's career explicitly showed how a teacher and author could influence the educated few and so influence history. As headmaster of Rugby, Arnold taught his students that their lives had consequence, that they could influence men to lead better, more godly lives. His later pamphlets on English social problems explained that the cause was the rich who were avoiding their responsibility to the poor. He urged all men to realize their responsibility to their fellow men and to activate the "Christian spirit" so that England would become a "Christian kingdom."[43]

The scholar, although wielding influence as a teacher, also intervened in public events. When Porter was a young man, he was full of enthusiasm for the democratic revolutions of the 1840s, and he imagined that the scholar could articulate the inchoate hopes of the people. The scholar wrote "a few words of power" that declared "the thought that every man has been thinking, but which till now, no one has fitly spoken; arguments concerning the rights of the citizen or Christian, which everyone has felt were convincing, but which no one has shown to be true; a people's glowing and fury which seem to gather and concentrate the fire that has been burning in ten thousand hearts, into one burning tongue of flame." The scholar had this power because he could marshal all "the splendor and the force" of human language. When Porter was middle-aged, he began to complain of the scholar's isolation. At his most optimistic, Porter could say merely that the scholar had to live in a world of his own but be "contented with that world . . . satisfied with the supposed satisfaction which it imparts." Porter's younger colleague Fisher interpreted this isolation from practical life as an advantage. From an "elevated point of view," the scholar could judge "the turmoil of practical life" with detachment. So by the 1880s, Porter's optimistic view that the scholar could and should express the will of the people had given way to Fisher's new notion that the knowledge of the scholar corrected the lessons that people learned from participation in events. Fisher's scholar bore in mind "the experiences of mankind, the analogies of history" which served "as aids to the silent drift which the busy actors are apt of overlook."[44] From Porter's youthful enthusiasm to Fisher's dispassionate analysis, the scholar as common man had become the scholar as expert.

Despite Fisher's and Porter's different emphases, they and the other New Haven scholars looked to Theodore Dwight Woolsey as an exemplary scholar. His career stood as "a signal example of the dignity, as well as the usefulness of a purely academic career."[45] During his career, Woolsey was a Yale professor and president (1846–71). His *Introduction to International Law* and *Political Science* (1877) were contributions to scholarship and attempts to educate the vital few. He also applied his ideas to current events when he helped arbitrate the U.S. naval claims against Britain after the Civil War, and he served the liberal Republican cause during the 1870s. In addition he wrote two books that specifically addressed current social issues, *Divorce and Divorce Legislation, especially in the United States* (1869) and *Communism and Socialism in Their History and Theory . . .* (1880). Because of his political involvement and timely concerns, Woolsey seems to resemble the Progressive disinterested expert. Yet Woolsey's definition of the useful scholar is far different from the politically involved Charles Merriam, who brought social science to the service of government through the Social Science Research Council. Woolsey's overriding purposes were religious: he hoped to reveal how different theories produced conditions that undermined evangelical hopes. For example, he argued that Rousseau's social-contract theory and communism each gave rise to a totalitarian state that deprived people of the freedom necessary for them to bring about the millennium.

The other New Haven scholars shared Woolsey's concerns and, as academic specialists, tried to correct false and evangelically counterproductive theories in their disciplines. In psychology, Porter attempted to refute the theories of John Stuart Mill, Alexander Bain, and other scientists who argued that human behavior resulted from the automatic response of the mind to external or physical stimuli. Porter thought that these theories denied free will and argued instead that people could act as they wished and make their world a better place. In church history and Biblical criticism, Fisher disputed the claims of the Tübingen school. Whereas David Frederic Strauss argued that New Testament miracles were myths and Ferdinand Baur disputed the historical accuracy of the first four gospels, Fisher maintained that the New Testament was a historically true account of miracles that were actual historical events. Although philologist Whitney rebuked scholars who used their

knowledge to confirm or deny religious and scientific theories—
such as Darwin, for his explanation of the origin of species or
Adam and Eve as the parents of the entire human race—he did
use his knowledge of philology to argue for beliefs consistent with
religiously based New Haven values. For example, he said that
philology proved that human beings had a social nature. This fact,
he stated, refuted the social-contract theory because it proved that
the state of nature upon which the theory rested had to be a man-
made myth.[46]

All the New Haven scholars were combating what they called
the New Infidelity found in contemporary literature, political theory, history, natural science, and psychology. This infidelity replaced both "the railing" against religion that Timothy Dwight
deplored in Thomas Paine's *Age of Reason* and the errors that
Taylor's generation of ministers found in the doctrines of Unitarians, Episcopalians, and rival Congregationalist sects. Now "infidelity appears in better dress and in better company than of old,"
Fisher wrote. "It takes on the function of the educator and social
reformer; it prefers a compromise with Christianity to a noisy
crusade against it; but the half friendly attitude it assumes may
render the task of exposing it all the more difficult."[47] The New
Haven scholars assumed the responsibility of exposing it and assumed that their scholarship gave them power to recognize the
atheistic implications of theories that appeared in secular guises.
In this new battle, the college had replaced the church; professors,
ministers; and college students and educated readers, congregations. To prepare for the millennium the New Haven scholars had
a defensive and offensive strategy: they refuted wrong ideas that
men might encounter, educated men who supposedly would be
receptive to right ideas, and hoped that their right thinking would
correct public opinion. Scholarship, books, and the college promised that New Haven religious beliefs and values would prevail;
voices that unknowingly popularized atheistic and antievangelical
messages would not gain cultural authority. Belief in the power
of ideas was at the heart of the New Haven scholars' activism.
Their scholar neither manned the barricades nor wrote for a mass
popular audience. His public service consisted in putting New
Haven ideas into circulation among the educated few.

Unlike Emerson, who saw the scholar as a rebel from both old
ways of thinking and established institutions, New Haven scholars
sought new means to make their traditional faith apply to the
future. Practically this meant the combination of the German craft

of scholarship with an evangelical vision of scholarly vocation. Yet their vision depended on the education of the few; it was not the vision of an evangelical preacher such as Lyman Beecher, who sought to convert the many. The New Haven scholars perceived that the college offered them a receptive audience of a few men whose ideas would then influence the many. Thus they sought to reform Yale College.

4
The College, the Scholar, and the Liberal Man

"It is necessary that it should be a school of Christian gentlemen."

Thomas Arnold of Rugby

The college promised a means for the New Haven scholars to reform American society. Among his colleagues Noah Porter gave this theme its fullest development. He proposed that the college could produce men who would be agents of social reform and that through these men the New Haven scholars would influence society. To the Yale-educated few, the New Haven scholars imparted an understanding of the past and so ensured that its traditions would shape the future. Porter predicted: "The higher education in mastering the past and sympathizing with the present, *will wisely forecast and direct the future.* The men whom it trains are men of the future, and to a large extent have the future of the country in their hands. Hence the relations of this education to the future take up into themselves and control its relations to the present and the past."[1]

College presidents inaugurated during the third quarter of the nineteenth century shared Porter's vision of the college as an institution that promoted social reform. Charles W. Eliot at Harvard, James McCosh at Princeton, and James Burrill Angell at Michigan also thought that the college could solve social problems arising from the rule of materialistic values over public life and the cultural fragmentation caused by religious sectarianism and partisanship. Typical of this consensus was Porter's complaint that "plenty of cheap glitter, of tawdry bedizenment and showy accomplishments; plenty of sensational declamation, coarse argument, and facile rhetoric; much moral earnestness which needs tolerance and knowledge, and religious fervor which runs into dogmatism and rant" suffused American life. Porter and other educators looked to college-educated men to heal these sores. College had cultivated and refined their moral nature and freed them from narrow, bigoted, and selfish interests. These men would be independents in politics, religion, and career.[2]

The college presidents disagreed, however, over the means that the college might employ to make a man cultured or liberal. Eliot proposed the elective system and abolition of Greek and Latin as required courses for undergraduates. At Cornell, students could earn a bachelor of arts degree after studying a so-called modern curriculum, which substituted modern languages for instruction in Greek and Latin. And it was a general complaint that colleges should offer a more practical (what we could call preprofessional) education. Porter contended that only colleges maintaining a required curriculum, study of classical literature, and required chapel and church could produce truly liberal men. To become cultured, and therefore liberal, students had to read extensively rather than specifically in an elected discipline, and learn how to think historically rather than scientifically. Extensive reading and historical thinking formed the basis of what Porter called "Christian culture."[3]

Porter's evangelical commitment and vision of an educated elite's leadership role were at the root of his disagreement with his fellow college presidents. According to Porter and his New Haven colleagues, this elite led through moral example and by providing a source of religiously based right ideas. Because the scholars started from an organic conception of society, they saw the college and an educated elite as bound up in the life of society in the fullest sense. In their opinion, practical education in Charles William Eliot's sense could not satisfy this deep social need. Exponents of practical education did not share the New Haven social vision and thus the sense of a college as embedded in social life. Instead, the vision of practical education implied that specifically trained professionals could serve society. Popular literature in the post–Civil War period pictured religion as irrelevant if not destructive to scholarly and professional life. Many educated Americans typed the religious man as either a sentimentalist, ruled by his heart, or a coldly logical theologian, ruled by his head. Religion seemed to be an accessory to life and, if brought to the center of public life, a force capable of dividing educated men. At Harvard, Eliot made religious services voluntary. At The Johns Hopkins University,

Gilman took care that religious sectarianism should neither divide academic life nor separate the college from the Baltimore community.[4]

For the New Haven scholars and educated readers in Britain and America, Matthew Arnold made the classic statement of the antagonism between religion and culture in his *Culture and Anarchy* (1869). Arnold associated narrow, illiberal cultural tendencies with religion and called them "Hebraic." He embraced what he called the "Hellenic impulse," which cultivated both aesthetic and intellectual natures. Arnold's Hellenism was a secular ideal that promised renovation of the life of the individual and the nation. For Arnold, *culture* referred to a secular process of human development resulting from study of, in his now classic formulation, "the best which has been thought and said."[5]

In response to Arnold's indictment of religious belief as narrow and Hebraic, the New Haven scholars defended their faith and educational ideals. They conceded that their Puritan ancestors had at times been Hebraic but insisted that New Haven religious belief now promoted self-development. Individuals could realize their full development, religion could unite all men in religious faith and intellectual conviction, and national life could become whole.[6]

Porter responded to Arnold's charges in an address delivered at Wellesley College in 1880. He argued for the New Haven middle way between extremes of sectarian dogmatism and liberal culture as a secular ideal. Porter denied that the religion he spoke for led to extremism, sectarianism, or competition among "rival houses of worship." These problems originated in the provincial village church, which discouraged liberal views with "its hard and scholastic statements of doctrine; . . . its narrow judgments of character; . . . its scrimping parsimony in some directions and criminal luxury in others; . . . the tenacity with which it adheres to old errors, and the credulity with which it runs after the latest sensationalism." In the college were none of these irrational extremes, for it was the home of a liberalizing religion. Students met the true God, the Christ of history, who was the heart of a nonsectarian, nondogmatic religion capable of uniting all educated men. Not Hebraic, this religion drew on knowledge from all fields. The relationship between religion and knowledge was symbiotic. Learning could reveal the full effect of Christianity on an individual, and only an individual with great knowledge could fully understand the ideal of Christianity. For Porter, the liberalizing effects of study "of the best" in art and literature did not occur automatically but

depended on religious values. Christianity and a Christian education alone could satisfy "the nobler capacities of man" and "the
severer judgment of God."[7] Art and literature had the power to
liberalize men only when they were studied from a New Haven
perspective.

Science, too, provided an inadequate educational rationale and
an insufficient source of values. Scientists who did not bring religious values to their work could know merely facts about this
world. This single-minded pursuit would make professors and their
students into egoists, who no longer had the essential scholarly
quality, "the docility of the child." Cut off from God's truth, scientists and their students would think of themselves as the creators
of truth. Only religion provided scholars and students with "a
resource of creative energy." Science, with its "atheistic tendencies," and modern culture, with its "frivolous but decorous tem-
per," threatened, Porter concluded, to "dry into barrenness and
comparative impotence the youth of any college in which they
should rule."[8]

Porter's Christian college stood at the threshold to a cosmopolitan world of ideas and guaranteed continuity between it and
the world of traditional family- and community-based values. Porter assumed that college-bound students came from families whose
love, examples, and simple teachings had instilled religious faith.
Having no intellectual basis, this automatically learned faith was
vulnerable to potentially atheistic ideas found in contemporary
thought. The college safely introduced its students to the works
of John Stuart Mill, Herbert Spencer, and Charles Darwin and
provided protection against undesirable messages.[9] A rite of passage, college marked the transition from childhood to adulthood,
from a traditional world of parents and village to a world of modern
thought with its basis in European and American colleges and
universities. Religious faith infused both worlds, but college students had armed themselves with a more profound understanding
of their faith than they had commanded as children.

Porter likened the college to a "fusing crucible," into which
students threw their traditional beliefs. There they mixed with
ideas from the fields of history, philosophy, literature, and science.
The result was an amalgam that he described in almost mystical
terms. Some students chose to refuse the product and saw it as
"worthless dross or base alloy." But those who reaccepted their
traditional faith found that it leaped "forth in purer metal and
brighter luster." Besides ensuring continuity, the process guar-

anteed wholeness of values in adult life, for the college graduate
had no "chasm between his practical and intellectual life."[10] Because of his own and his colleagues' experiences, Porter knew that
this process worked. They had brought their religious faith to
college, where the new thought of the 1830s, German idealism,
had challenged it. In response, they had discovered a historical
way of thinking and the understanding that religious faith was based
on an inherent need for God. This result was practical insofar as
it furnished the New Haven scholars with means to interpret their
world.

In the early twentieth century, cultural critics such as Van Wyck
Brooks disdained a theocentric world view, criticized the gentility
of their nineteenth-century predecessors, and redefined practical
education to mean one that prepared students to understand social
and economic facts. Then Porter's interpretation of the liberal arts
college seemed but an astute analysis of why this college was a
socially irrelevant institution. For example, Brooks accused nineteenth-century educators of perpetuating two irreconcilable worlds,
one with practically based values and the other with theoretically
based ones. He proposed that socialism could heal this split.[11] For
Porter, Christianity had no secular substitute. Education in a Christian college assured that men would have the one value system
that could guide public and private lives.

Porter's comparision of the college to a "fusing crucible" that
prepared young men for manhood suggests that the college could
restore tribelike cohesion. The college resembled the place, and
its education the ritual process, which prepared young men of
primitive tribes for manhood. In this rite, young boys left their
families' homes and entered a special isolated hut. There priests
and honored men of the tribe took charge. They performed the
circumcision rite and, while the wounds healed, recounted the lore
of the tribe. Then a priest delivered a final lecture that advised
initiates on their duties as men and warned them against temptations that they would encounter. Circumcision had symbolically
opened the boys to their elders' lessons, and the wounds' healing
symbolized the initiates' assimilation of their elders' knowledge
and entry into the moral world of men.[12]

Like the primitive tribe, the college prepared its students for
manhood by means of a patterned ritual. It included the prescribed
curriculum, religious practice, and the community life among the
students. The curriculum first opened the mind and rendered it

susceptible to the view of the world that professors would teach. During the first two years at Yale, study of mathematics, Greek, and Latin made students' minds receptive. In the third year, courses in natural philosophy, physics, and astronomy began to reveal the natural world. In the senior year, professors imparted their vision of a moral, natural world through courses in chemistry, geology, anatomy, and physiology. Seniors also learned that the world was moral in courses on the history of philosophy, mental and moral philosophy, natural theology, evidences of Christianity, American and English constitutional law, and political and social science.[13] The final lesson was the baccalaureate sermon, which instructed the graduating seniors on their duties and cautioned them about the particular temptations that the New Haven scholars perceived in their contemporary world. Theoretically the college ritual had promoted self-development. Graduates were expected to be liberal men who would eschew materialism and the atheism implicit in contemporary ideas. These were men prepared for the modern world, not merely for careers. This is what Porter meant when he said that college graduates had acquired "not erudition, so much as culture; not facts, not reflection, not feats of memory, not even the mechanical mastery of abstraction, but the power of subtle and ready thought, and of apt and finished expression."[14]

Just as the social life of the initiation lodge was an informal but vital part of the primitive ritual, so college life complemented the curriculum. College theoretically was the student's first experience with life beyond his family's control. Porter said that its rules replaced "the public opinion of the little community which has hitherto formed [the student's] aspirations and his hopes, his principles and his prejudices." The college, like any community, contained a variety of men. Some achieved eminence for scholarly ability, while others became known for their wit or their way with the "ladies." But unlike natural communities, the college gave young men the experience of living in a community where men valued men for their real worth; nowhere else "are the factitious distinctions of life, as of wealth, birth, and manners, of so little account in comparison with intellect, generosity, and openheartedness. In none do the rich and poor meet together on terms more honorable to the rich and more acceptable to the poor, than on the arena dignified by the presence of earnest intellectual labor, and cheered by the sunshine of youthful generosity." Friendships and acquaintances provided types, or lessons, that the student could use after college. "Its loves and its hatreds, its triumphs and defeats," Porter said, "are those by which he ever afterwards reads and interprets society and literature, politics and history."[15]

Religious faith and practice also guaranteed that the college would be an institution of self-development. Public observance included the daily worship service led by the president. It symbolized and reaffirmed the connection between faith and learning, as it made manifest the act that students and faculty were all men before God. Christianity was a force in students' private lives as well. Its ethical precepts allowed students to monitor their own behavior and inspired them to study industriously. Further, Christianity gave the curriculum its common purpose, for all disciplines testified to divine truth. Because the Christian scholar knew that his discipline never could reveal the fullness of divine truth, he never became one-sided or arrogant in his knowledge. Commitment to Christian truth knit scholars in all disciplines into a corporate whole and united students and faculty. No single value system, such as knowledge for its own sake, separated the Christian college from the world; the college community shared Christian faith with men and women in everyday, nonacademic lives. Thus, merely the two specialized functions of the college distinguished it from other social institutions: it both prepared young men for the contemporary world of ideas and action and provided a home for scholars, with their specialized means of perceiving divine truth.[16]

To transform the college into their ideal institution, the New Haven scholars had to reform the college of mental discipline, which they had inherited from their teachers, the authors of the Yale Report. The New Haven college reforms fit into a historical context when we remember the close friendship of Porter and Horace Bushnell. In the antebellum period, each man found American society wanting. Porter observed "the trickery of business, the jobbing of politicians, the slang of newspapers, the vulgarity of fashion, the sensationalism of popular books, [and] the shallowness and cant that dishonor the pulpit and defile worship." Looking beyond the doctrinal debates dividing American Protestants, each friend searched for a religious faith that Christians shared and for institutions untainted by sectarianism or episodic emotionalism. Their training in the moral-government theory of the Scottish philosophy and Nathaniel Taylor suggested that the church was just one among many institutions, including government, the family, and schools, that God had established for the purpose of nurturing his people. To Bushnell the family, and to

Porter the college, appeared as an institution organically connected
to the life of the nation and able to secure evangelical progress.
Bushnell rethought the relationship of the family to children's
religious development in his famous *Christian Nurture,* and Porter
saw the college completing the religious education that Bushnell's
ideal family had begun.[17]

Reform of Yale into a college of Christian nurture may also be
seen as part of a larger trend among New England colleges. Historian David Allmendinger explains that in the antebellum years
colleges ceased trying to govern all aspects of students' lives and
began to use academic measures as disciplinary levers. Either a
student performed adequately in the classroom or he was dismissed. Allmendinger attributes this change to an awareness among
college authorities that revivals no longer were effective means of
maintaining order.[18] Among the New Haven group, we have seen,
questions arose about the efficacy of revivals, but this questioning
did not stem from their experiences as teachers or college admin-
istrators. Rather, these men objected to revivals—and specifically
to college revivals—because of their experiences as students and
their perspective as liberal evangelicals. As students they had been
deeply disturbed by the college of mental discipline. Its curriculum
had taught merely the intellectual foundations of religion and had
left some students unsatisfied, while extracurricular college revivals
had won some students' hearts and offended others. To end this
split between head and heart, curriculum and extracurricular revivals, the New Haven scholars discouraged college revivals as
means of securing faith and used their scholarship to transform
the curriculum so that it would embrace all students in Christian
nurture.

Thus, the purpose of Christian nurture guided the New Haven
scholars as they reformed Yale from 1846 until the mid-1880s.
In describing the history of Yale during these years, historians
George Wilson Pierson and Brooks Mather Kelley recognize only
those changes that they see as progress toward Yale's evolution
into a modern university in the first years of the twentieth century.
These changes include: the introduction of history and political
science as new courses, the development of a graduate department,
the granting of the first American Ph.D. degree (1861), and the
founding of the Yale School of Fine Arts (1869). In fact these
changes and others in the *substance* and *style* of education were the
New Haven scholars' attempts to make their ideal college a reality.[19]
Consequently, the New Haven scholars tried to reform the teach-

ing of Latin and Greek, to reconceive the purpose of the recitation method of instruction, and to reform the vocation of college professor.

Porter's lifelong friend and colleague at Yale Theodore Dwight Woolsey announced the beginning of these reforms in his 1846 inaugural address. Departing from the goals of the 1828 Yale Report, President Woolsey argued that college should develop students toward true freedom and wholeness. This new idea supplied a middle way between two imperfect religious ideals—the do-gooding Arminian, who paid little attention to self-improvement, and the ascetic antinomian, who ignored his social responsibility. Woolsey's college promised that the student could undergo a renovation of self more complete and long lasting than the psychic cataclysm of Taylor's and Beecher's revivals.[20]

Woolsey's reference to "true freedom" and "wholeness" showed his adoption of an imported educational ideal. He and his colleagues learned it from German evangelical humanistic philosophers and philologists, such as August Boeckh, at the University of Berlin. These German humanists taught that the uncorrupted text gave access to the spiritual achievements of classical civilization.[21] Historians of German intellectual life describe the resulting ideal as self-development (*Bildung*)—inner growth achieved through "full and harmonious training" provided by a curriculum of mathematics, classical languages, and history. Students' natural faculties developed until they reached a "stage of completeness or wholeness" that signaled their having become new men.[22] The crux of this education was study of the human spirit or creative nature as it had expressed itself in the past. *Bildung* suggested to the New Haven scholars how they might transform Yale College into a nurturing institution. The goal of self-development thus influenced what subjects the scholars thought should be in the curriculum and how they thought each subject should be defined.

History, philosophy, literature, and politics now appeared as the proper center of the curriculum, for they were "the fountains from which cultivation is to be derived." These subjects gave students role models and taught the rules by which men lived. Self-development united these subjects; they were not divided, in the modern sense, between the social sciences and liberal arts, because all these subjects concerned the study of man. If, however, history became the mere study of "mechanical masses" or historical forces, then it no longer promoted self-development.[23] Thus the scholars saw some courses as more valuable than others. Although all courses testified to universal truth, only some courses promoted self-development. Consequently, study of natural sciences and mathematics now was of less educational value than study of history, literature, philosophy, and politics. In contrast, in the college of mental discipline all courses had testified to divine truth and trained the intellect. Self-development thus did not provide a comprehensive rationale for the college curriculum and in fact destroyed its previous unity. In the mid-nineteenth century the demise of the college curriculum unified in purpose did not await the advent of social-science courses but began with the reform efforts of the New Haven scholars.[24]

Study of Greek literature promised knowledge of Greek civilization, the major source of self-development. As advocates of classical study, the New Haven men imagined an ideal Greek who was a prototype for their liberal man, and they saw Greek civilization as the birthplace of modern ideas. Fisher argued that there was a "genetic connection" between Greek "literature, philosophy, ethics, and jurisprudence" and those of modern civilization. Greek civilization promised negative examples as well. Porter observed that students would learn about modern materialism and spiritualism in Greek literature, since these modern phenomena merely repeated the errors of the Epicureans or "the mythical constructions of Plato."[25]

In Greek literature, students found the most liberalizing lessons. In Greek classics they could discover a model man who was "always intellectual, impressive, and intelligible, because he is the perfection of the natural and earthly in its purest and noblest manifestations." Students of modern literature never benefited from this lesson, for they met only models of imperfect modern men and so could not enlarge their "conceptions of the forms which humanity may assume." The model Greek found in literature taught by correcting nineteenth-century men's "special defects of thought, of sentiment, and of action, by the clear rationalism, the simple emotion, the manly behavior which it always sets forth. It even preserves us against its own peculiar errors by the very distinctiveness with which it avows them, and the consistent energy by which it acts them out."[26] Whereas the scholars' teachers had emphasized that study of Greek grammar had provided an unparalleled source of mental discipline and formed the basis for the command of modern languages, they viewed study of the Greek language as less important than study of literature, for the latter was a means to self-development.

The New Haven scholars' evocation of Greek as a source of cultivation is another example of their taking the middle way. At one extreme, Eliot abolished Greek and Latin as required courses at Harvard and denied that classical languages had any special power to impart liberal culture. At the opposite extreme are the concerns of the six Presbyterian ministers and six laymen who served in 1853 on the board of trustees of recently founded Westminster College in western Pennsylvania. To promote the college's purpose of "mental and moral training," its faculty proposed a course of study that the trustees accepted "with the understanding that the expurgated editions of the heathen Classicks be read."[27]

As a source of self-development, the teacher was as important as the subject, for he was a living role model. Porter probably drew this idea from the writings of Thomas Arnold, the English evangelical educator and historian, whose *Life and Correspondence* his friend Henry Barnard (Yale, 1830) had lent him in 1845. Arnold's *Life* had an immediate, powerful impact on Porter, who read the book intensively, repeatedly consulting it for inspiration. In 1847 Porter wrote a strongly favorable review of the *Life* for the *New Englander,* and in 1870 he drew the epigraph of his *American Colleges* from it. Arnold inspired a style of teaching that historian Sheldon Rothblatt calls "saintly" or "Christian." The saintly teacher made loyalty to him, not impersonal rules, the force behind college discipline. Because the force of this system derived from the words and example of the teacher, he may be said to have had charismatic power. He wanted to capture students' minds so that he could shape their character. This teacher had power, Porter explained, to "reach the inner life of the pupil by what he says and does, as no other person can."[28]

The recitation method of teaching allowed the saintly professor to exercise personal influence. A give-and-take occurred as the student prepared passages from the assigned text for the instructor's in-class examination of him. Measured in terms of their contribution to self-development, the benefits of the recitation, Porter found, often exceeded the value of the information imparted. The relationship between student and professor enabled each to appreciate the other's mind. The bond between them included mutual affection, from which friendship might blossom, making "real the ideal of friendly guidance on the one hand and of grateful docility on the other." In contrast, the lecture was a one-dimensional, one-way teaching method that required students to take notes passively and merely to memorize their contents.[29]

Through students and research, college professors had two means of influencing national life. Students learned what made past civilizations imperfect or successful, and professors ensured that these lessons would be applied when they gave examples of how the past influenced the present. Professors sent their students forth, Porter envisioned, to "mingle in the concerns of life," to act as a leaven in the life of the nation. The influence of college graduates served to "soften our controversies and dignify our discussions, refine upon our vulgarities and introduce amenities into our social life."[30]

The college professor also contributed to national self-development in his role as researcher; his advances in scholarship balanced the expansion of the American economy. The New Haven scholars imagined national development in much the same way as they imagined individual development. Like the student who developed his moral, intellectual, and aesthetic nature until he became liberal or whole, the nation that developed both its material and its intellectual sides became whole and capable of true freedom. Whereas in 1846 Woolsey had thought of culture exclusively in terms of individual self-development and had conceived of a cultured nation as merely the sum of its liberal citizens, now in 1871 Porter considered individual and national self-development separately. Going beyond Woolsey, he thought of a fully cultured nation as an institutional entity.

Yet, in the mid-nineteenth century it was not certain that the college was or should be the exclusive home of learning. On the negative side, the scholars' own experiences as Yale professors showed that teaching and college duties often left little time for anything else. Like Porter in the 1850s, a professor tied to teaching but trying to write often was left in a state of nervous exhaustion.[31] On the positive side, the scholars' situation in New Haven showed that a college could provide a home for a community of men whose shared commitments inspired intellectual endeavor. Still, challenges to the college came from several directions. In "The American Scholar" Emerson implicitly rejected the college and looked to a vocation of solitary thought. Other nonacademics such as John Stuart Mill attempted to refute ways of thinking, such as the Scottish philosophy, upon which most colleges based their ways. Even though they often were allies of the college against theorists like Mill, museums, historical societies, and lyceums claimed equal status with the college as homes of learning. The college thus had no automatic title to preeminence. To assert its claim, the New Haven scholars had first to establish the authority of the university-trained scholar and his scholarship and then to show that only the college could be his home.

In his 1871 inaugural address, Porter set forth the reasons that the college should have claim to the first rank. He drew on his colleagues' and his experiences in New Haven and at Yale and attempted to integrate his understanding of the new demands of scholarship with the idea of education as culture, which Woolsey had introduced twenty-five years before. *"For the general culture of the country,"* Porter argued, it was obvious *"that our colleges should be seats of learning."* Although historical and scientific societies did advance learning, they were adequate only "for the special or the occasional student." In other matters these organizations deferred to colleges and universities, depending on them "for support" and referring "to them as authorities." Among learned institutions, only colleges could support the full-time, professional scholar who devoted his energies to "the twofold activity of acquiring and imparting" knowledge. In a college he found an ideal setting for his work. He had colleagues to provide intellectual stimulation, as well as "the sense of responsibility and of social excitement which are essential to the highest success." Even more, the college should and could provide the scholar with all the resources that his research required, such as first-rate libraries, collections of art, and specimens from natural science. The college-based scholar had to have time for his work; so Porter recommended that a senior professor be allowed to teach less and that graduate fellowships supply both a continuous supply of apprentice scholars and the staff to discipline undergraduates. Porter wanted to bring to Yale the example that he had seen or knew existed in Germany, that of eminent professors such as Boeckh and Ranke, who went "from the lecture-room to the study to prosecute the researches which have made them authorities in the world of learning and lights to mankind." For Porter, the charismatic teacher who contributed to the self-development of his students and the scholar committed to furthering research could be the same person. A home of teaching and scholarship, the Christian college promoted "the organized and persistent pursuit of science and learning." Its professors moved "hopefully and eagerly forward, to greet every new discovery, to welcome every new truth, and to add to past contributions by new experiments, invention, and thought."[32]

This close look at Noah Porter's idea of the Christian college reveals that in the nineteenth century, at least at Yale, the modern university did not immediately succeed the college of mental discipline. Instead, higher education in the nineteenth century may be divided into three periods: the college of mental discipline (1795–1846), the Christian college of the New Haven scholars (1846–83), and then the modern university. In this scheme, the college of mental discipline belongs more to that period of intellectual history identified by Henry May as the Didactic Enlightenment, and the New Haven scholars' Yale belongs more to the Romantically influenced mid-nineteenth century.[33]

Although historians have not noted the college reforms of the New Haven scholars, their contemporaries and former students did. Timothy Dwight the younger saw the 1840s as the beginning of "the modern time," when Woolsey first encouraged scholarship and a scholarly spirit. Daniel Coit Gilman found that the college enjoyed a "new life under Woolsey," and William L. Kingsley said that a "broader culture and truer scholarship" came to Yale in those years. Andrew Dickson White admired the teaching abilities and scholarship of his professors. He estimated that Hadley might have drawn "throngs of students" at Berlin or Leipzig. In philosophy, "Porter opened students' eyes and led us to do some thinking for ourselves." While noting that "colleges are dull places at the best, and the professors sometimes become as dead as any tooth in the brass wheels of the public clock," Theodore Parker told Porter that it gave him pleasure to hear from students "that you keep a live soul in the dull routine of a college, and not only instruct but also inspire your scholars." In Dana's lecture room, White felt "himself in the hands of a master." Julian Monson Sturtevant, president of Illinois College and a former Yale student, perceived that at mid-century study of Greek and Latin had become more than the "intellectual gymnastics" of mental discipline. Teachers now brought their students "into sympathy with the classic authors as models of literary excellence."[34] As Yale graduates Daniel Coit Gilman and Andrew Dickson White exemplify, advocates of the modern university often accepted and built upon New Haven scholarly lessons while bracketing their teachers' religious ends.

Other former students of the New Haven scholars appraised their Yale education less favorably. In the late 1860s a New York–based movement of young alumni—the "Young Yale" movement, as it came to be known—campaigned to gain alumni representation and to reduce the number of ministers on the Yale Corporation, the governing body of the college. Alumnus William

Walter Phelps (Yale, 1860) startled his former professors at an alumni dinner in 1870 when he said that the college should be governed no longer by the "Rev. Mr. Pickering of Squashville, who is exhausted with keeping a few sheep in the wilderness." Alumni on the Yale Corporation could give the college a "knowledge of what is wanted in the scenes for which Yale educates her children." Members of the Young Yale movement hoped that their college would start preparing men for careers and stop preparing them for lives as Christian gentlemen. The criticisms of publisher Henry Holt (Yale, 1862) show how this generation viewed their education. Even with "the most diabolical ingenuity," Holt expected, his professors could not "have done more to make both religion and scholarship repulsive." Writing in the 1920s, he accused his Yale professors of "Puritanism." Through this charge, he identified the New Haven scholars with their seventeenth-century forebears who had executed witches, and he divided American history into two periods—a past where religion ruled and a present where it did not.[35]

The rise of the Young Yale movement was one indication that the composition of the student body was changing and that tensions were arising between social reality and the New Haven college ideal. During most of the antebellum period Yale students came from New England and New England areas of settlement in the Midwest. These students' fathers might be professionals, merchants, or town businessmen. Other students, such as William Graham Sumner, came from families of mechanics with little or no wealth. Beginning in the 1850s, however, increasing numbers of students whose families tended not to come from New England and not to be Congregationalists or Presbyterians entered the college. Yale was ceasing to be an institution of regional importance where cohesion stemmed from deeply held and shared religious and social beliefs. When Porter and his colleagues attended college in the 1820s, the question was what sort of Protestant religion would give unity to the college. By the time of the disparaging remarks about Mr. Pickering of Squashville, the question was arising whether religion deserved a central place in college life and studies at all. The advent of students from large metropolitan centers such as New York City and Chicago meant that an increasing proportion of the student body was not inclined to share New Haven ideas of success and influence, namely, that a man of culture could distinguish himself and gain leadership status in a community who respected him because of who he was, not what he had done. These young men tended to define success in terms of business achievement and acceptance by the new institutions of metropolitan life—social and athletic clubs. Henry Holt identified 1856 as the year when "the first group of the younger sons of New York business magnates" entered Yale bringing a "revolutionary quantity of new clothes."[36]

The Young Yale movement found a supporter in William Graham Sumner, who was then hoping for appointment to a Yale professorship. His comments on education supply a context for evaluation of contradictory charges of Yale admirers and critics. Favorably reviewing Eliot's inaugural address, Sumner wrote that "the secularization of education is going on all the time, in spite of all which is done or said against it. It is to be classed with the advance of democracy as one of the inevitable things which we have got to undergo." Sumner here implies that secularization is a process that eliminates the control of religion over public life and affairs. Because he thought of the college as an institution of public or national life linked to government and its policies, he denied that religion should have any authority over it. This view established the terms in which Sumner evaluated the worth of education. Speaking to parents in 1880, he said that students should learn "the best science and thought of the day." Then they would become "practical in the best and only true sense, by making them efficient in dealing intelligently with all the problems of life." National and local governments, as well as trades and professions, he concluded, needed this kind of citizen.[37]

This statement suggests that Sumner and his Yale teachers agreed that educated men should play an important role in American life. But their agreement existed only on a surface level, for Sumner rejected the overarching unity provided by divine truth and, rolling back or ignoring the authority of religion, relied on the secular value words *practical* and *efficient*. In contrast, Sumner's Yale teachers believed in divine truth and so thought of family, college, and government as unified in their ultimate purpose. All were divinely established to promote moral development, and the education imparted by the first two ensured a continuity of values between youth and adulthood and between private and public life.

Like Sumner, some Yale students moved away from the religious idealism of their teachers by denying religion authority over public life. Gilman, for example, was able to unbundle New Haven teachings, keep religion for private life, and draw on scholarly lessons in his public career. Other students, as Holt's previous comments show, thought religion damned anything with which it was connected. For him, New Haven scholarly practice and religious thought were inextricably combined; if you wanted to get rid of religion, then you had to throw out the whole package. For some, New Haven lessons were stepping stones; for others, barriers.

Until recently, modern historians have listened sympathetically to critics of mid-century Yale. Historians of the college criticize Porter and his colleagues for not reorganizing Yale into a university. Most historians read Porter's inaugural address as a defense of the old-time college and compare it unfavorably with Eliot's inaugural address of two years before. Educational historians view Porter's defense of classical studies as a defense of mental discipline. They further assume that teaching reforms inspired by Thomas Arnold and the German-inspired model of the professor as researcher were mutually exclusive.[38] In fact the New Haven scholars were among the first Americans to argue that research in addition to teaching was the responsibility of the college professor. While we remember Porter for his opposition to Eliot's elective system and his defense of Greek and Latin as required courses, we may also remember him for seeing the college as the home of scholarship. The founding of the Johns Hopkins and Clark universities did not first establish the purpose of scholarly research in America. Rather, their founding signified departure from the religious framework of the New Haven Christian college, for knowledge and its pursuit now existed for their own sakes.[39]

The concept of the college as an institution of individual and national culture was behind the New Haven scholars' collegiate reforms. They argued for a curriculum of required courses that furthered self-development and against innovations that had other rationales. For instance, Eliot contended that the elective system was a forward step in the march of liberty.[40] This was not the future that the New Haven scholars imagined. They foresaw "a future kingdom of God that shall be built up under the guidance of an Almighty power, and shall be neither more nor less than a human society transformed, by means of social agencies, into a tabernacle in which God shall, indeed, dwell with men and wipe away all tears from all eyes."[41]

5
Science: Observing a Fact, Knowing the Divine

Truth, though so glorious in itself, aye, heaven-born, how it is feared and fought against and often persecuted by self-deluded man! Give the trilobites a chance to speak, and they would correct many a false dogma in theological systems!

James Dwight Dana, 1857

Alone the word *science* usually refers to a natural or physical science. To change its meaning, we add an adjective such as *social* or *behavioral*. Even then *science* denotes knowledge of the physical world gained from observation and induction. The New Haven scholars, in contrast, thought that a science was "knowledge," "truth," or "a branch of knowledge having a certain completeness." In 1865 Theodore Dwight Woolsey called all college subjects sciences and divided them into the mathematical, physical, and moral sciences. In the last category he put history and political science, as well as the study of art, literature, and metaphysics. He further assumed that all science "is man's arrangement of the thought of the infinite God."[1]

The New Haven scholars had unshakable confidence that their research would continue to affirm divine reality despite the fact that starting in the 1830s, shifts in natural science, Biblical criticism, and philosophy jarred the certainty that the Bible and the natural record told the same story and that man could know about God. Charles Lyell's *The Principles of Geology* (1830–33) and Robert Chamber's *Vestiges of the Natural History of Creation* (1844) challenged the accuracy of the Biblical record. D. F. Strauss's *Life of Jesus* (1839) showed that the New Testament was merely a historical account. John Stuart Mill contended in his *System of Logic* (1843) that man could know nothing but the ideas that the physical world "impressed" upon his mind. Historical determinists such as F. P. G. Guizot stripped history of its providential framework and argued that material forces governed progress. Finally, the theories of Charles Darwin, when popularized by scientists such as Thomas Huxley, expelled God from the physical universe and left man an unthinking animal at the mercy of nature.[2] Whereas educated Protestants previously had taken Biblical inerrancy and providential history for granted, now they had to choose among several conflicting theories.

These challenges to the Biblical account of Creation did not affect the religious belief of the New Haven scholars, because their faith had a different basis from belief in the inerrancy of the Bible. During their college years, the scholars had learned from Coleridge that religious truth lay beneath both doctrinal debate and the facts of natural science. Study at German universities and the lessons of the historical school then had given this belief a systematic and methodological foundation. The result was New Haven science. It retained the empirical dimension of the Scottish philosophy but assumed that every observable fact of this world had an idealistic correlate. This synthesis freed the New Haven scholars from the dilemma that had troubled their teachers, Yale professors such as Silliman and Taylor. Following the Scottish philosophy, both Taylor and Silliman had encouraged empirical study of the observable world. Silliman had argued that nature was as much God's book as was the Bible, and Taylor had contended that social and political institutions were part of God's moral government. The investigator collected facts, analyzed them using his common sense, and reached conclusions that could only accord with the preexisting record of God's work found in the Bible. According to Silliman and Taylor, new geological discoveries had to confirm the account of Creation found in Genesis. Since discoveries brought into question the Mosaic account, Silliman and Taylor had had several alternatives: they could question whether scientists had correctly followed the procedures of common sense, they could call natural scientists atheists and reject their findings altogether, they could modify the new scientific findings to conform to the Bible, or they could find a new basis for their religious faith. Taylor had rejected natural science altogether, Silliman had modified its findings, and their students, the New Haven scholars, found a new basis for their faith and a new way of explaining the connection between this world and a divine reality.[3]

The New Haven scholars gave facts an idealistic correlate. For historian Fisher, political events, art, and literature were correlates of national character; for psychologist Porter, language was the correlate of thought. In New Haven science the mind acted creatively to make theistic sense out of the world that was the visible part of a divine universe. For the theistic New Haven scholars, there was no inevitable conflict between science and religion. If discoveries in natural science revealed that customary views of Biblical history were wrong, then, Fisher argued, "the aim should be to eliminate that error, and to do it, if possible, forthwith." Natural science was, after all, "a branch of human knowledge to be hailed as an ally and a friend." As long as the scholars believed that it was scientific to know God, they could read the physical world symbolically for its divine meaning and feel no tension between their scholarship and their faith. Geologist James Dwight Dana urged ministers to join with natural scientists and "encourage research with a willingness to receive whatever results come from nature." Porter promised that we "would cast off our Christianity as a filthy garment if we loved it better than we love the truth." Even if scientific investigation were "carried to the farthest bound," Fisher predicted, "it will never be able to dispense with God. It is plain that the world is a cosmos—a beautiful order."[4]

The New Haven scholars were confident that scientific investigation would never undermine their religious belief, since they had accepted German idealistic thought. In *The Human Intellect,* Porter traced the history of the theory of innate ideas from Kant to William Hamilton, Schleiermacher, and Fichte, thus demonstrating how German thought, which Silliman's and Taylor's generation had feared, provided a basis for evangelical faith.[5] Faith preceded observation of either the natural world or the Bible and came from knowing that God had created the physical world and man in his image. In his *Human Intellect* Porter tried to prove "that there is an uncreated thinker, whose thoughts can be interpreted by the human intellect which is made in His image."[6] Thus, Porter's work is the central text of New Haven science, for it justifies as the true way of knowing the process by which geologist Dana, historian Fisher, political scientist Woolsey, and art historian Hoppin collected and analyzed the facts of this world and then related them to a divine whole. New Haven scholarship promised that lessons could and would affirm the spiritual dimension of human existence. Further, *The Human Intellect* illustrates the dilemma of theistic scholars in an increasingly secular world. They wanted to establish the authority of scholarship to explain the facts of this world to an audience of well-educated men from every Protestant sect. In other words, the New Haven scholars wanted to throw out the false theories of metaphysicians and the doctrinal debates of ministers without throwing out God too.

The argument of *The Human Intellect* justified New Haven science as a way of knowing at the same time that it established psychology as a scientific study unrelated to metaphysical speculation and exempt from the agnostic or atheistic conclusions of philosophers such as John Stuart Mill and Herbert Spencer. Porter started his text by defining psychology as "the science of the human soul." But it was the whole soul, comprising what we now call "mind," as well as man's spiritual attributes. Porter learned this definition from Adolf Trendelenburg, his professor at the University of Berlin. *Psychology* replaced the terms *mental science* and *moral philosophy,* which were prevalent in America and England to 1860. For instance, writing in the 1830s, Brown University president Francis Wayland had defined his subject as "moral science" and, much like earlier Scottish philosophers, had studied the mind as a collection of "faculties." Porter found the term *psychology* preferable because it treated the mind as a whole and implied that it had active, creative powers.[7]

Porter's psychology was a middle way between the metaphysician, who claimed a priori knowledge of God, and the materialist such as Mill, who claimed that man could not know God at all. Rejecting the claims of the metaphysician, Porter argued that psychology was "simply a science of observation and of fact." Only the scientist could discover "what conceptions and relations are philosophically valid as the axioms and postulates of scientific knowledge." Still, the theistic scientist "considers and records facts as he finds them, whether they do or do not square with his philosophy."[8]

The facts that Porter sought to study came from language, which he considered to be the outward manifestation of consciousness. Associationist philosophers had argued, however, that language proved that the mind merely received external stimuli, which then caused it to produce ideas. The literal meaning of words proved that the material world "impressed" "images" for the mind to "store." By referring to the etymologies of these words, Porter showed that their original meanings had described physical actions; only later had the words come to define mental processes. The use of historical etymology thus helped Porter refute an implication of the Scottish philosophy that nineteenth-century English associationists had carried to an extreme.[9]

In choosing the language of common life as a reliable source for the study of psychology, Porter was adopting the lessons that he had first learned from Coleridge and that his study in Germany had made more systematic. To the modern scholar, Porter's use of language seems far from a laboratory study of how the mind responds to certain conditions. Still, Porter was moving from purely theoretical discussions toward more empirical study. He rejected the language of scholarly discourse as a basis for psychological study by arguing that for this purpose it was totally unreliable. It was prejudiced by all those "influences which spring up on the soil and within the limits of speculation, from the influence of preconceived theories, whether fondly cherished by their originator, or traditionally accepted from revered teachers; whether adopted or defended through the pride of opinion, the tenacity of consistency, or the heat of controversy."[10] Thus, Porter tried to move beyond the theoretical arguments of the past. His psychology did not merely refine or clarify the previous speculation of others; it was a science based on observation and induction from facts. Psychologists since William James have defined psychology as "the science of mental life." They assume that the mind is a physical entity and that scientists can draw no conclusions about man's spiritual nature from the study of the mind. For Porter, in contrast, affirmation of man's spiritual nature was the essence of psychology. Therefore, he could accept the work of scientists such as Alexander Bain, who argued that the functions of the brain were localized in the mind. But Porter denied that Bain's findings proved that the brain was the same as the soul. "The excitement of a nervous organism [the brain]," Porter argued, "does not and never can be made to signify the same thing, as to feel, to know, or to will." With concerns different from those of cerebralist Bain or associationist Mill, Porter assumed that there was a God, "a creating Spirit, who originated and controls matter." Therefore, he wanted to investigate the "created spirit [the soul], which is intimately connected with and affected by a material organism [the brain], or which, perhaps, is itself the organizing agent." The believer would find, Porter argued, "a unity of purpose and intention in the order and beauty of these arrangements."[11] Whether geologic formations or the development of species confirmed or denied Biblical history was irrelevant when psychology could show the fundamental unity in man, God, and the natural world.

Porter's explanation of inductive method in the conclusion to *The Human Intellect* supported this belief. First the scientist observed a particular group of things, and then he concluded that they shared a certain characteristic. He assumed that this characteristic was a constant, that is, that it had not varied in the past and would not vary in the future. Induction, however, did not stop here but included an analogy which confirmed that God had informed the world with his meaning. An image that Porter used in a popular lecture explained this vividly. He asked his audience to consider a mountain, with its top hidden by clouds and its foundation buried in the earth. Scientists used analogy to interpret "the inaccessible by the suggestions indicated in the portions which we measure and scale. For the rest, we cannot believe that what we shall hereafter discover will belie what we already know. . . . When we essay to construct into an harmonious whole the unseen foundations, the accessible slopes, and the unapproachable summit, we are not disturbed that we know and judge of each by a process peculiar to itself."[12] In *The Human Intellect* Porter used more technical language to make the same point:

> We analyze the several processes of knowledge into their underlying assumptions, and we find that the assumption which underlies them all is a self-existent intelligence, who not only can be known by man, but must be known by man in order that he may know any thing besides. In analyzing a psychological process, we develop and demonstrate a metaphysical truth, and that is the truth which the unsophisticated intellect of child and man requires and accepts, that there is a self-existent personal intelligence, on whom the universe depends for the beings and relations of which it consists.[13]

In this more complex statement, the totality of the human soul and God is like the mountain; the soul is the visible, and God the invisible, manifestation of one whole. Porter had analyzed the soul through classification of its various thought processes apparent in the historically correct understanding of words. In each thought process he had found the assumption of a "self-existent intelligence." This conclusion demanded that scientists recognize not only that God existed as an ontological necessity but also that there was a God whom they could know. Like the mountain, the invisible God was knowable because the scientist fitted observed facts into a preconceived pattern of a theistic universe.

The mountain analogy may help to explain New Haven science, but it obscured the fact that God is not like a mountain. The scientist can predict what the top of a cloud-veiled mountain is like because he has seen the whole mountain on a clear day. Even though the scientist had never seen God, he could still know him, for he assumed that God had arranged the universe according to certain principles. In contrast to Darwinians, who viewed natural processes as random, wasteful, and savage, Porter's scientist conceived of nature as orderly, uniform, and neat; its means were adapted to ends according to the rules of harmony, beauty, and grace. With these assumptions, induction depended on belief not merely in God but in a God who behaved in predetermined ways. "Induction," Porter reasoned, "assumes that the *rational methods of the divine and human intellect* are similiar, and that the human intellect is therefore capable of judging of the principles and aims by which the universe was constructed and its laws can be known. More briefly expressed, induction is only possible on the assumption that the intellect of man is a reflex of the Divine Intellect; or that man is made in the image of God."[14]

Knowing nature meant anthropomorphizing it and ascribing to God qualities that the New Haven scholars in particular, and Victorian culture in general, deemed positive. In the mountain analogy, the inscrutable other, the shrouded summit, is merely a continuation of a very stable natural feature and hence is not so inscrutable after all. Similarly, because God had made man in his image, man was, Porter thought, just as orderly and predictable as God. Porter's psychology suggested that men could act in constructive ways, while it stripped from God his mysterious attributes and left him the essence of a cultured man.

While the sources of Porter's idealist method are easy to find in Coleridge and Trendelenburg, it is more difficult to trace the idealism of geologist James Dwight Dana back to German thought. First-rate education for natural scientists in antebellum America did not include study at German universities. The best training of the age included an apprenticeship in the laboratory of an established scientist and then an expedition to an unexplored area of the globe, such as Charles Darwin's voyage on the *Beagle* and Thomas Huxley's exploration of the South Sea Islands. Dana received his training in the Yale laboratory of Benjamin Silliman. Then he sailed to the South Pacific with the famous United States Exploring Expedition of Captain Charles Wilkes.[15]

Throughout his career Dana both popularized and advanced scientific knowledge. His authoritative texts, especially those in mineralogy and geology, won him a place in the first ranks of American scientists. The *Manual of Geology,* published in 1863, reached its fourth edition in 1895, and his *Manual of Mineralogy,* published in 1849, reached its nineteenth edition in 1977. In editions through 1894, Dana said that classification of minerals showed the design of God in the universe. Editors since then have deleted Dana's theological statements while leaving his valuable data, and present-day professors still may require their students to read edited versions of this text.[16] As the former student and son-in-law of Benjamin Silliman, Dana succeeded him as editor of the *American Journal of Science and the Arts,* which he transformed into an outlet for American's preeminent scientists—Alexander Dallas Bache, Joseph Henry, Benjamin Peirce, Oliver Wolcott Gibbs, and John Frazer. Dana also was a fellow of the Royal Society and a correspondent of leading British and Scottish scientists, including Charles Darwin.[17]

Dana's 1855 presidential address to the American Association for the Advancement of Science illustrates the dual role of popularizer and contributor to scientific research. The conclusion and introduction affirmed that nature was God's work and one part of his revelation. He asked his audience to realize that nature per se was not atheistic; a natural scientist who remained humble, docile, and "forgetful of ambitious self, shall find the truth and feel its benign influence." Then, introducing the body of his talk, Dana switched his concerns to those of the natural scientist with a specific field of expertise. He acknowledged that American science had made many advances in research over the past year and disclaimed any intent to "roam over others' territories." He promised to speak only about the advances in his field of geology as they pertained to the natural history of the United States.[18]

Dana's position as a popularizer is best seen in his response to Tayler Lewis's *Six Days of Creation* (1855). Lewis, a professor of Oriental languages at Union College, denounced natural science because he thought that Christians should accept the authority of the Bible despite discoveries of geologists or Biblical critics, who used the modern techniques of philologically based criticism. Science, Lewis argued, could not answer ultimate questions. Replying in the *Bibliotheca Sacra,* Dana agreed that science could not explain ultimate questions but denied that the Bible answered all questions accurately. He warned that antagonism between the Bible and natural science could be counterproductive to true religion. If theologians confronted the believing natural scientist with this supposed antagonism, then the scientist might choose nature, "God's acknowledged works, *versus* the Bible, 'the Book.' " Maintaining that religious and scientific research championed "the unrestricted, objective pursuit of science," Dana thus reassured ministers and religious readers of the *Bibliotheca Sacra* that science would not attempt to supplant the authority of religion, while he claimed for science an area of investigation independent from religion.[19]

Benjamin Silliman taught Dana the method of Baconian science, which reigned in both English and American scientific circles until Lyell's *Principles* called into question the Biblical account of Creation. The Baconian scientist drew meaning from facts through identification and classification of natural phenomena—minerals, fossils, or species. Assuming that the world of God and the world of nature comprised a unity, the scientist expected to discover God's lessons as he investigated the natural world. Silliman saw himself as "the honored interpreter of a portion of . . . [God's] works."[20] He read nature much as the trained minister read the Bible.

Because Silliman did not integrate German idealism into his scientific method, he believed that the natural record supported the Biblical story of Creation. For example, when Silliman prepared an American edition (1829) of the *Introduction to Geology* by British scientist Robert Bakewell, the standard text in American colleges until publication of Dana's *Manual,* Silliman added an appendix that reconciled geologic history with Genesis. He conceded merely that a day in the Biblical account was longer than twenty-four hours. In spite of the publication of Lyell's *Principles,* Silliman held to his belief in the accuracy of the Biblical account. To his 1833 edition of Bakewell's *Geology* he added an essay, "Consistency of Geology with Sacred History," that contained a chart entitled "Coincidence between the Order of Events as Described in Genesis, and that unfolded by Geological Investigation."[21]

Dana followed the Baconian method of his teacher to the extent that the substance of his work was identification and classification. But Dana described the relation between God and nature in a new way: now the truth of God subsumed the lesser truth of nature. He read God's truth, not Biblical history, in nature. Dana explained that the mineralogist learned about God as he pursued science:

> To learn to distinguish minerals by their color, weight and luster, is so far very well; but the accomplishment is of a low degree of merit, and when most perfect makes but a poor mineralogist. But when the science is viewed in the light of Chemistry and Crystallography, it becomes a branch of knowledge, perfect in itself, and surprisingly beautiful in its exhibitions

of truth. We are no longer dealing with pebbles of pretty shapes and tints, but with objects modeled by a Divine hand; and every additional fact becomes a new revelation of his wisdom.[22]

In this statement, Dana used the word *truth* to mean scientific truth as well as a revelation of divine wisdom; hence both *science* and *truth* had transcendent meanings. Science did not reveal a God like Voltaire's *horloger,* who had set the machinery of nature in motion. Neither did it reveal the transcendentalists' God, who was immanent in nature and visible to every man. Dana's God was visible to the trained scientist, who through methodologically correct study came to an understanding of the world. He read in it the presence of God. This God stood behind nature and revealed his wisdom in its forms. By combining idealism and realism, Dana avoided the transcendentalist heresy of pantheism, of seeing nature as God. Dana's Romantic science also protected his religious views from the challenge that scientific discoveries could pose, for he had divorced his faith from the literal truth of the Bible. This was an intellectually complex middle way, one shared by his New Haven colleagues, who saw the universe as a theistic whole from which they could read God's meaning or truth.[23]

The processes of induction and analysis that Porter's psychology vindicated were crucial to Dana's search for truth. When the scientist compared the facts of nature that he had classified, he was not limited to facts from one scientific field. Dana assumed that all the sciences were unified; each "sheds light into the precincts of the other, and all combine in harmonious exhibitions of truth. More than this, common ideas underlie the whole system of the universe, declaring a unity of nature, parallel with the unity of the Infinite Author." When the scientist appealed to the "general principle" of his discipline, he was not acting as a narrow specialist. He was appealing "to the deepest and widest range of knowledge."[24]

Dana's 1857 article "Thoughts on Species," written for a ministerial audience, illustrates his method of analysis. It is important to know, he argued, whether man was of one or of several species, for this information would justify the view that God had created man. To demonstrate this, Dana created analogies between the inorganic, physical, and organic worlds. Observation of the inorganic world showed that distinct "molecules" represent separate elements. (We would use the word *atom* instead of *molecule.*) But in the organic world each animate thing develops from a "germ cell," or seed, which contains specific plans for its growth. Because this process gives a living thing a historical dimension, no one species embodies the species itself. For example, what is a horse— a foal, a mare, or a stallion, or an Arabian, Clydesdale, or Percheron? Although there is no one embodiment of a species, this does not mean that a species does not exist. To prove its existence, Dana referred his reader back to the fact of the inorganic world: that every element has its own molecule. This comparison was valid, he argued, because the ideas of God "pervade the universe" and give it "unity and universality beneath and through diversity."

An essential attribute of speciesness, Dana argued, was the ability to vary in nature without loss of intrinsic properties. Water, after all, can be ice, steam, or liquid, but it remains water, whereas water is different from the hydrogen and oxygen that compose it. In the organic world, the horse and the donkey are species and have as a vital property the power to reproduce themselves. But their joint progeny, the mule, is not a species because it lacks this essential attribute. This analogy led Dana to his conclusion that man is one species. The races are variations of one species because they can interbreed and produce fertile progeny.[25] Dana's theory was consistent with current geologic and catastrophist theories of natural history and was a more satisfying answer than Louis Agassiz's idealistically based theory that God had created each race separately because he did not intend them to interbreed.[26]

Dana's argument contained both conclusions from empirical research and conceptualizations based on idealism. Because Dana thought that no human of any race or either sex embodied the human species, he concluded that a species was not an actual thing but an ideal contained in the germ cell, or seed. In other words, a species was real, but the ideal of it "exists only as a result of logical induction," not of empirical observation. Dana thus cut a middle way between the nominalist position that species and all the other products of the mind were real and the idealist position that the idea of the species itself was real. Like Porter, he had made language a correlate for thought in his idealistic formulations.[27]

From Dana's call in the 1850s for scientific research through the reception of Charles Darwin's *On the Origins of Species* (1859) and *The Descent of Man* (1871), Dana and his colleagues remained convinced that religion and science spoke ultimately to the same truth. In 1883 Dana said, "Let science dig, and dredge, and work in her laboratories. She is searching for God's truth." The scholars explained how Darwin's books actually supported their theistic beliefs. Like a model Baconian scientist, Darwin seemed to have accumulated a mass of data and then interpreted them by induction. According to both Porter and Fisher, the resulting pattern was a teleology in the natural realm that neither commented on the existence of God nor in fact had any bearing on it. Darwin's theory left plenty of room for God to set evolution in motion. The fact that evolution had occurred, Porter argued, could not "drive the fact of design out of the universe, nor dispense with the assumption of design as one of the axioms of science."[28]

James Dwight Dana gave more thorough consideration to Darwin's theories in a series of lectures that he delivered to an audience of nonacademics and nonscientists at Yale in 1883. Now Dana revised earlier antievolutionist ideas implicit in the 1857 article on species. In that article Dana had shown that he was a catastrophist; that is, he believed that new animal species originated only at times of natural catastrophe. But Dana had also accepted Charles Lyell's uniformitarian theory that plants could vary or adapt to natural conditions. This position prepared the way for later acceptance of evolution.[29]

Dana put the Darwinian theories of natural selection and evolution within a New Haven perspective. He found that other factors besides natural selection had caused adaptation, and he emphasized the importance of the Lamarckian idea of the use and disuse of limbs, as well as the roles of inheritance and environment in adaptation and evolutionary change. He could not accept, however, the view that the struggle for survival was a blind, random process. Struggle was part of God's plan for the harmonious development of the world and rewarded the most vigorous, adaptable, and creative animals. In this benign process, greed and brute strength were vanquished, and might did not mean right.[30]

Dana also could not agree that man was descended from an animal. Darwin had not based his conclusion on rigorous scientific reasoning. Because the geologic record contained no fossil evidence to link man with any form of inferior life, man's descent from animals was a mere theory. Cephalization, an accepted theory in the nineteenth century, suggested a different conclusion. Limbs connected with thinking—arms and hands—were more developed in the higher animals. Change through time could not account, Dana concluded, for the different structures of man and ape, which could not be related.

Dana also found that evolution neither absolved people from their God-given responsibility to improve their character nor explained the development of society and civilization. Only lower animals, he believed, could accumulate and genetically pass on knowledge about how to survive. Man, in contrast, needed to learn these techniques and more from his education so that he could develop himself to a state of culture or wholeness. Although biological evolution might explain change among animals or in prehistoric times, since humans had existed their ability to accumulate knowledge and consciously transfer it from generation to generation had been the major force in history. Dana portrayed man as a creation of God whose free will explained the development of his character and his society.[31]

Just as the New Haven scholars rejected the ideas of natural development as a random, brutish process and of human development as independent of human will, so they rejected application of these ideas to social development. Responding to the imagined comments of a social Darwinist defending late-nineteenth-century imperialism, Porter wondered whether it was necessary "in the struggle for existence" for the weakest nations inevitably to "go to the wall." He criticized the prediction "that the intelligent should compel the ignorant, the civilized should displace the savage, and the Christian and refined should subject the lawless and rude to obedience and civilization, and do this, if necessary, by violent methods,—and by wholesale massacres and bloody lessons which centuries of horror and hate shall not forget."[32]

Porter found this social-science thinking cold-hearted and defective, for it excluded considerations of feeling or sentiment. Feeling "directed by knowledge and judgment," he argued, "is practical wisdom, common sense, sagacious insight, scientific genius." The wise social scientist should recognize that all laws and social institutions that promoted "the gratification of the nobler and better sentiments" were good. Any theory that violated the "fellow-feeling which makes the whole world kin" or "gives spur or rein to the appetites which we have in common with the brutes" was false. Consequently, social science need not exclude religion; the social scientist should consider man's longing for immortality and his belief in God. The "emotional fires" that "a firm belief in truth" often ignited were real facts.[33] Porter and his colleagues thus called for what we might term a holistic appreciation of man and his society. They accepted implicitly the idea of an active or positive government, and they criticized explicitly those scientists and philosophers who in the last half of the nineteenth century argued that people were mere products of the physical universe.

Specifically, the New Haven scholars attacked the psychological and social-science theories of Auguste Comte, John Stuart Mill, and psychologist Alexander Bain. These "materialists" denied that man had a spiritual nature and argued that the mind was a physical organ. In *The Human Intellect* Porter traced the error of Mill and his school to their misreading of John Locke. They selected certain of his "leading doctrines" and then interpreted them "in a narrow spirit." As a result they falsified Locke's thinking and developed theories that attributed human knowledge to experience. Even more serious was their claim that the scientist could know nothing but the facts of this world. Mill contended that the scientist could know facts in their relation to other facts. For the positivist, a fact was not an ideal construction, such as Dana's germ of a species, but an actual thing or event. Porter considered this definition of science and what scientists could know to have metaphysical implications. Postivists saw human progress as the result of material causes and not as the creation of man.[34]

The moral implication of these theories drew the New Haven scholars' thorough condemnation. A theory of the human mind that denied the existence of a soul "with sublime attributes," thus distinguishing "it from matter," destroyed human responsibility. "In truth," Fisher argued, "it is fatal to the higher life of man. It gives the lie to consciousness which testifies to our freedom, and to our guilt for wrong choices." Materialists, it seemed, could truly know nothing. Their theory "destroys the difference between truth and error in mental perception; for both are equally the result of the molecular action of the brain and equally normal. It destroys science, for who can say that the molecular movement by which science is thought out, may at any time change its form, and give rise to conclusions utterly diverse." In the world of the materialists, right was relative and social institutions of family, state, and law were merely conventions. The results, Porter found, were "caprice in morality, tyranny in government, uncertainty in science." The materialist's science promised a false salvation—"painted and gilded machines that at a distance seem to reveal the mysteries of the highest truth, and on a near approach vanish like the vapor before the sun." Because these painted machines absolved the individual from responsibility for self-improvement, the new science promised to "shut and bar forever the brazen gates which seem to lead into His inner sanctuary."[35]

Positivism, far more than Darwinian theory, modified the New Haven scholars' role as advocates of science. Until the late 1850s they had been straightforward advocates of scientific research and had reassured audiences that science could never overthrow religious truth. Properly trained scholars such as Dana and Porter could expound the true relationship between God and nature. Starting in the late fifties, the works of Mill and Alexander Bain in psychology, Huxley in natural science, Henry Thomas Buckle and F. P. G. Guizot in history, and Herbert Spencer in social theory put theistic scholars on the defensive, not merely because of their scientific theories but also because of their claim that science was at war with religion. Historian John W. Draper, for instance, suggested in *The Conflict of Religion and Science* that Christianity inevitably "view[ed] with disdain . . . the progressive intellectual development of man." Spencer, it seemed to Porter, betrayed an arrogance unbecoming of a true scientist. It was bad when Spencer claimed that social evolution—which to Porter's mind denied man's free will, responsibility, and agency in ensuring that development be moral—was an axiom that men of science "worthy of the name" ought to accept. It was worse when he denied theists scholarly authority, saying that none could "accept sociology in any scientific sense of the term." Now, the New Haven men had to explain that some science was false—its theory was illogical, its hypotheses and conclusions denied the reality of religion, and it transformed man into a one-dimensional creature of exclusively material needs and desires. Nonetheless, they did not defend all theistic theory, for some violated the tenets of their scholarship. For example, philologist William Dwight Whitney criticized Oxford University professor Max Müller for using language to prove that the human race could have descended from Adam and Eve.[36]

In the now classic *Victorian Frame of Mind* Walter Houghton suggests that doubt afflicted British intellectuals. Confronted with the discoveries of natural science, Victorians became skeptical. Such was not the case for New Haven scholars. Their way of knowing, as we have seen, allowed them to accept discoveries in geology and physics and still see design and order. Their science did mean, however, that they rejected *theories* antithetical to the New Haven way of knowing. Porter, for example, rejected Bain's theory of mind. By denying the spiritual aspect of mind, or that the soul was an actual part of the body, Bain also denied a fundamental assumption of New Haven science—that man, a creation of God, could truly know this world and its relationship to the divine. Today we see Bain's theory as a stepping stone along the path of what psychologists call cerebral localization. In the 1870s, not having the benefit of our twenty-twenty hindsight, Porter saw Bain's theory as a stepping stone toward anti-intellectual nihilism. Even though Porter deplored that "men of knowledge took for granted that Christian theism is doomed to banish before what is called modern science and culture," still he did not doubt. He had faith that the people would find that Christianity was "a fact of life," despite the theories of Mill, Bain, and Spencer, which suggested otherwise.[37]

The New Haven scholar who did begin to doubt was an exception among the group. In Theodore Dwight Woolsey's response to the method and findings of modern science we find a New Haven version of Tennyson's *In Memoriam.*

> Yes, wisdom now is built on sense;
>   We measure and we weigh,
> We break and join, make rare and dense,
>   And reason God away.
>
> The wise have probed this wondrous world,
>   And searched the stars, and find
> All curious facts and laws revealed
>   But no Almighty mind.
>
> From thinking dust we mould the spheres,
>   And shape earth's wondrous frame:
> If God had slept a million years,
>   All things would be the same.
>
> O give me back a world of life,
>   Something to live and trust,
> Something to quench my inward strife,
>   And lift me from the dust.
>
> I cannot live with nature dead,
>   Mid laws and causes blind;
> Powerless on earth, or overhead,
>   To trace th' all guiding mind.
>
> Then boast that I have found the keys
>   That time and space unlock,
> That snatch from heaven its mysteries,
>   Its fear from the earthquake shock.

Better the instincts of the brute
  That feels its God afar,
Than reason, to his praises mute,
  Talking with every star.

Better the thousand deities
  That swarmed in Greece of yore,
Than thought that scorns all mysteries
  And dares all depths to explore.

Better is childhood's thoughtless trust
  Than manhood's daring scorn;
The fear that creeps along the dust
  Than doubt in hearts forlorn.

And knowledge, if it cost so dear
  If such be reason's day,
I'll lose the pearl without a tear,
  And grope my star-lit way.

And be the toils of wisdom curst
  If such the mead we earn;
If freezing pride and doubt
  And faith forbid to burn.[38]

Although doggerel, Woolsey's poem makes the same charges as his colleagues' prose. Porter, too, argued that rationalism untempered by faith made scientists arrogant, and he despaired of Spencer's social science, which seemed to kill sentiment. Woolsey goes further in this private expression and describes the emotional impact of science. He rhetorically considers the unreasoning faith of the brute and the thoughtless trust of the child as alternatives to a cold world created by atheistic, scornful reason. The *if*s of the last two stanzas save Woolsey from these anti-intellectual fates by offering another alternative: New Haven science. It neither prohibited intellectual inquiry nor prevented satisfaction of spiritual needs. Woolsey's poem clarified the choices that a person living in this age of choice could make.[39] There was Comtian positivism, Mill's psychology, blind faith, or New Haven science.

    Woolsey's doubt, while atypical among the New Haven scholars, may have been typical of a theistic layman's response to new scientific discoveries and theories. Laymen shared neither the New Haven scholars' profound understanding of their epistemology and their ability to rebut contradictory theories nor the supportive milieu of New Haven, where a scholar met other experts who most probably agreed with him. Though the New Haven group thought of themselves as what we call cosmopolitans, their cosmopolitanism was based on participation in a world of evangelical scholarship. From our secular perspective and the perspective of nonevangelical Americans in the late nineteenth century, the New Haven men appear as provincials. For example, New York University professor B. N. Martin, who had reviewed *The Human Intellect* for the *New Englander,* advised future economist Richard T. Ely (Columbia, 1876) to seek advice about graduate studies in philosophy at German universities from Porter, who was "the man who knew most about Germany." In Germany, Ely found that few people had heard of H. Ulrici (1806–84), the professor at the University of Halle whom Porter had recommended.[40] From his stance inside the world of evangelical scholarship, Martin had one view; from outside Ely had another. Even though Porter could not help Ely, in his role as popularizer he may have helped other evangelicals. For laymen, New Haven scholarship functioned much like New Haven college reforms; both mediated between a traditional belief system and the cosmopolitan world of scholarship. Each helped evangelical believers negotiate the transition to a modern secular world. New Haven science encouraged research while insisting that its facts revealed an ultimate world of reality. New Haven scholarship thus pointed toward our modern definitions of scholarship while making advances in natural and social science acceptable to nineteenth-century theistic readers. The scholars absorbed new discoveries and theories, and their science pulled a sacred canopy of meaning over all.

In the last third of the century, some natural and social scientists began to define science in a new way, by "the hard *objective* character of the material and the method."[41] Scientists also began to exclude consideration of first or final causes, whether they were expressed in New Haven theistic terms or the secular terms of a Marx or Spencer. Even at Yale, Porter's successor as professor of psychology, George Trumbull Ladd, moved from New Haven science toward the new definition. Ladd's psychology bridged the span between Porter and idealist confirmations of the divine, on the one side, and James and his empirical understanding of the mind, on the other side. Ladd introduced Americans to the work of German scientists Hermann Lotze and Wilheim Wundt, who were then pioneering laboratory research as the method of psychological study. This method could provide data that allowed the scientist to describe the working of the mind, Ladd said, but it could not reveal the "first and last things of the mind."[42]

James established the first laboratory for psychological research in America at Harvard. Whereas Porter had defined psychology as "the science of the human soul," James called it "the science of mental life." For James, science did not include the New Haven process of induction and analogy that led to a realm of divine meaning. He argued that after the scientist had collected his facts and "ascertained the empirical correlation of the various sorts of thought or feeling with definite conditions of the brain," he must stop. If he proceeded, he became a metaphysician.[43] Even though James agreed with Porter that the mind was an active agent and that the world was rationally intelligible, James excluded divine truth from what the scientist could know as a scientist.

Although twentieth-century intellectual historians see connections between the psychologies of James and Porter, *The Human Intellect* is not a source for James's thought.[44] His *Psychology* ignores Porter and his *Human Intellect*. Further, James continued to worry about the impact of science on religion. He did not vindicate religion until *The Varieties of Religious Experience* (1903), when he argued that religion must be real, since it produced observable effects, the frenzy of a Shaker dance for instance, that scientists could study. Porter's work could not have been known to James, for Porter had reached a similar conclusion twenty years earlier. The scientist should see as real facts, Porter argued, the "emotional fires" that "a firm belief in truth" often ignited.[45]

Unlike James, who merely ignored New Haven science, William Graham Sumner both directly criticized his teachers' methods and explained the new method in the social sciences. The social scientist, Sumner wrote, should abandon traditional or dogmatic methods of explanation and strive for "strictness of definition, correctness of analysis, precision in observing phenomena, deliberation in comparison, correctness of inference, and exhaustiveness in generalization." In this call for strict empiricism he sounded like a New Haven scientist. But then he went on to say that the social scientist wanted to know "*reality*" beyond everything else." He did not want to know the truth, with its implication of divine meaning, because he did "not know where or how to get it." To Sumner, truth and reality were antagonistic concepts. The former seemingly belonged to a world of ministers, amateurs, and mystics. The latter denoted the scientific world of scholars, whose method,

Sumner said, "shall descend to a cold clear examination of facts and build up inductions which shall have positive value."[46]

The New Haven scholars, Sumner's teachers at Yale, saw themselves as scholars who could know truth. Their scientific method called for the close examination of facts and then permitted idealistic conclusions. The New Haven scholars moved from Sumner's cold, hard fact to affirm the existence of a theistic universe. Their world was a beautiful order, an expression of divine truth.

6
History: From Fact to Providence

G eoffrey Tillotson's remark that the nineteenth century was the first to give itself a number suggests the profound historical consciousness of the age. The New Haven scholars all used and advocated a historical method of explanation. In the introduction to his *International Law,* Theodore Dwight Woolsey mentioned that a historical treatment had "naturally" suggested itself. "As linguistics is a historical science," William Dwight Whitney explained, "so its evidences are historical, and its methods of proof of the same character." Calling for an improvement in literary scholarship, Noah Porter found modern criticism to be "a most important adjunct to history, and for that reason," he said, "eminently deserves to be called historical criticism."[1]

With the rise of historical thinking, historians began to organize their field as a separate discipline. In European countries, national archives and public record offices were established. In the United States, state and local historical societies proliferated. Historians began to see themselves as scholars. They received an increasingly standardized course of university training, found employment in a university or one of the newly established archives, and followed generally accepted methods of historical scholarship. They published articles in journals that devoted themselves to furthering research. At Yale, Woolsey introduced history into the undergraduate curriculum in 1847, a professorship of history was established in 1865, and Fisher became professor of history in the

Theological Department in 1861. Appreciating these changes as part of the larger phenomenon, Fisher said that "history in general is taking all over the civilized world, a high place among studies."[2]

For the New Haven scholars, historicism replaced mechanical, static conceptions of the universe and society inherited from the Scottish philosophers, who had drawn their social and psychological theories from postulates about common sense. For instance, Adam Smith's ideal man was the creature of his self-interest and acted predictably in all historical situations. With its sources in German Romanticism and idealism, historicism introduced a dynamic and potentially relativistic way of understanding. As the philosopher Maurice Mandelbaum explains, historicism contends that "an adequate understanding of anything and an adequate understanding of its value are to be gained by considering it in terms of the place it occupied and the role it played in the process of development."[3]

In the practice of history, as in science and education, the New Haven scholars took a middle way between the extremes of Romantic and scientific history. In finding this way, the scholars moved beyond the practice of history as it had existed in the previous generation. John Stuart Mill's introduction of French historian Jules Michelet to readers of the *Edinburgh Review* in 1844 explains these three types of historians. In the preceding era, historians had understood the past only in terms of the present. Historians of this type had had an idea of what a society or ruler should be like and had measured past societies and rulers against this standard. The second type of historian recreated the past through empathizing with his subject. The third type stood apart from the subject and saw history as a series of causes and effects.[4] Mill's first type resembles the Enlightenment historian, whose work the New Haven scholars had moved beyond; the second type is the Romantic or literary historian; and the third is the scientific historian.

Romantic or literary historians, including Michelet, Carlyle, and Charles Kingsley as well as Americans George Bancroft and Francis Parkman, emphasized the uniqueness of the individual. They attempted to recreate his spirit or character and to place it within history conceived as a whole. In Carlyle's writings history became the story of the acts of great men. For Bancroft, history was the progress of democracy.

The scientific historian tended to be more interested in the study of society and, in the second half of the century, was often a university-based scholar. He could see merely a fragment of the past, which he discovered through his study of original documents. Whereas the literary historian was the subjective recreator of the past, the scientific historian objectively analyzed a particular institution or nation. Progress became regular and uniform because history was predictable, the result of known effects, not of capricious individuals. The scientific historian usually was a secularist to the extent that he denied that history revealed an unchanging divine reality, and he often placed his facts within a framework based on nineteenth-century natural or social-science theories. For example, Auguste Comte's positivism and sociological theories underlay the histories of Renan, Taine, and Buckle. Darwin's idea of struggle inspired Herbert Spencer's idea of historical progress, and Henry Adams grounded his historical theories in the laws of physics.[5]

New Haven criticisms of Bancroft and F. P. G. Guizot illustrate the scholars' middle way. Bancroft, Porter wrote, filled his narrative with "specious generalization[s]" about the rights of man. Besides engaging in political polemics that supported theories in fundamental disagreement with New Haven theories of natural law, Bancroft engaged in "aesthetic demagoguism." Porter wrote Woolsey that Bancroft was "a scamp—or rather a fool in his philosophy." Fisher conceded that Bancroft was accurate but criticized his rhetorical style, with its "episodes of ornate disquisition" interrupting the narrative.[6] Although Guizot's *General History of Civilization* was scholarly in style, Woolsey had major reservations about the author's viewpoint and selection of subject matter. Guizot had described "the *mechanical* side of human improvement" and so included merely economic, social, and political events and progress. These developments represented only one side of history and had not necessarily caused progress. Woolsey called for the historian to study religious and literary culture, which could reveal "the influences over the individual of truth, religious and moral, and science and of beauty in all its various forms." These sources enabled the historian to see through the mechanical, external facts to the internal, spiritual life of man.[7]

New Haven history was neither entirely Romantic nor entirely scientific. Like scientific historians, the scholars were university-trained and dedicated to an academic career, but they rejected scientific history when its theories violated their ideas of human agency and providence. Their history emphasized the uniqueness of the individual and his power to determine events but contained disapproval of Carlyle's hero worship and Bancroft's rhetorical flourishes. In short, while aspiring to practice history in a scholarly manner, the New Haveners rejected the implied secularism of scientific history.

In his 1898 presidential address to the American Historical Association, George Park Fisher summed up the New Haven approach to history. He rejected Taine's formulation that the individual was a "spiritual automaton" and the positivist notion that the individual belonged "to the category of effects." History was not "the growth of that impersonal being called society" but a drama in which the individual was an actor. When the historian wrote about this drama, he assumed a scholarly style. He avoided bias, either religious or political, and did not resort to descriptive embellishments and paradoxes to make his work interesting. Even though speaking shortly after the Spanish American War, Fisher chose not to comment on it and instead addressed the more important topic of the historian as a judge of the moral worth of historical figures. The historian stripped the laurels from the unworthy and rescued the worthy from defamation. He thus corrected the conclusions of an unschooled public opinion, put good men on their pedestals, and so filled the past with proper role models.[8] From a New Haven perspective, Fisher's history was useful in the same sense that Porter's college professor was useful. Each gave educated men models for their own self-development, but the historian extended the lesson. His interpretation of the relationship of educated men to historical change suggested that educated men would affect the present, for what had been true in the past might be true again.

The New Haven scholars learned their historical method from two related sources: the German historical school and Thomas Arnold. The philologist Boeckh taught his students how rigorous criticism of classical texts could lead to the discovery of the spirit of an age. Although Woolsey was the only New Haven scholar who attended Boeckh's classes, his lessons reached them all. Boeckh's students developed the implications of his method for other disciplines. For example, he taught G. B. Niebuhr, the first historian to apply the critical reading of sources to Roman history. In turn, Niebuhr influenced Thomas Arnold, who continued Niebuhr's work in his *History of the Later Roman Commonwealth* (1838–42). At the University of Berlin, historians Niebuhr and Ranke, jurists Savigny and Eichhorn, philologists Boeckh and Bopp, and theologian Schleiermacher formed what is known as the historical school. The New Haven group learned of their work both through journals such as the *British Quarterly Review* and the *New Englander* and through their study in Germany, especially at the University of Berlin. Fisher's comment that the classics should be studied in Arnold's sense, as an introduction to ancient history, suggests a method of historical study as well as a line of influence. It ran from Boeckh to Arnold and embraced the historical school.[9] These sources had three lessons for the New Haven scholars: how to relate a fact of human history to a larger whole, how to describe the crucial role of the individual, and how to see progress in history as the development of people and nations toward full self-development or wholeness.

The historical school taught that historians should first accumulate facts and then use them as the basis for deductions about a larger metaphysical reality. This method had at its core the idea that fact and generalization, physical world and whole world, existed in a microcosmic-macrocosmic relationship extending throughout history. The macrocosmic reality that members of the historical school such as Ranke sought to know was theistic. This historian, most famous for his insistence on the central importance of facts, also believed that "God dwells, lives, and can be known in all of history. Every deed attests to Him, every moment preaches His name, but most of all, it seems to me, the connectedness of history in the large . . . stands there like a holy hieroglyph. . . . May we, for our part, decipher his holy hieroglyph!"[10] Thus, the trained historian gained knowledge from his study of the facts of the past, and this knowledge made evident the relationship between each fact and the divine whole. In essence, New Haven historical and scientific methods were grounded in idealism. Like scientist Dana and psychologist Porter, the historian, too, assembled facts and induced their connection to a divine reality. Through their idealistic methods, the scholars were able to combine secular and theistic ways of understanding. Judged by the criteria of contemporary historian Dorothy Ross, New Haven history was secular, but only to an extent. The scholars argued that history was divided into periods both distinct from each other and distinct from the present. And they considered change from period to period real, as more than "random variations, the surface appearance of essentially unchanging things or the recurring cycle of an endless wheel." Their past was "both decisively different from and causally linked to the present."[11] When the scholars thought historically, they were secular authorities finding value and meaning in the secular world. Still, when assessing the relative merit of historical periods, they resorted to a theistic strategy. Whereas totally secular historians keep the relativism of their historicism within bounds by judging events against social-science theories of, say, the just society, New Haven historians appealed to their theistic values and beliefs. Institutions, laws, and people could be understood in the context of their age, but they also could be measured against an unchanging divine standard.[12]

From the historical school and Arnold the New Haven scholars learned that the individual had a determining role in history. Events flowed forward until a moment of choice appeared; then the decision maker drew upon tradition, made his choice, and directed the course toward the future. His decision affirmed the value of the past while it established continuity with the future. Further, the individual was morally responsible for his choices, since he was acting within the larger framework of providential history. For the individual, New Haven history cut a middle way between free will and determinism. Reforms and revolutions resulted from human decisions and actions, Fisher explained, and not from economic, political, or social forces. "Great men are not puppets moved by the spirit of the time. To be sure, there must be a preparation for them, and a groundwork of sympathy among their contemporaries: otherwise their activity would call forth no response."[13]

The third lesson of the historical school was the definition of progress. For Ranke, divine purpose was the "universal principle" of world history.[14] To evangelical scholars such as the New Haven group, universal history was a postmillennial reading of the past and a prediction for the future. Progress appeared in history as each successive civilization provided increasingly more opportunity for self-development of its citizens. Since the Reformation, George Park Fisher argued in his *Universal History,* men's minds had been increasingly free from domination by the Catholic Church and absolutist governments. In the present day there were even more reasons for evangelical hope; inventions, cultural developments, and philanthropic movements showed that people were putting their freedom to good use. Human history, Fisher thus predicted, was moving toward its ultimate goal of "unity in variety." By this he meant that "the development and growth of distinct nations, each after its own type, and, not less, the freedom of the individual to realize the destiny intended for him by nature, are necessary to the full development of mankind,—necessary to the perfection of the race. The final unity that is sought is to be reached, not by stifling the capacities of human nature, but by the complete unfolding of them in all their diversity."[15]

Fisher's vision was the New Haven version of the nineteenth-century liberal dream—that history was moving from an unfree past toward a free future. American authors such as Emerson, Thoreau, and Whitman shared New Haven hopes for social perfection. These Romantics found possibilities for individual fulfillment through escape into American nature, whereas the New Haven men and European authors such as Guizot and John Stuart Mill located their vision of individual fulfillment within society. These European thinkers' visions of the free or perfect future were, however, unacceptable to the New Haven men. Guizot, for instance, described this future but defined it in material terms: his free future consisted of freedom from physical want and political tyranny. John Stuart Mill, in comparison, hoped for liberty from the restraints of inherited religious and political institutions and social conventions. Guizot's and Mill's hopes left the New Haven scholars unsatisfied and worried, for their emphasis on the spiritual aspect of human nature meant that material plenty alone could not produce an ideal society. Mill exemplified the dilemma of the unbelieving nineteenth-century liberal: when people were free from the domination of church and monarch, how would they rule themselves? Mill's solution in *On Liberty,* that discourse among wise and learned men would replace the restraints of the past, seemed insufficient.[16] These New Haven descendants of the Puritans doubted human reasonableness; even educated people needed an absolute against which to judge their actions. Believing that religion could supply such a measure, the New Haven men found the German ideal of liberty through self-development (*Bildung*) congenial, for it did not exclude religion. When Fisher celebrated diversity, he understood that diversity was contained within the bounds of accepted moral standards and Biblical laws. The restraints of Christianity allowed for the true freedom of human life and prevented the false freedom of a purely hedonistic life. Human self-development was possible only within civilization.

By identifying individual with national self-development, the New Haven scholars continued a major theme of Puritanism, which historian Sacvan Bercovitch discusses in his *American Jeremiad.* As nineteenth-century descendants of the Puritans, the New Haven men thought that the more self-developed individuals became, the more their national life—government, literature, art, science—would show the entire nation to be self-developed. Individual and national growth were compatible, inextricably linked through mutual dependence. Nevertheless, the scholars were unlike their Puritan forefathers to the extent that their writings inspired hope and not the anxiety of the jeremiad. Bercovitch finds that Puritans depended on engendering a sense of insecurity in order to guarantee the outcome of their mission. The more one feared for the promised future, the harder one would work to bring it about.[17] As Fisher's optimistic view of human progress shows, his intent was quite the opposite; he looked for human accomplishments to prove that God's promise was being fulfilled.

To discover the extent to which a civilization had nurtured the self-development of its people, the New Haven scholars chose for study those aspects of the past that they believed revealed the character or inner essence of a people, that is, their literature, religion, philosophy, art, and architecture. This concern explains why Woolsey accused Guizot of offering an incomplete picture of human progress. Political changes, "the public doings of states," were not primary issues for New Haven scholars. Fisher explained that good modern historians increasingly concerned themselves with "the character of society." They wanted to know "how men lived from day to day, what their occupations were, their comforts and discomforts, their ideas, sentiments, and modes of intercourse, their state as regards art, letters, invention, religious enlightenment."[18] Government, nevertheless, could restrict and influence human activity. For example, the despotic governments of Arab countries, Fisher found, inhibited self-development. "The counterpart of tyranny in the ruler was cringing, abject servility in the subject. Humanity could not thrive, man could not grow to his full stature, under such a system." Consequently, Arabic literature was "monotonous," and Arabic architecture projected "magnitude without elegance." Arabs, Fisher concluded, might be "apt interpreters and critics, but they produced no works marked by creative genius."[19]

Religion, too, could limit human expression. Spanish painters of the Renaissance, thought art historian James Mason Hoppin, produced no great paintings. Their work lacked originality and had a "rigid character." The cause, Hoppin found, was "a cowled monk standing behind [every painter] directing every stroke."[20] When the principles of Protestantism were incorrectly applied, then it might limit self-development, too. Critical of New England theology in the eighteenth century, Fisher described how it began to dominate intellectual life by stifling the potential of the human mind to give "birth to the higher forms of imaginative literature and art" and causing a split "between the understanding and the aesthetic nature." Drawing on the same figures as Van Wyck Brooks in *America's Coming of Age* twenty-three year later, Fisher complained about the extremes represented by Benjamin Franklin and Jonathan Edwards; the former, "a typical burgher," was an empiricist concerned only with the material side of life, while the latter "discoursed from his own enraptured experience on the reality of spiritual light."[21]

Certain historical periods exemplified the human potential for self-development. Among primitive Christians, Fisher found, religion had had the ideal relation to human life. Their religion had supplied "the spirit of a new life." People had not needed "to avoid the world, but only the evil in it. Religion was not to be something apart, but rather a leaven to permeate all things." Medieval and Renaissance Catholicism had destroyed this ideal by erecting barriers "between things sacred and secular, between priest and layman, between religion and human life."[22] Art historian Hoppin discovered another ideal epoch for self-development in fifteenth-century Florence. Its citizens had partially freed themselves from the domination of Christian medievalism but had not yet become the subjects of despotic rule. In this Renaissance city, artists had received encouragement, not from aristocrats, "but from that intelligent social organism of freemen in whose tastes and sympathies they lived and were nourished and formed an integral part." Free to pursue their own ideas, artists had discovered the inspiration of the Greeks and had returned to study forms from nature. These artists had produced great work because they had looked "beneath the form of things and [drew] the soul out of natural objects."[23]

Surpassing past civilizations, the New Haven scholars thought, Athens of the fourth and fifth centuries B.C. had permitted the fullest human self-development. At the battle of Marathon the Greeks had proven the strength of a free people. The battle "was a mortal conflict between the East and the West, between Asia and Europe,—the coarse despotism under which individual energy is stifled, and the dawning liberty which was to furnish the atmosphere required for the full development and culture of the human mind."[24]

The Greeks' educational system, of all aspects of their civilization, drew the praise of the scholars, for it had produced the men responsible for Greek cultural achievements. Hoppin explained that although the Greek curriculum had contained fewer subjects than the present-day curriculum offered, its courses had been "more philosophic, reaching deeper, training the nature symmetrically, making intelligent and habile men, citizens ready for every public work, art, and need." The Olympic games symbolized this excellence; celebrating the achievements of body and spirit, they stood for the ideal of the whole man.[25] Despite this perfection, Greece had declined when aristocratic governments had arisen after the death of Pericles. Writers and artists then had started to imitate nature and strive for decorative display. "After freedom was lost," the more ornamented Corinthian order had flourished, replacing "the stern simplicity of the Doric" and "the softer and more graceful character of the Ionic." The Olympic games also had changed, becoming a formalistic exhibition "of overtraining and sheer muscularity."[26]

In the New Haven ideal of Greece there was both warning and promise. On the one hand, it promised that nineteenth-century America was becoming more like Greece, containing ever more potential for self-development. When political scientist Woolsey, for example, praised the union of Greek city-states as natural, not imposed but arising from circumstances, he immediately suggested a favorable assessment of the American colonies' origins.[27] Not by imitating but by realizing in themselves the principles of Greek art and architecture, Salisbury thought, would Americans create "harmonious art." When Hoppin extolled Greek education, he implicitly extolled the New Haven ideal college and the reforms stemming from it that were instituted at Yale. Because Porter wanted college students to gain culture (*Bildung*), he encouraged them to study Greek literature and to learn from the examples of manhood that it contained. On the other hand, the Greek example warned that a civilization could not maintain its greatness if there were no external controls to "uphold the moral interest of society." Only Christianity could preserve a civilization. Although Greek philosophy had encouraged a higher ethical life, it had been imperfect and incomplete as an ethical system because it had not contained the perfect model of Jesus Christ, which drew people toward the development of their higher nature. Undirected by the model of Christ, Greek men had given play to their baser nature and let their imaginations and desires run free. Philosophy ran into the excesses of Epicureans and Stoics; moral standards declined until even homosexuality was accepted.[28] The fact that Greece had had its glory and then had declined taught that the greatest achievements were transitory when true religion did not secure their permanence.

The New Haven scholars' adoption of the Greek ideal resembles their adoption of the college. Both show how the scholars found secular substitutes for religious ideas and institutions that no longer appealed to a wide audience of educated men and so had become dysfunctional. Infusing the secular with evangelical meaning, they made Greece and Yale College into New Haven means to the millennium. In the evangelical scheme, the college was the primary institution for teaching the new gospel of Greece. If the college did not teach Greek history through its literature, then from the New Haven perspective, the college was a church without a Bible. If the millennium was to be a certainty, then courses in Greek literature could never be elective. History, the Greek ideal, and the college enlarged the scholars' audience beyond New School Presbyterians and Congregationalists to embrace most Protestants in the educated Victorian reading public. By finding evangelical lessons in Greek history, the scholars were at once participating in and using for their own purposes the popular Greek revival of the mid-nineteenth century.[29] Thus, they matched their message to their media, the literature and educational institutions of Victorian America.

For church historian Fisher, the discipline of history opened new approaches to religious questions of the day. By seeing himself as a *historian* and by side-stepping issues that had caused division within Nathaniel William Taylor's generation, he could reach a broad reading public. Fisher assured readers of his *Reformation* that he did not intend it "as a polemical work." He accepted, and expected readers to accept, that Protestant reformers were not "exempt from grave faults and infirmities." Wanting to discover "the real truth," he would be impartial but not indifferent and would avoid both the "carping spirit that chills the natural outflow of just admiration" and "the spirit of hero worship." Also, because Fisher and his generation saw themselves combating the "new infidelity," the previous generation's concerns had become beside the point. By the 1850s, it seemed to Fisher, the public mind had turned from questions of natural and moral ability to new questions—"the relations of religion to the discoveries and conjectures of natural and historical science, the miraculous life of Christ, and his work among men and for them."[30] Drawing on lessons that he had learned at Halle and from his reading of Thomas Arnold and

John Henry Newman, Fisher addressed the new issues. He responded to Biblical critics who, by challenging the truth of miracles, seemed to undermine the accuracy of the entire Bible, and he tried to vindicate heroes of the Protestant reformed tradition under attack for supposed illiberalism.

Fisher's approach to the question of Biblical miracles illustrates his overall strategy in arguing for the Bible as a historical document. Drawing on the research of other historians, he contended that the Apostles had actually existed and that Biblical miracles had been actual historical events. Evidence from Biblical narration supported this contention. Fisher said that he was justified in taking evidence from the Bible itself because it had scientific, scholarly authority; "the laws that determine the credibility of history are respected in the composition of the sacred books. Contemporary evidence is furnished; and the departures from this practice are the exceptions that prove the rule."[31] Fisher thus refuted Renan, Strauss, and Baur, who from their argument that the miracles were not actual historical events proceeded to contend that Christ himself was not divine. In contrast, Fisher saw miracles as actual events providing further proof that Jesus was the Son of God. Proper understanding of the miracles showed the relationship of God to this world; He stood behind nature and intervened in natural processes through the agency of his Son.[32]

Fisher's reason for vindicating the historical truth and divine nature of Biblical miracles was not the same as that of Taylor's generation. The older generation of New Haven theologians and Yale professors had rested their Christian faith on the irrefutable fact of Biblical inerrancy. Doctrine had been revealed completely in the Bible. It was therefore a static, abstract entity refined and debated by successive generations of Protestant ministers. As we have seen, the younger generation of New Haven scholars believed that people had an innate need for God that only the Christian religion could satisfy. Therefore rebuttal of Biblical criticism of the miracles was irrelevant to their faith. Fisher, in fact, said that he did not expect to persuade the nonbeliever; he wanted merely to show Christians that Biblical criticism did not have to undermine faith.[33] Even though Fisher's scholarship might confirm traditional belief, it still could not eliminate the fact that believers now could choose from among several interpretations of the Bible. No matter how powerful or true Fisher's history was, his New Haven scholarship could not turn back the historical clock; readers and students had to live in a world of choice.

Although Fisher did not need the Bible to be literally true for reasons of faith, he did need it to be true, and thus authoritative, for the practical reason that its commandments and description of Christ's behavior linked faith to ethical teachings. In the Bible the trained scholar discovered God's revelation of not only the origin of things, the purpose of history, and the nature of evil but also "the nature and the chief end of man" and his relation to the world. Since the initial revelation of Christian doctrine in the Bible, Fisher learned from Cardinal Newman, doctrine had developed as successive civilizations began to practice increasingly advanced meanings of Biblical truth. In Fisher's words, "The ethical relations of Christianity are by degrees unfolded." Thus the cruel entertainments of ancient civilizations, the slave trade, and slavery itself had disappeared. "The treatment of the poor, of the insane, and of the suffering and afflicted classes generally, which failed to shock the Christian sense of a former day, is now felt to be inhuman."[34] The idea of development was thus a source for criticism, but it held this criticism within the bounds of what was perceived as Christian. For all periods, the example of Christ was an absolute ethical measure. In New Haven practice, Christ and Biblical teachings were the idealistic correlates that historians used to judge the morality, the degree of self-development, of men and nations.

The New Haven Christ, however, was particular—he was the New Haven ideal man perfectly realized with intellect and emotions, heart and head, fully developed and in balance. Christ as model man confirmed that individual self-development could not be undesirable, for the vision of all men become Christ-like was integral to millennial thought. When the New Haven scholars replaced the stern arbitrary God the Father of Puritan theology with a more approachable, gentle, and loving Jesus the Son, they were participating in a change found generally in nineteenth-century Protestantism that some historians refer to as the "feminization" of American religion. But replacement with the quintessence of the New Haven ideal man was a specific modification. For New Haven men Christ became the super role model, the standard against which historical figures could be measured. The scholars' modification of the nature of Christ shows us that men were active participants in the humanization of the deity and that the term *feminization* describes only one-half the process. When we compare the moral lessons of the New Haven scholars and women sentimental authors of the same period, we find that both celebrate moral power. Both groups made heroes and heroines of moral individuals, but each spoke to its own sex-defined audience. From New Haven scholars and authors of sentimental novels, Victorian men and women learned that their moral power would triumph over materialism. But while women's lessons appeared in a domestic entertainment form, the novel, and limited women's moral power to private life, men's lessons appeared in the form of scholarship and suggested the public influence of moral men.[35]

To prove that model men had influenced events, Fisher turned to Luther and Calvin, the central figures of the Protestant tradition. That they had changed history no one in the nineteenth century denied, but these men needed vindication. Frequently contemporary historians and popular opinion associated intense religious belief with a narrow, illiberal spirit that inevitably led to persecution in the state and censorship of literary and artistic expression. Even when writing Noah Porter a thank-you note in 1879 for his "pleasant words," Oliver Wendell Holmes could not help twitting his New Haven friends. First, he assured Porter that though his letter was written on a Sunday, it was written after sundown. Then, admitting to "partial acceptance" of predestination, Holmes said that his beliefs "would have made [him] a candidate for the kind offices of the Genevan turnspit."[36]

The historical figures whom Fisher described were a far cry from Holmes's intolerant Puritan. Luther was an example of culture, or *Bildung* and showed that even an intensely religious man could lead a full human life: "At home and with his friends he was full of humor, was enthusiastically fond of music, and played with skill on the lute and the flute; in his natural constitution the very opposite of an ascetic." The concept that ideas developed over time allowed Fisher to excuse Calvin for his harsh rule in Geneva. As a man of his times, Calvin had ideas of the state far different from ideas prevailing three centuries later. In seventeenth-century Geneva, or in any other European country of that day, the idea of a state limited in its purview over private life and belief had no meaning. As a result, persecution for religious belief and severe forms of punishment were common, but even then, Genevan magistrates were merely following the precedents of Catholic magistrates. Moreover, the times demanded firm rule. People were accustomed to "freedom and little fond of restraint"; only Calvin's followers were committed to "order, independence, morality, and temporal prosperity." In comparison with other Puritan leaders, Calvin was no extremist. He neither supported John Knox's "iconoclastic measures" nor made any comment upon Anglican ceremonies and customs that were anathema to "a more rigid Puritanism." In short, Calvin was able to take advantage of a historical moment and prove that individuals counted in history. He provided systematic thought and action "when the ideas of the Reformation were widely diffused, but when no adequate reduction of them to a systematic form had been achieved."[37] Fisher's accounts of Luther and Calvin freed the New Haven scholars from the stigma of descent from seventeenth-century Puritanism and allowed them to teach that an evangelicized world would bring to perfection and permanence the intellectual, political, and artistic achievements of Greek civilization.

Role models found in historical figures such as Luther and Calvin, and in ideal scholars such as Niebuhr, Arnold, and Woolsey, also taught that power to direct events stemmed from ability to put ideas into action. This tenet of New Haven belief shows the extent of their idealism. It describes both how they perceived the world and its relation to divine truth and how they perceived power and social change. Change occurred, not because of impersonal laws, but because of the influence of men. Real power was not the moral influence of women, the aristocrat's ability to triumph in battle and win a throne, the capitalist's ability to make money, or Emerson's Napoleon's ability to lead the people; real power belonged to the intellectual man of action with a firm religious belief. This lesson may have given the New Haven scholars confidence about their own role in American society and encouraged students to choose professions, such as the academic, yielding only modest material rewards. Provided there appeared fully self-developed liberal men, social theories based on materialistic conceptions of power and change would not take hold. Mankind's understanding of the vital principles of liberty and republican government would continue to grow. Implicitly the New Haven scholars taught that the material developments of the nineteenth century— steam engines, factories, and railroads—could not impede this spiritual progress. Men such as the New Haven scholars and their role models determined the course of history by ensuring that material things served providential ends.

7
Political Science:
The State as Means
to Self-development

T he New Haven scholars' political science was the necessary
partner to their idea of history. Progress in history implied
not only progress to the present but also progress toward
individual and national self-development. The absolute control of
government and religion over people seemed to be diminishing;
thus, in the present age people enjoyed increasing degrees of
freedom and had to learn how to govern themselves. To guide
development along its proper course, Christian truth and the example of Christ provided general principles; political science sketched
in the details with regard to the government of nations, while
social and cultural criticism (the subjects of chapter 8) dealt with
other, equally significant areas of individual and national life. When
men followed proper New Haven theories in their political and
private lives, self-development or full human liberty could be realized in present-day America.[1]

Woolsey introduced political science into the curriculum of Yale
College in 1847. This event began the New Haven scholars' transformation of the purpose of the college curriculum from mental
discipline to self-development. The beginning of the college of
mental discipline and the influence of the Scottish philosophy in
the American colonies is usually dated from the inauguration of
John Witherspoon as president of Princeton in 1768. Moral philosophy, he explained, "not only points out personal duty, but is
related to the whole business of active life. The languages, and
even mathematical and natural knowledge, are but hand maids to

this superior science."[2] When the German-influenced Woolsey started to teach political science, he began a new period in the history of American higher education by dividing Witherspoon's *duty* into two categories, each taught in its own course. While Woolsey lectured on man as citizen, introducing students to theories of natural rights and the state and explaining the application of these theories to current political questions, newly hired Yale professor Noah Porter addressed questions of duty in the more private areas of life in his classes on mental and moral philosophy. For example, Porter discussed duty toward family, self, friends, the physical world, God, and even animals.[3]

From a present-day perspective, to the extent that Woolsey and his colleagues divided the study of duties among academic specialties, they were compartmentalizing knowledge and furthering modernization of the college curriculum. Historians explain that political science was only the first of the social sciences to emerge from moral philosophy; history, sociology, and anthropology followed. Woolsey, however, understood his discipline in other terms. The college, he thought, had three groups of sciences or disciplines: the mathematical, the physical, and the moral; and history, political science, and metaphysics were in the last category. The political scientist concerned himself with man's actions in the state and was not, Woolsey insisted, like a minister. Whereas a minister considered actions *and* the motives behind them, the political scientist considered actions and their consequences for the state only. Because the political scientist did not concern himself with questions of individual morality, he was a secular scholar. Nevertheless, the ultimate purposes of Woolsey's political scientist still were religious, for he believed that God had established the state to accomplish his ends.[4]

Woolsey's religious framework appears not to have prevented his cooperation with his contemporaries, including other mid-century college professors and reformers who belonged to the American Social Science Association (ASSA). But the next generation excluded religion from social-science discourse while continuing Woolsey's methods of comparative historical analysis and institutional interpretation of state and society. Woolsey was among the prominent college professors and officials, including Francis Lieber of Columbia and the Reverend Thomas Hill, president of Harvard, who lent their names to the ASSA at its founding in 1865, and for one year Woolsey served as head of the Department of Economy, Trade and Finance. Like Woolsey, members of the association believed that social harmony, a state in which all individuals' interests blended together without friction, could exist. It did not exist in the present because people did not know the facts necessary for the running of government, the economy, and social institutions. When the facts were known, all people would agree and would set society on its way toward its natural harmony.[5] For Woolsey, of course, the presumed social harmony was an aspect of divine truth. And it was this framework that decisively differentiated his mid-century Romantic understanding of political science from that of the social-science-minded next generation. For example, superficial comparison of Woolsey's political thought and social criticism with those of William Graham Sumner reveals that the two men agreed on many issues, including the origin of the state and political rights and the threat that Jacksonian democracy posed to sound government. But when the basis of their thought is compared, it becomes evident that Woolsey's religious and moral interpretation of historical progress differs fundamentally from Sumner's social perspective. The relationship between teacher's and student's thought may be understood in terms of secularization. Both Woolsey and Sumner assumed that societies progressed according to fixed laws, but Sumner discarded Woolsey's religious idealism and saw these laws as exclusively social and economic. Woolsey's concern was the relationship of the state to moral progress; Sumner's, its relationship to economic and social progress. Denying that morality belonged to the realm of reality that social scientists studied, Sumner opened the door through which a renegade former Yale graduate student, Thorstein Veblen, could enter and begin to criticize the moral underpinnings of Victorianism. In his *Theory of the Leisure Class* (1899), he rejected the idealism of thinkers such as the New Haven scholars and questioned whether acquistion of things really served moral purposes. In Veblen's mental world, what was real were the social and economic motives lying beneath a camouflage of moral cant.[6]

In the 1840s, however, Woolsey's political science represented an intellectual advance. He drew from the lessons of the German historical school to modify the political thought of Timothy Dwight and Nathaniel William Taylor, much as Porter modified their religious and philosophic thought and Dana modified Silliman's science. Dwight's Federalist political theory had roots in Scottish philosophy, and he drew on it to criticize the theories that he believed lay behind the excesses of the French Revolution. In *The True Means of Establishing Public Virtue* (1795), he contrasted the definition of liberty in social-contract theory with the definition derived from a theistic conception of human nature and found that the latter was true liberty. Taylor developed Dwight's thought further by arguing that God was a moral governor who ruled over God-given social and political institutions. To the arguments of his Yale College and Theological Department teachers, Woolsey added a historical dimension and methods of analysis derived from philology.[7] When Woolsey read the laws of civilization so that they revealed its spirit or character, he looked below the surface of events, just as philologists did with classical texts and historians did with facts of the past. In Woolsey's political science, for example, Greek texts showed how the Greek state had been ruled. Its practices were of primary concern to the political scientist because, Woolsey believed, concepts of rights and government had evolved from them. Influenced by the historical school, his political science was thoroughly historicist. Theories of rights and government had developed over time, and man had always lived within history, in society, under a government.[8]

Continuing the concern of Timothy Dwight with political theories associated with the French Revolution, Woolsey drew on his historicist political theory and his organic concept of the state to develop a critique of antebellum Democratic party political theory. He rejected the maxim that the voice of God was the voice of the people and the theory that true freedom existed in a state where government governed least and assumed no responsibility for the moral development of its citizens. Rather, he assessed governments by the relativistic principle that a proper form of government should fit the historical situation of a particular people. A democracy was not necessarily a more desirable form of government than a monarchy. Although monarchs might have absolute power in theory, they rarely possessed that much power in fact. Popular institutions, religious influences, and the advice of counselors checked and limited royal power. Because none of these checks operated to restrain a pure democratic government, an absolute democracy was more to be feared. The will of the people, whether it expressed reason or passion, became the will of their government. Restating Dwight's concern with Rousseau, Woolsey pointed out that the contemporary theory of unlimited democracy resembled this theory of the French Revolution. "Starting from freedom and making freedom inalienable, it ends in a slavery of the individual to the mass, which is much worse than despotism as the mass can never die while the despot happily is not immortal."[9] The reciprocal surrender of rights between citizens and state did not protect individual rights if the votes of the majority of individuals could "send one to the guillotine." Social-contract theory, with its "enormous absurdities," made the state "a great abstract totality that has swallowed up all individuals and so has a great stomach but has no head nor heart." Woolsey hoped that his historically based political theory would overturn the arrogant spirit of the present day, which taught that "no one knew anything until we were born, that the world has been misgoverned and only misgoverned until now, that a great light has arisen in our age, country, and party, before which the world was involved in darkness." Critical of social-contract theory, Woolsey taught that a state of nature was a fiction. His students learned that people had always lived in society and that rights had their origin in human nature. Man did not enter society when he chose to alienate some of his rights; he entered history when he was born into the family, the fundamental social institution. Governments, even though primitive, had existed always; their purpose, rarely fully realized, was "the protection of all a man's liberty and power, for gaining all the ends for which reason pronounces that he exists."[10]

Considering the Declaration of Independence and its basis in social-contract theory, Woolsey noted that its exclusively political emphasis meant that it ignored the fullness of human nature. People, he thought, were more than political animals; they had physical, moral, social, and religious characteristics, and happiness resulted from the development of all of them. Thus, "rights" comprised "the powers and prerogatives with which the individual is invested for the purpose of developing his nature, which other individuals are bound to leave undisturbed."[11] Woolsey's theory that the state existed to promote individual self-development implied that the state had rights and powers intrinsic to its own purpose. As a necessary means or condition for moral improvement, the state had to have powers that would establish the means by which citizens could improve their moral natures.[12] In contrast, the negative state of social-contract theory had the power merely to "define, protect, and redress individual rights" because an increase of its powers was thought to reduce individual freedom. Besides promoting human freedom, defined as moral self-development, Woolsey's positive state also had the power "to guard by law and penalty the morality of the people" and "to promote the public good when rights and moral conduct are not immediately concerned and by means which are no violations of rights or prejudicial to morality." To guard morality, the state could define the rights to worship, free speech, free association, and property, as well as rights emerging from the tendency to form families, such as the rights to marry, divorce, and inherit.[13] To promote the public good meant provision for "intellectual and aesthetic wants, and for the cultivation of the moral and religious nature of [the state's] subjects and citizens." This state was a facilitator, a means for the community to "do its appointed work in the world." The main limit on state power was the realm of private activity; a state should not do what an individual or private association did or could do. For instance, the state should not replace private industry or charity but only complement it.[14] The state always allowed sufficient freedom for human self-development, restricted public behavior counterproductive to self-development, and established institutions to promote self-development.

To promote morality, Woolsey said, the state could use its power in the areas of education and poor relief. His discussion of these topics shows how he visualized the role of a positive state and also how he foresaw the need for limits on state powers. Woolsey found education to be such an indispensable precondition of self-development that he supported compulsory-education laws and a state-supported system of grade school education.[15] Just as college education protected society from the rule of selfish elites, public primary education protected it from "the evils coming from an ignorant lower class in all, especially in free, states." Without education, citizens and especially laborers had no capacity to make choices beneficial in the long run. Education gave the lower classes a chance at upward mobility and so freed them from their employers' domination; at the same time, it showed that indulgence of "low pleasures" was not the sum of happiness. Thus, education was moral because it promoted "the industry, morals, loyalty and quiet of the class."[16]

Because of these overriding moral interests, schools, Woolsey argued, should be public. The interests of religious denominations were no barrier to the teaching of morality, for they would compromise and choose a mutually agreeable text. Their compromise would not include atheists, because their rights conflicted with the state's need for moral instruction. Still, their children could be exempt from moral instruction.[17] State support for higher education, however, was a different matter. Because Woolsey thought that it would encroach upon individual rights, he opposed it. A true university, he argued, contained a school of theology. If one denomination controlled this school in a state university, then the rights of excluded denominations would be violated. Furthermore, the state should not sanction the one version of God's truth that the professors of a denomination inevitably would teach. There was also the increasing likelihood in the postbellum years that professors would teach atheistic, materialistic theories. The neutrality that a state-supported university should assume on these issues conflicted with the interests of the state, because it would be supporting theories that were, according to Woolsey, antagonistic to its proper moral purposes. Education that did not allow for the possibility of God implicitly denied his existence.[18]

Despite his advocacy of a morally active state, Woolsey did not support increasing the police power of the state through legislation such as state prohibition of alcoholic beverages or the federal Comstock Law. In these instances, the state exceeded its powers, invaded the area of private rights, and left no room for individual choice. When balancing the wrong of immorality against the individual right of self-development, Woolsey always sided with freedom. If government restricted individual liberty too severely, then citizens would perceive it as an enemy. Immorality, if it "does not obviously or seriously threaten the existence or well-being of society, must be endured for the sake of freedom, and be left to society and opinion to correct."[19]

Citizens would also be tempted to extend state power too far on account of their natural desire to aid the poor. Woolsey wanted such aid to be limited in scope—supplementing the efforts of families and private organizations—and limited in purpose—assisting the needy and not those he called the "vicious" poor. Charity, Woolsey advised, arose from a feeling of humanity, not from the right of the poor to receive aid. He found the claim that the poor had a right to state relief dangerous. It portended the enlargement of state power, for if the state had the obligation to aid the poor, then it also had concomitant rights and could extend its control. Laws might punish people who merely squandered property or require workers to pay part of their wages as guarantee against the future. The state might even claim the right to preserve itself "against the increase of a class that cannot support itself" by prohibiting marriage until a couple could support themselves. Thus, Woolsey cautioned against the increase of state power at the expense of individual freedom and family privacy that Progressive Era eugenicists espoused and in some cases practiced. Responsibility for freedom, however, rested with the individual. A citizen compromised his own true liberty, Woolsey cautioned, if he left every responsibility to the state. "If he thinks that the end of government is to support him, to point out to him ways of industry, to lead the way in every enterprise, he remains a dependent, undeveloped citizen; he is not a freeman in his spirit."[20]

Woolsey's political science shows, therefore, how the New Haven group modified European definitions of liberty to emphasize individual liberty and limit the powers of the state. Although Woolsey had learned of self-development (*Bildung*) from the German historical school and had borrowed its methods of analysis and historical argument, he retained the particular emphasis of Anglo-American liberalism on the individual, never seeing, as some Germans did, individual freedom as subordinate to the purpose of creating the wholeness of the state. Still, the religious Woolsey defined *liberty* differently than did Mill. Woolsey thought that the English liberal had gone too far. It was less important to call forth "the qualities of the individual, his full and free personality, to the greatest possible extent" than to cultivate "the moral nature by the discipline of justice."[21] Thus Woolsey forged a middle way between idealistic-historicist and realist-empirical interpretations of the state and power.

Woolsey was a pessimist when he viewed political events in the United States from the 1830s through the 1870s. In the earlier period, theories of Jacksonian democracy destroyed the checks that the founding fathers had established on the powers of the federal government. In the post–Civil War era, the appearance of professional politicians and enlargement of the federal government's powers suggested that the state had become hostile to individual self-development. "We move in masses," Woolsey accused. "We obey orders whom to vote for, we exercise our passive natures as though we were Mohammedans in politics."[22]

But Woolsey praised the period from 1787 to Jackson's inauguration as a kind of American golden age when theories of democracy drawn from Greek and Roman models had prevailed. Until Jacksonian innovations, American democracy had worked; its constitution, suffrage qualifications, and system of representation had limited the power of the majority. The community had granted the privilege of the suffrage "to those who would be likely to use it in consistency with the public welfare, and as a trust committed to such as had intelligence and integrity enough to vote for good magistrates." The Jacksonians' demand that representatives enact the voters' will portended further tyranny. French Revolutionary theory had come to the United States, Woolsey warned. Political privileges now were co-extensive with rights of citizenship, and "both were deduced from the rights of man."[23]

Woolsey opposed universal male suffrage for practical and theoretical reasons. Enfranchisement of unpropertied or uneducated citizens meant that elected leaders would be demagogues. Government then would not promote the interests of all, and two political parties would arise. On one side, a party of the demagogue would support the interests of the foreigner and the poor and would base itself on the misunderstood principles of "liberty and equal rights." Its opponent party would stand for "property and civil order," and both parties would be "intensely selfish and equally one-sided." The result of their competition for power was a debased political life—platforms that were merely vote-getting promises, inferior candidates, and patronage and payoffs.[24] Theoretically, universal suffrage was based on the false notion that the suffrage was a natural right similar to the right to acquire property or to form a family. Woolsey argued instead that the suffrage was a political privilege conferred by the community on those men it deemed able to secure its true interest. Suffrage qualifications should allow those men to vote whose level of education or possession of property showed that they had a long-term point of view. Woolsey hoped for a constantly expanding leadership as more men acquired property or education.[25]

The enfranchisement of unpropertied white men by the states during the antebellum years and enactment of the Fifteenth Amendment (1870) made Woolsey accept universal male suffrage as an unalterable fact of political life. He still hoped, nevertheless, that the state could serve as a means to individual self-development. The American environment itself might check an unlimited democracy from becoming a tyranny in fact. Because most citizens owned a small amount of land, they would resist the rule of demagogues and continue to pay taxes, educate their children, and practice industry and thrift.[26] While the American environment acted on the majority of Americans, education would create an influential minority of principled men who, through their example, would encourage politicians to change their ways and other men to follow their lead.

Education changed a man's perspective by allowing him to appreciate the long-term effects of his action, whereas property and material concerns narrowed his perspective to the short term. On the one hand, lack of property made poor men think merely of satisfying their present needs. On the other, wealthy men feared loss of what they had. For example, southern slaveholders practiced a blind conservatism that undermined their own rights. If they had the right to take from slaves their right to their own labor and lives, then their own freedom was not safe. "What is to prevent socialism from dividing up the property of a community among its members," Woolsey asked, "if we acknowledge that neither property, nor any other right, is Sacred?"[27]

In the 1870s, Woolsey found, men of the wealthier classes let their businesses consume their time. Was it honest, Woolsey questioned, "to get rich and give thanks for security and freedom without manifesting strong indignation against the evil that we see around us"? Were these men really laying "up treasures of security for their children, or [were] they not, by their listlessness, hastening on the corruptions of the country?"[28] Free from the merely narrow interests of property or tradition, educated men could seek out and follow the best ideas. These were men of honor who had the "independence" and "character" to renounce "all that is mean, base or unworthy of a man; above all, untruthfulness, unfaithfulness, cowardice, especially moral cowardice." They were "ready to do what is right in spite of all obstacles." The families that these men formed "preserved the nation from decay" and were "a source of health to the state," for they established a "standard of true excellence," purifying public opinion as they diffused "their own culture around them" and "propagat[ing] it onwards in families modelled after the idea of true virtue and religion."[29]

In the post–Civil War years Woolsey put his faith in no reform such as Civil Service or the Mugwumps. Whereas Sumner had faith in laws and reforms restricting special interests, Woolsey counseled always that "the cure of political evils must come, not from any measures or influences affecting large masses at once, but from sentiments that grow up in individual minds." He warned that if honorable men seceded from an existing political party to form another, they would accomplish nothing. The third party probably would have conventions and caucuses, and inevitably its members would be "corrupted by negotiations with the others." The honorable man had to act independently. For Woolsey this meant voting according to principles and refusing to support an "improper" candidate. When enough men acted this way, a party would have to reform itself and start to nominate honorable men as candidates. In the meantime, honorable men should offer themselves for office, Woolsey suggested, much as candidates did in present-day England or ancient Rome. Finally, honorable men could try to persuade voters through journals and newspapers that rose above partisan politics "to ferret out the secret corruption of legislators," to lead public opinion, and "to give their readers large views, outside of the party horizon, of the great interests on the success of which the country's hopes depends."[30]

Beginning in the 1870s, Woolsey began to analyze and criticize the history and theory of communism and socialism, for he believed that these theories promised an all-powerful state and a false utopia. His criticism reveals how he defined social improvement as a process that could not exist without an intellectual elite and private property. A communist state would enlarge the scope of its activities until they pervaded all areas of life. Its citizens, Woolsey argued, would have even less freedom than the slaves on a southern plantation had enjoyed; its rulers would be more despotical than any tyrant of ancient history, whose power could not "have crushed individual rights to an equal degree." They would destroy liberty in order "that equality of condition may take its place." Though the theories of communism and socialism promised cooperation, in actuality they destroyed all motive for the individual to work for others and left the individual an isolated unit in society. Without private property, men would have no motive to work for something larger than themselves, such as the family, which held their loyalty to this and future generations. It concerned Woolsey that the independent opinion of citizens would not act as a countervailing power to the self-interest of the state. The state, he predicted, would grow "strong and uncontrollable" as its functions grew and citizens lost power "to oppose, or correct, or enlighten the state in favor of the interest of general society." For the lower classes, there would be sameness and loss of diversity; without the traditional upper classes, comprising the rich and "highly trained persons," society would stultify in its present condition, for there would be no learning or intellectual progress. Upper-class and educated elites allowed for progress by maintaining the idea "that there is something better than material good . . . that cultivation of soul and mind is better than utilized results of knowledge." "An opulent class" did not exist merely for its own pleasure. When its members moved forward in "a course of hard thinking . . . toward some ideal goal, they awaken others who would have slumbered amid empty hopes."[31]

Most of the scholars' methods of analysis combined with evangelical hopes to produce optimism about the future of American society. But Woolsey was a pessimist, as his poem about science and his response to Jacksonian democracy show, and republican political thought inherited from his Federalist college teachers supplied a vocabulary for expression of his fears. He did not believe that history was only moving forward, toward a future of self-development. Instead, he concerned himself with the question of whether republics must decay. History seemed to show that all great states had declined, and analogy to the life of a man suggested inevitability. Millennialism saved Woolsey from total pessimism. He advised that economic growth and increasing concentrations of wealth did not automatically cause national decline. Although material prosperity brought certain evils, it also brought cheaper commodities, greater personal industry and thrift, the spread of charitable institutions, and the development of community resources that could be used in hard times. Having dismissed material things and conditions as insufficient in themselves to destroy a republic, he pointed to the real cause—"the weakness and shortsightedness of human nature working on a large scale." Because Woolsey believed that the actions of educated elites shaped a society, he expected that signs of national decay would first appear in their values and beliefs. If the upper classes were responsible for moral improvement, they could also encourage moral rot. Woolsey's religiously based criticism always cut both ways. Instead of being honorable and independent, men in a nation with a decaying moral fabric would have a "tendency to self-indulgence" and lose their "sterner self-asserting virtues." They would show no interest in political life, refuse "to exert themselves for the public good," begin to sneer "at heroic virtues," and doubt "the worth of things valued in olden times," adopting instead "the cosmopolitan feeling that owns no bonds of country."[32] Christianity offered hope, but not unconditionally. Historical examples showed that Christianity was powerless when morals had deteriorated too far. For the Romans, Christianity came too late; only invasion by German barbarians could alter the course of history. Other post–Civil War social critics such as Henry George (1839–97), Edward Bellamy (1850–98), and Henry Demarest Lloyd (1847–1903) shared Woolsey's republican fears and millennial vision. All hoped that the American nation might avoid the historically destined fate of all republics if there occurred a general moral revival, what Woolsey termed "the revived prevalence of Christian faith." Nevertheless, these postwar critics differed from Woolsey in their proposed means of reform, for their anticipated moral revival was a precondition for more fundamental changes in American society and economy, to be realized through implementation of either the single tax, the industrial army, or socialism.[33]

With its emphasis on morality and individual self-development as means and ends, Woolsey's political theory can best be understood in the context of the antebellum Whig party. Like Whig politicians, entrepreneurs, and reformers, Woolsey rejected the Democratic party definition of freedom as the unfettered pursuit of material wealth and territorial expansion. Whigs saw the future in terms of the moral development of the nation and its citizens. While Whig politicians supported policies that would make the nation an arena for individual moral development, the New Haven scholars concerned themselves with the moral development of men. The New Haven reform agenda started with the scholars' role as college teachers and publicists who nurtured a self-controlled elite and disseminated right ideas among them. Members of this elite acted in their communities as moral magnets drawing less well-educated men to their example of self-control and advocacy of right ideas. From this elite flowed policies designed to promote individual and national development. Woolsey's positive state, which promoted moral development and did what individuals could not do for themselves, could justify both state support for primary and secondary schools, his chief interest, and a system of federally financed internal improvements, such as Henry Clay's American System. In terms of what Woolsey rejected, his independent man of honor in politics resembles the self-controlled ideal man of temperance and moral reformers. These evangelical reformers saw people's potential for true freedom compromised by lack of self-discipline and passion for things mundane. When, however, people threw off their attachments to substances like alcohol and institutions like political parties and southern slavery, they would obey God's word, which God-given natural institutions such as family and school had prepared them to hear, exercise self-control, and develop their moral natures. On this general level, Whigs and the New Haven scholars agreed that the self-controlled individual was a precondition for a moral world. In current sociological terms, we can express their agreement by saying that all Whigs and antebellum reformers saw the self-control of individuals as means to social control.[34] Yet the term *social control* should not suggest the same negative implications as it does when applied to a modern totalitarian movement that has a single purpose and the power to bring it about. Though agreeing on the need for individual self-control, both Whigs and reformers advocated different means to this end. The scholars, for instance, opposed the immediatism of abolitionists and other perfectionists. Unlike these extremists, the New Haven men intended their message for a male educated elite and proposed more gradual institutionally based reforms with a nurturing emphasis.

Because New Haven political science was intended for a small audience of men who wished to belong to an educated elite, Woolsey could shape his message accordingly. Unlike Whig politicians and popular reformers, he did not have to win men of various social, economic, and religious backgrounds to his cause. While Whig politicians implicitly supported the role of an elite, Woolsey could make this message explicit to his selected audience of Yale students and college-educated readers—the "young men of liberal culture" who "in a republic like ours are in a degree responsible for the measures of government." Nevertheless, even among the college-educated, Woolsey's evangelical emphasis reduced the audience for his views. For example, when Woolsey gave the Phi Beta Kappa address at Harvard in 1875, he chose to discuss "The Relations of Honor to Political Life." Although Woolsey and President Charles William Eliot of Harvard agreed that college-educated men should lead the country, they defined this leadership differently. Eliot felt that college-educated men could lead by finding places in government through its civil service system or by entering a profession.[35] Always, Eliot defined *useful* in a more pragmatic, utilitarian way, whereas Woolsey emphasized the power of individual example and moral leadership. Yale students, who had heard George Park Fisher discuss the historical role of leaders such as Calvin and Luther and Porter describe the ideal scholar, probably would have more fully understood, if not appreciated, Woolsey's description of the honorable man in politics. The westward spread of evangelicalism during the course of the nineteenth century should have meant extension of Yale ideas to a national audience. But increasing pluralism in American society and advancing secularization limited New Haven ideas to an audience of like-minded educated evangelicals living in a period when it was acceptable to cast political hopes in religious terms. It was Eliot's more secular thought that caught the imagination of future generations.

Woolsey's reaction to the effects of the Civil War shows the critical power of his political theory and his perception of the period after 1861 as a new age. He now had doubts about an active government and questioned the extent to which government should take responsibity for the moral welfare of its citizens. After the war, the powers of government seemed to be qualitatively different and threats to liberty. Inventions and advances such as the telegraph and transcontinental railroad suggested new responsibilities for the federal government. Further, the war had opened the possibility of extending the domain of federal law and vastly increased the amount of patronage. The Union seemed to be growing into "so great a tree, with such thick foliage, that the states, like shrubs, will lose their healthy growth under its Shade; that instead of being protected, they will wither." The federal government also faced peril from its suspension of specie payments and funding of the war debt. These financial measures had caused accumulation of great fortunes and the eclipse of middle-class virtues such as "thrift, moderation, and forethought." A result was discontent among all groups. Laborers sought to redress grievances through strikes, and western producers, feeling "oppressed by transporters," attempted "by legislation [to] change the laws of profits." Great corporations had arisen. With their vast resources and the "increased venality" of congressmen, they could buy votes and divert the course of government from furthering individual self-development. For Woolsey, the transition from antebellum Whig to postbellum Republican was neither smooth nor complete. The evangelical strain of New Haven thought remained uneasy with a positive government concerned merely with the material development of the nation. Woolsey's uneasiness, however, was personal and not general among his colleagues. Speaking in Buffalo on 29 December 1876, Noah Porter urged Yale College graduates to vote Republican, since that party favored education.[36]

An appreciation of the New Haven scholars and other mid-century groups will revise our understanding of the shift in social thought from the late nineteenth century to the early twentieth. When we compare the social thought of William Graham Sumner with that of Progressives such as Herbert Croly, we are describing movement away from a government policy of economic laissez faire. But when instead of Sumner's political and social thought we take as a basis of comparison New Haven scholar Woolsey's, in which government was an active moral agent, the shift appears less absolute and more relative. Whereas Woolsey thought of the state as a means to freedom in an evangelical sense, Progressives emphasized the power of government to create a socially desirable present. Finding in Christian thought or German idealistic conceptions of history the idea that the state could actively promote realization of an ideal society, Progressives reshaped, or made secular, the Whig emphasis on moral development. Without hope for the millennium of nineteenth-century evangelicalism, the Progressive generation of Jane Addams, Herbert Croly, E. A. Ross, and John R. Commons rethought and redefined what the powers of an active government should be in the secular twentieth century.[37]

8
From Whole Man to Whole Society

*We would not recall those times when art was for the few, and the
great multitude lived in the misery and squalor of serfdom. . . . and
in no other country in the world are tasteful, comfortable, and
happy homes so abundant as in our own.*

Edward Elbridge Salisbury, *"Principles of Domestic Taste,"* 1877

The concept of self-development (*Bildung*) gave the New
Haven scholars a critical tool for describing their ideal individual, their ideal society, and the relationship between
them. Self-development implied, first, an individual free from
mundane dependencies and able to realize his dependency on God
and, second, that institutions of law and education, which the
scholars understood as God-given, were intended by him to promote individual self-development. Therefore, analysis of the family
or of a nation's political system could reveal the extent to which
it promoted individual self-development and thus was part of the
divine plan. Consequently, desirable change or reform meant making institutions promote self-development and, as a result, God's
purpose. The New Haven scholars assumed that they were merely
reading this message *from* the thing that they were analyzing, when
actually they were reading *into* the thing their understanding of
its long-range purpose. Perception of the world in terms of self-
development thus filled it with theistic meaning and allowed the
New Haven group to see its future in evangelical terms.

To describe self-development, they drew on a vocabulary full
of organic imagery. They described college graduates' self-development in terms of *wholeness* and *culture,* because college had
developed students' *nature.* The process of education resembled the
growth of a tree. It does not bear fruit, George Park Fisher said,
"until time has been allowed it to grow, to send down its roots
and assimilate the elements that nourish it." In contrast, men who

had received the wrong kind of education had not developed all sides of their nature; they were *one-sided*—religious sectarians, bigots, political partisans, materialistic businessmen, or geniuses. Their education might be called *hothouse,* because it *forced* education, just as a hothouse forces a bud to bloom before the proper season. The scholars also admired human creations as part of this organically whole divine world. To Noah Porter the achievements of modern civilization appeared as the "blooming flowers and ever ripening fruit of the ideas of God."[1]

Whether applied to personal or social development, organic imagery and self-development made progress seem regular and orderly and made the future appear as the continuation of the past. The present had grown from seeds of development, and growth proceeded according to laws contained within the seeds. The human mind, Fisher said, was "a germ which education provokes to unfold." Woolsey compared the growth of the state to the growth of a tree. Dana interpreted natural selection and the struggle for survival as divinely ordained processes. In history, a revolution was merely the moment when men selected the strands from the past from which the future would develop. Seen through New Haven eyes, the world was a beautiful order.[2]

When men were fully self-developed, they enjoyed true freedom. For the New Haven scholars, this freedom did not justify a romantic, self-indulgent flight from the responsibilities of civilization; it brought an intensified awareness of citizenship in a divinely ordained community. Liberty was not, as nineteenth-century liberals such as John Stuart Mill thought, an end in itself but a means. Free men recognized their ultimate dependence on God, strove to improve their moral nature, and accepted duties and responsibilities stemming from their human rights. They respected the rights of their fellow men, obeyed the laws of the state, and protected their families.[3] It followed that institutions of American life—family, state, church, school, and college—could contribute to human freedom insofar as they promoted self-development. Books, art, and architecture also were liberating to the extent that they were morally didactic or could be perceived as such. The New Haven view of history gave hope that in the nineteenth century the entire world would enjoy true freedom. External restraints from despotic governments and absolutist religions seemed to have almost disappeared. The Protestant Reformation had freed the human imagination from control by Catholic priests. Now the demise of absolute monarchies and the spread of representative governments promised that states would allow individuals sufficient political freedom for self-development. A group of evangelically committed educated men taught in colleges and helped to create an elite who would counsel less-educated men on their proper social and political responsibilities. Missionary work promised that this new enlightenment would spread from western European countries, and economic abundance promised that poverty would no longer bar self-development.[4]

With this view of history and interest in culture as *Bildung*, the New Haven scholars asked two questions of their contemporary world: what historical survivals still threatened true freedom and what new phenomena portended destruction of the nineteenth-century promise. In the first category they put southern slavery, Catholicism, and poverty, and in the second, the rise of what we now call an industrial work force, professionalism, and a consumer-oriented marketplace. Unlike more popular nativist and antislavery lecturers, they analyzed forces that, on the one hand, limited self-development of enslaved blacks and free workingmen and, on the other hand, tempted middle-class men into new forms of material dependence and slavery. While the New Haven men were aware of the social realities of their time, such as the effects of urban life on working people and the growing numbers of Catholic immigrants, these were not major concerns. The explanation lies in New Haven social theory, according to which the existence of the few, an educated elite, was a precondition for the millennium. Therefore, the scholars worried most intensively and extensively about how contemporary society affected the creation of this elite and, to a far lesser extent, how this elite should address the material and moral condition of nonelites.

For example, the New Haven scholars' response to Catholicism shows their definition of social problems in terms of independence and self-development. Although he deplored nativist political parties, political scientist Theodore Dwight Woolsey observed that immigrants tended to "act in masses" and support political bosses, whom he called "demagogues." Woolsey criticized immigrants' tendency to maintain loyalty to their homelands and to resist adopting American ways of political independence. Given his special interest in education, the Catholic problem meant to Noah Porter the consequences of Catholic education for intellectual progress. Whereas he compared Jesuit colleges unfavorably to formal French gardens, with pruned bushes conforming to mathematical designs, he likened Protestant colleges to English parks, with landscape designs that enhanced the beauty of their existing natural features. Protestant colleges encouraged "the freedom and independence of individual man," while Catholic colleges required "obedience and dependence." Jesuits were "casuists" whose understanding of a problem never deepened. The religion of Protestant scholars, in contrast, encouraged their contemplation of human ends and did not require adoption of a narrowing ascetism. Not confined to monasteries, Protestant scholars belonged to families and participated in everyday life. These relationships disciplined naturally, discouraging flights into mysticism and making thought practical to human concerns.[5]

For the New Haven scholars, industrialism and slavery were more serious threats to wholeness and freedom. Slavery deprived men of their freedom to develop themselves morally, and industrialism posed new threats to independence.

To discover New Haven opinions on slavery, it is necessary to consult articles written by ministers for the *New Englander*. (See appendix 4.) They argued that the southern system denied slaves their natural rights to keep the products of their labor, form and support families, and educate themselves. The South, with its slave labor system, appeared as the antithesis of self-development, an atavism in the nineteenth century. An oligarchy ruled the South and was trying to expand its power by westward expansion. Immediate emancipation, however, was no answer, for it would merely abolish the institution of slavery without remedying the other conditions that made men slaves. Immediate emancipation promised neither to destroy the slave oligarchy's power nor to make slaves truly free men; it merely would deliver uneducated, propertyless slaves into a new form of servitude under ex-slaveholders.

Despite their insight, *New Englander* writers after the Civil War opposed plans of radical Republicans. Instead, they supported education for freedmen and women and predicted that the law of supply and demand would turn freed slaves into free laborers and ex-slaveholders into agricultural entrepreneurs. When white southerners obstructed this progress, Woolsey urged southern gentlemen to act as a responsible elite, to encourage their fellow citizens to obey the law and to recognize that all men were equal before it.[6]

Until the late 1870s the New Haven scholars did not dwell on the effects of industrialism, simply because they did not think that it undermined the true freedom and moral development of American workers. Industrialism in the United States, they thought, differed from industrialism in England. English laborers worked under the "penumbra of feudalism," with artificial restrictions such as the apprentice system, limiting their chances for upward mobility. Without hope of material improvement, English workers lived "degraded" lives and were often intemperate. American workers, in contrast, were well paid, well fed, and respected as valuable members of their communities. They had the opportunity to become educated and to own land. Nevertheless, the scholars did not see the American future in terms of industrialism. Rather, they looked forward to a time when each family would have its own farm and land would be more and more evenly distributed.[7]

Painter John Ferguson Weir, whom Yale president Woolsey hired as the first director of the Yale School of Fine Arts, expressed the vision of working men as independent individuals in his *The Gun Foundry* (1866). The painting shows a scene in a factory that produced cannons for the Union army. Apparently without supervision, workers cooperate to pour molten iron into a cannon mold. In the heat of the foundry, they have removed their shirts. Their poses reveal well-muscled forms that would have reminded educated nineteenth-century viewers of statues of Greek heroes. At the side of the foundry, ladies and gentlemen admire these free workers of the North, whose labor they hope will destroy the slave power. Light emanating from the molten iron visually unites the workers and their audience, illuminating the former and dazzling the latter. Given the New Haven idea of a divine reality embracing the world, the light seems to surround the workers' mundane task with divine meaning. Weir used his art to make evident the New Haven idea of the nobility and individuality of the worker and his moral equality with the obviously prosperous spectators.[8]

It was probably the labor violence of the 1870s that caused the New Haven scholars to change their opinion and perceive industrialism as a problem. Recognizing that a new age had arrived, Woolsey explained that "the days when the workman was the proprietor of his machines and products, the days of home-work and cotton looms, have given way to vast engines and vast manufactures." Compacting laborers into masses where men lost their individuality, factories now seemed to threaten the dignity and freedom of workingmen. Whereas the interest of the individual worker had formerly served the larger interests of society, now the massed force of workingmen opposed this general interest.[9]

The Gun Foundry (1866) by John Ferguson Weir. Reproduced by permission of the Putnam County Historical Society, Cold Spring, New York.

To the New Haven scholars, poverty appeared as a problem because of the ways it affected morality and because of the false reforms that the need for its solution called forth. Reform had to solve the problem of poverty, Noah Porter explained, because "the stomach must be appeased, the body must be clothed, the family must be sheltered, the supply for future need must be secure at least for a week, or a man cannot hold that dignity and independence which are the conditions of moral development and quiet self-culture."[10] While the scholars believed that the poor could better themselves in New Haven terms, they condemned the poor in their present state as "vicious," "sensual," and "materialistic." They meant that the poor were given to what we would call immediate gratification and did not practice self-restraint, a precondition of self-development. The burden for solving the problems that poverty presented fell both on the poor themselves and on the rest of society. Never writing tracts for the poor to explain how they could be moral and industrious, the New Haven men told their educated readers that they should realize their twofold Christian duty to prevent and relieve poverty.

Although the scholars expected American economic progress and the fair treatment of labor to solve the problem of poverty, they called for recognition of workers' right to the product of their labor and their right not to be sacrificed for production. Specifically, they supported the ten-hour day, low-cost mortgages, and vocational education, reforms that they thought would make it easier for workers to better themselves. These reforms seemed no more than the application of "the gospel to social life."[11] Socialism, or any reform that destroyed the right to private property, was not a true reform. It made "the rich poor without making the poor rich," for the poor lost their right to own homes and accumulate property, major incentives to self-improvement. The New Haven scholars thus believed that true reform harnessed men's inherent acquisitiveness and interest to their wish to provide for their families. If men had no desire to rise, then they would give themselves to "far grosser and more abandoned sensuality" and consume "the abundance provided for [their] use."[12]

Although it is clear that the social turmoil of the 1870s troubled the New Haven men, it is difficult to know exactly where they stood with regard to the Social Gospel movement and the issues it raised. All but Fisher had died by 1907, when Walter Rauschenbusch published *Christianity and the Social Crisis,* and so none could have had any idea of the full meaning of the movement. Nevertheless, we can assemble a credible case that they would have supported the Social Gospel movement to a certain extent.

Historians find roots of the Social Gospel in the social thought of mid-century liberal Protestants, especially Horace Bushnell, his disciple and biographer Theodore Thornton Munger (Yale, 1851; Yale Theological Department, 1865), and Newman Smyth. Bushnell's connection to the New Haven group is already evident, and it can be noted that both Munger and Smyth supported the scholars on religious matters, held pulpits in influential New Haven churches, and, like the scholars, studied in Germany and received inspiration from idealism and historical methods of Biblical criticism.

On issues of social policy, the New Haven group were not the sort of conservatives who stressed the primacy of economic rights. On the one hand, Porter defined private property as "an arrangement to which man has a natural right which is sanctioned by the nature of men and the will of God," and he considered that a professor, journalist, minister, or politician committed the moral crime of demagoguism when he argued that "property in itself is . . . robbery." On the other hand, Porter and his colleagues never thought that natural right to property meant that property rights were absolute and inviolable under all conditions. The right to it, Porter's friend Woolsey recommended, should never be pushed to extreme limits, "for ethical truth is as peremptory and exact as physical truth." It is also evident that the New Haven scholars did not support social policy based on laissez faire, for they consistently supported a morally active government, and their religious values served as a basis for criticism of social injustice. Porter, for instance, called for social scientists' recognition that human life should be more than brute struggle and invoked "the law of love, which, were it perfectly obeyed, would be quick to interpret and prompt to regard the teachings, and apply the lessons, which human experience must gather from social observation and experiment." And a *New Englander* writer contended that the labor problem of the 1870s could not be solved "by any science, falsely so-called, which is developed solely from the principles of selfishness."

From these views it follows that the New Haven men could support reform measures such as state regulation of railroads' rights of property. However, they never recommended socialism or any other form of state-directed corporate ownership, for it would have too severely compromised individual freedom. Unlike several other late-nineteenth-century social scientists, namely, Richard T. Ely and Herbert Carter Adams, the New Haven scholars found no bridge to socialism in either liberal Protestant thought, which emphasized social progress, or German idealistic conceptions of history, which interpreted progress as a gradual realization of an ideal.[13] They always believed that possibilities for universal self-development existed within the established property arrangements of the American economy.

Whereas the New Haven group hoped that upward mobility would make possible the self-development of workingmen, they feared that the side effects of upward mobility threatened to divert men of the middle classes from this purpose. Political partisanship, religious sectarianism, false political and philosophical theories, excessive devotion to business and professional interests, and indulgence in luxury were temptations that could lure these nineteenth-century equivalents to Bunyan's Pilgrim from the path to self-development, their heavenly city. The New Haven group adopted the plight of these men as their special concern, for they were candidates for the elite that the scholars believed was a precondition for the millennium. As the New Haven scholars described their hopes and fears for these men, they were in fact coming to terms with one of the dilemmas of nineteenth-century liberalism. If there was freedom from the narrowing effects of doctrinal religion and traditional political institutions, then what forces would restrain human behavior? The New Haven scholars observed the political and intellectual life of Jacksonian democracy and concluded that the rule of *vox populi, vox Dei* did not work. In worrying about the individualism of antebellum politics and revival-oriented evangelicalism, the New Haven men were in accord with their friend Horace Bushnell. He proposed that *Christian Nurture,* a process of family-based education, could naturally develop the intrinsic Christian goodness of children. The New Haven ideal college really extended and completed the Christian nurture that Bushnell's family started. Nevertheless, whereas Bushnell's family was a universal institution for all, the college was for a few men. The college was a democratic institution because the education of the few was supposed to serve the interests of the many, not because it reflected the dominant values of society and opened its doors to the many.[14]

New Haven lessons prepared college students for leadership defined in social and cultural terms far more than in political and economic terms. For example, in political science classes Woolsey lectured on academically current and respectable theories of natural rights and the state that countered more prevalent and popular beliefs. Further, role models selected from classical literature and history, the example of the scholars themselves, and their explicit criticism of material pleasures taught that economic success did not necessarily promote self-development. College education brought the process of human personality development to a stage of completeness and did not, in a utilitarian sense, provide either a degree to serve as a ticket to a job or training that qualified a student for a profession. Graduates, the scholars expected, might continue their studies and prepare for a specific profession, for no one profession was the sum of a useful human life. Neither was one profession, say, business or government service, more or less useful than another, such as journalism or engineering. Rather, values derived from a college education guaranteed that members of all professions would be useful, for they would not become single-mindedly obedient to a code of behavior unrelated to comprehensive spiritual values. The values absorbed in college provided "the broad link among cultivated men of all professions." College education gave the future professional "large views of [his profession's] relations to society and the universal source of knowledge" and countered his tendency to defer "to mere technicality and unintelligent tradition."[15]

Because college graduates were supposed to act as models for other men, all aspects of their lives had to give evidence of their self-development. *Taste* was the word from the vocabulary of organicism that suggested self-developed men's ability to act properly in the marketplace as consumers. Taste made college graduates into complete bourgeois Christian gentlemen who could select from the abundant marketplace purchases that had an organic, or tasteful, relationship to moral growth and self-development. Taste transformed the world and its goods from things that would compromise self-development into things that acted as means of grace to promote this process. Once again, Horace Bushnell explored the connotations of taste, while the New Haven scholars applied them to specific fields, in this case art and literature.

Taste, Bushnell explained, implied choice governed by internalized values, whereas *fashion,* its opposite, implied obedience to external authorities, most probably foreign and related to the aristocratic social orders of France and England. For example, Major Effingham of James Fenimore Cooper's *Home as Found* was a fashionable hero because he was "drawn from the arbitrary rules and customs of a cold-hearted artificial foreign society." The fashionable person ignored local sources of authority such as neighbors, minister, and parents to pattern himself after models, such as the Major, derived from magazines and books. The fashionable man was no more than his exterior affectations of manner and dress. "His soul is on the outside of him," Bushnell said, "a change there, changes all there is of him."[16]

The New Haven scholars found fashion to be antidemocratic for the reason that it threatened social cohesion. Fashion encouraged the rich to isolate themselves from the less well-to-do and to deny their membership in a moral democracy. Theodore Dwight Woolsey described how the rural cemetery, a new phenomenon in the 1840s, destroyed social wholeness "by making brotherhood in wealth . . . the principle of admission." In earlier years a graveyard had adjoined a church and welcomed all its members. Now Mt. Auburn in Cambridge and Laurel Hill in Philadelphia created family unity in death at the expense of "brotherhood in faith, or the brotherhood of human kind or both." Wealthier Christians who purchased plots were "driving out perhaps the poor disciple, whose glorified form now beholds its Savior, and admitting a bloated slave of lust, whose end no one loves to think of." The architecture of the monuments in these cemeteries appeared to be fashionable and tasteless, presenting the "embodied littleness" of a "gothic cathedral, Doric temple, little gothic castle in clapboard, imitations of the pavilion at Brighton, and sundry eclectic non-descripts which by the juxtaposition of parts have become monsters, all going up as if to create a sensation."[17]

Taste, in contrast, perpetuated moral order. It was an innate tendency that nurture promoted; no reader could consult a magazine and acquire it instantly. God, Bushnell said, had created a universe in which everything was fitting and harmonious, and so tasteful things, whether man-made or natural, manifested a part of the divine order. Because Americans were politically free from the rule of Europeans, they could choose to follow the guidelines of taste rather than obey the dictates of fashion. Bushnell urged America to "dare to be republican" so that the country might be a realm of taste where "the graceful dress of our people, their fine truthful manners, the genial glow of their society, their high-toned liberty and tasteful piety, [would] combine to show the dignity of our institutions." In a society ruled by the principles of taste, material things such as the architecture of houses suggested social unity. If tasteful designs were followed, the cottages of common men would be "sprinkled over the hills and blended with the elegant mansions of the rich."[18]

Noah Porter was the New Haven scholar most concerned with the relationship between taste and the literary marketplace. Books, he thought, had the power to strengthen readers in their religious faith or to "reduce the soul to barrenness and waste." The publishing revolution of the nineteenth century created many of the problems of which Porter complained. New techniques of manufacture and distribution made possible an American literature national in scope made up of books, newspapers, and magazines suited to various interests and pocketbooks. For instance, Oliver Wendell Holmes intended his *Atlantic Monthly* column, "The Professor at the Breakfast Table," for a national audience and often poked fun at local peculiarities, such as the religious beliefs of more theologically conservative groups. Although conceding that Holmes had the liberty to say what he wanted at his own breakfast table, Porter warned that Holmes should not be so impolite as to ridicule his religious faith when the *Atlantic Monthly,* figuratively speaking, came into Porter's house as a guest. He feared that even if readers avoided Holmes's ridicule of religion, they still might unknowingly choose a book by an atheistic author. Comparing the author to a godless scientist, Porter said that he was as apt "to set himself forth in independence of God, as is the scientific oracle. Both are Creators in their way, and both are tempted to imitate the thunder of the Deity, by tricks like the would-be Jupiter of olden time." Whereas the scientist created his "universe in thought, after the laws of nature," the atheistic author presided "over the world of fancy, of imagery, of expression." The popularity of atheistic authors and what Porter called the "satanic school of poets" was "gigantically fearful" and "insidiously subtle."[19]

The relatively inexpensive cost of books and the abundance of the nineteenth-century literary marketplace encouraged a new way of reading that Porter called "mechanical dawdling." Previously books had been a scarcer and dearer commodity; a family was likely to own the Bible and then possibly Bunyan's *Pilgrim's Progress* and an almanac. Readers, most often men, consulted their books over and over and drew from repeated readings new applications for their lives. Nineteenth-century readers, who were mostly women, read less intensively and more extensively, rapidly consuming one book after another. To these readers books were diversion or escape, not keys for unlocking the divine meaning of everyday life. What was even more serious, not even educated elites were to be trusted as guides. They were becoming, Porter found, "intellectually blasé, enfeebled in their capacity of judging with moral earnestness, through the distracting influence of the numberless objects that the wealth of modern science and the activity of modern literature and modern life pour out before their mental vision."[20]

Other Victorian educators agreed with the New Haven scholars. George Ticknor encouraged the founding of the Boston Public Library because he believed in the power of books and perceived the marketplace as a source of inexpensive, immoral literature. Bostonians Charles Eliot Norton and Charles William Eliot tried to control the choice of book buyers by controlling the marketplace. They encouraged publication of inexpensive moral books packaged in distinctive covers; consumers had only to select books from Norton's Heart of Oak series or Eliot's Five Foot Shelf and they had taken a first step toward moral growth.[21]

The New Haven scholars supported this strategy, but their response left consumers a larger role. They were expected to learn not only how to choose tasteful books but also how to read their moral message. Noah Porter's *Books and Reading,* subtitled *What Books Shall I Read, and How Shall I Read Them?* taught these lessons. (In case the reader remained unsure of what books to read, the book contained an appendix that was a list of acceptable books chosen by the librarian of the Boston Public Library.) Porter phrased his recommendations in the language of organicism. Good literature was nurturing, and the reader read it actively to avoid "the intellectual dyspepsia which is induced by a plethora of intellectual diet, if that may be called intellectual which is the weak dilution of thought." His comparison of good literature to nourishing food implied its connection to life; bad literature was merely a snack, an insubstantial activity for leisure time. Intelligent readers would choose "nutricious," "succulent" reading, a balanced diet with no excess of novels. Overabundant novel reading was "a kind of intellectual opium eating." Readers most especially should not select novels with sensational plots and prose styles which did not conform to canons of taste. They could easily avoid these books, for their authors had inflated "the English language till it almost bursts with the expansion."[22]

Porter recommended a reading diet of poetry, history, and newspapers, as well as proper novels. Good novels had a "fitting" style, and their plots connected readers with a larger world. Novels by Walter Scott, Thackeray, and Harriet Beecher Stowe, for example, taught readers about foreign lands and history while affirming timeless moral principles. Histories offered similar benefits, provided their authors were not secular determinists like George Bancroft, Richard Hildreth, and Thomas Carlyle. Niebuhr and Thomas Arnold were preferable; their books illustrated "the permanent laws and forces in humanity." Porter told readers not to waste their time with entertaining, quickly read novels, known as "railroad reading." Poetry could be read as easily, and it had moral value. Good poetry was "simple in phrase" and "lively in imagery." Wordsworth was Porter's favorite poet, and he also recommended verse by Americans Richard Henry Dana, James Russell Lowell, John Greenleaf Whittier, William Cullen Bryant, Ralph Waldo Emerson, and Henry Wadsworth Longfellow.[23] Implicitly, he rejected poetry that created an autonomous private world through its language and use of symbols.

Porter's approach to literary criticism showed the effect of German philosophy and philology, which distinguished his approach from that of ministers who also reviewed for the *New Englander*. They asked merely whether authors wrote in tasteful style and whether their ideas supported New Haven religious, political, and social views. For example, Nathaniel Hawthorne won praise for his *Twice Told Tales* and *Mosses from an Old Manse,* although *The Scarlet Letter* never was reviewed. Hawthorne's writing appealed because his style was "the simple clothing of his thought," and he had correctly seen human character with "its universal fountain of corruption." Writing about poorer folk, Hawthorne penetrated "the humble exterior of poverty" without playing on mawkish sentimentality, "hobby-riding upon humanity," or preaching "philanthropic cant." Another reviewer criticized Melville for unflattering descriptions of missionaries and religious awakenings in his travel books *Typee* and *Omoo.* A true record, the reviewer argued, would show that missionaries had taken law, the Constitution, and morality to Polynesia. Dickens, still another reviewer concluded, was a fashionable writer whose books followed formulas. "Mr. Dickens," this reviewer said, "seems to have done like those preachers who sometimes give us the same sermon on different occasions, under different texts, and in different covers."[24]

While Porter did not disagree with the substance of these reviews, he contended that literary critics should appreciate literature for different reasons. Rather than merely saying whether a book was suitable reading, the critic should interpret the author to the reader in the same way as Carlyle and Arnold revealed "a man's character and moving principles." Rooted in German historical criticism, what Porter called the "new criticism" "not only interprets an author by means of his times, *but it interprets the times of an author by means of his writings.*" Therefore, this criticism was both philosophical and historical. The rise of this new literary criticism, Porter observed, showed that people now viewed literature not merely as "one of the accessories of culture and luxury" but "as the best and noblest expression of the best powers of the ablest men of an age."[25]

The career of the art critic among the New Haven scholars, James Mason Hoppin, followed the same transition from religious to academic vocation as did those of the rest of the scholars. Also, much like Dana and Fisher in their disciplines, Hoppin combined historical analysis learned during study in Germany and the associationism of the Scottish philosophy. Disturbed by theological controversies that seemed to limit the ability of ministers to preach effectively and persuade listeners of divine truth, Hoppin began to write and lecture about art in the early 1860s. In 1879 he left his professorship of homiletics in the Theological Department to become the first professor of art history in the Yale School of Fine Arts. During his subsequent career Hoppin earned a national reputation as a proponent of art education, an art critic, and a popularizer of Ruskin.[26]

From John Ruskin, Hoppin learned the associationist theory that upon perceiving an object, observers experienced a simple emotion. This inspired them to make a series of associations that encouraged appreciation of the object as beautiful. In short, observers first learned a vocabulary of associations. When they viewed an object, their imaginative act consisted in recalling the specific associations that the object in question expressed. Hoppin drew words to describe beauty from the New Haven vocabulary of organicism. For example, he said that beautiful art expressed order and unity. Echoing the beliefs of Noah Porter about the human mind, Hoppin said that art was beautiful when it corresponded to the order found in the natural world and the unity of the human mind and therefore displayed proportion, moderation, and grace. These qualities gave the work its intrinsic ethical nature and imbued it with moderation, which was, Hoppin explained, "the continence of conscious spiritual strength."[27]

Beautiful art, Hoppin thought, combined aspects of realism and idealism to reveal divine truth. He argued that the artist who painted nature as it was resembled the literary realist, whose works were merely "pieces of loose real life, without unity and plan." The realist was a slave, a mere copyist of the natural world, who exercised no independent judgment. The pure idealist, Hoppin thought, erred in another direction, for his art, too, had no relation to divine truth; idealistic art merely presented the artist's personal world of meaning. Neither idealist nor realist painter filled the true office of the artist as "a priest of the divine." A true artist combined aspects of idealism in much the manner as did New Haven scientist Dana and historian Fisher. He observed nature closely and was a realist to this extent, but then the artist idealized his subject by isolating it from "its accidental and perhaps degrading circumstances." The artist then "conceiv[ed] the object in its most complete, universal, perfect form." The resulting painting made visible the universal, divine meaning of the particular subject; it was "the true idea of the thing rather than the thing itself." The artist thus had transformed natural subject matter until it created associations of uniqueness and wholeness. Art mediated, Hoppin believed, between the contemplation of nature and of the divine and led "from all that is earthly up to the praise and glory of God."[28]

Hoppin's argument for the particular usefulness of art shows the major difference between his theories and those of Ruskin. The New Haven disciple saw art not as the source of morality but as a means to individual and social self-development. Since true education, Hoppin held, "produce[d] a harmonious development of the nature," education should include art education, for it was as much a part of mental development as was logic or mathematics. The lessons of divine unity taught by art, Hoppin believed, countered the materialism of the present age. Borrowing a phrase from Wilhelm Von Humboldt, Hoppin argued that art would raise Americans' sights "above the dead level of the actual" and take the place of an exclusively narrow, utilitarian conception of human life. True art built up "the spiritual side" of human nature and made people "more happy, loving, and contented awakening the sense of pleasure in beautiful objects that God has made . . ." and sweetening "the fountains of our social life." In the 1860s Hoppin saw "the evil and sceptical tendencies" in science as the major narrowing forces that art could oppose. By the 1880s his criticism of American life had broadened to include "our intense pursuit of wealth" and "the bitterness and hatred" stemming from "conflicts between capital and labor." The labor violence of the 1870s, therefore, caused neither Hoppin nor Woolsey to change his opinion that New Haven ideas were relevant to American society; violence was but another problem that self-development properly understood could remedy. Art, Hoppin insisted, was always a force for individuality and freedom.[29]

Like New Haven scientist Dana, historian Fisher, and psychologist Porter, art historian Hoppin practiced a scholarly method that was a middle way between pre–Civil War Romantic idealism, in this instance John Ruskin's, and late-nineteenth-century positivism, in this instance art critic Bernard Berenson's. When Hoppin analyzed the beauty of an artwork, he looked for one quality—*character*—whose importance his German lessons had taught him. If a work of art had character, then it had individuality, a uniqueness that distinguished it from the less beautiful or ugly. Character also showed the relationship between a work of art and the civilization to which it belonged. It was obvious to Hoppin that "the distinctive spirit of the period and history of the work is stamped on it." Hoppin's analysis of the statue he called the *Venus of Milo* illustrates his method. First he described the character of a particular period in Greek history. Sculptors of this period, he argued, had depicted man as man and not as hero because a spirit of skepticism encouraged them to make their figures less like idealized gods and more as individual men. Hoppin then analyzed the composition of the Venus and found that it followed these principles. On this basis, he attributed the statue to the sculptor Skopas.[30] Like the other scholars, Hoppin started with an object, which he carefully observed, and then related it to an idealized whole, say, the character of a civilization. Hoppin's method also illustrates the distinctive relationship between individuality and society that occurred in New Haven thought. Every New Haven scholar assumed that increased individuality led to social wholeness. Much as art reflected its civilization and was not an escape from or criticism of its conformity, increased individualism among people led to increased social responsibility and cohesion, not selfishness and anarchy.

At the same time that Hoppin was writing, the young Bernard Berenson was beginning to practice a method of art criticism that departed from Hoppin's use of idealized conceptions such as character. Berenson based his attributions of a work of art on observation of the painting technique displayed in the piece in question. Then he found a painting with similar technique for whom the identity of the artist was an established fact. For Berenson, painting technique was an objective observable reality, and the conclusions that he reached from its analysis neither confirmed nor denied any religious truth. Further, Berenson conceived of art history as a subject useful for understanding the relationship that one work of art bore to another in a historical series. Hoppin, in contrast, saw art history as an adjunct to history, and history as a subject that permitted understanding of the extent to which a civilization fostered self-development. Ernest Samuels, Berenson's biographer, explains that his method of art criticism originated in part in the lessons of William James, who taught Berenson at Harvard. When James studied psychology, he observed his subjects' responses to certain situations. Berenson observed how the artist responded to a canvas, and the evidence of his behavior was his technique.[31] Thus Hoppin's critical theory bears the same relationship to Berenson's as Porter's psychology does to James's. The New Haven scholars based their studies on facts but then went on to describe their subjects' significance in terms of their relationship to a divine whole.

Hoppin's evaluation of works of art from various historical periods reveals the optimistic view of historical progress typical of

his New Haven colleagues and contrasts sharply with the pessimism of Charles Eliot Norton, the Harvard art critic, who taught
that there had been no art worthy of consideration after 1600.
Hoppin and Norton agreed that artists of ancient Greece and the
Renaissance had most clearly depicted truth in natural forms. Hoppin, however, taught that artists since then had learned new means
to reveal truth in ways suited to the current age. For example,
Hoppin praised the pre-Raphaelites and French landscape painters
for returning to nature for inspiration and departing from the
formalism of Neoclassicists such as David. Pre-Raphaelite Edward
Burne-Jones had gone too far, however; his paintings appealed to
the eye, not the mind, and reproduced forms "not sufficiently
rooted in nature." The Impressionists, Hoppin thought, were "infusing new life into painting, catching the light and atmosphere of
heaven, penetrating the mystery of color and promising a true
advance in landscape art." French landscape painter Millet earned
Hoppin's special praise for depicting "the Roman simplicity" of
peasants. Millet's composition of peasants at work in a field suggested "the life of brotherhood of toil." Hoppin's comments reveal
that for the New Haven men, this painting contained several layers
of meaning. Hoppin saw the peasants as he and his colleagues saw
factory workers; they testified to the universal nobility of human
nature and dignity of work. Millet's peasants also had meaning for
the New Haven concept of self-development. Living in a state of
republican simplicity, the peasants led an intrinsically tasteful life
and consequently did not need to learn New Haven lessons. In
his admiration of Millet's painting, Hoppin suggested that Americans of the Gilded Age could return metaphorically to the simplicity of the peasants. Middle-class Americans did not have to
forsake the abundance of the marketplace if they merely applied
New Haven lessons.[32]

Art brought wholeness to life and could come in the form of a
photograph, a chromolithograph, reproductions of Italian masterpieces or Greek sculpture, and original paintings by members of
the National Academy or itinerants. Whether one viewed a popular chromolithograph or a sophisticated painting, both works of
art encouraged the viewer to think of the same moral whole.
Morality that led to a prudish censoring of art was narrow and
illiberal. Art critic Hoppin assured the New Haven Law and Order
League that a statue of a nude Greek hero or goddess was moral.
If the entire work was moral, it inspired viewers to think of the
ultimate reward promised their soul, not immediate gratification

of the flesh. Porter similarly instructed readers of Shakespearean plays to think of the moral message of the entire play. If a scene was part of this whole, it could never be immoral.[33] The New Haven men's response to popular art forms and Victorian prudery was consistent with their earlier refusal to join in the sectarian controversies of the 1820s and 1830s. Much as sectarian controversies destroyed the unity of religion, prudish censorship destroyed the unity of art.

In the field of art criticism and appreciation Hoppin pursued the New Haven goal of freeing divine truth from the confines of Scripture and sermon. Hoppin argued that art should be part of life and not the exclusive property of museums. Art served man's full nature; it supplied "wants that are real, houses to live in, churches to worship in, costumes to wear, and also above all, objects of the imagination and the affections to feed the higher nature." American art would be original and express the American character. It would grow from the American land, American "industrial energies," and "the ideas of freedom and equality." American artists, Hoppin predicted, would make manufactured products "truly artistic." As the nation's wealth increased, there would be more support for art schools, where artists would learn to build monuments and public works that were "the finest conceptions of the imagination."[34] Growth of American industry, the prevalence of manufactured goods, and the immense private fortunes that were accumulating could be means to American cultural wholeness.

Hoppin's comments about Impressionists Degas and Renoir show why the New Haven scholars' way of perceiving the world as a divine whole died with them. Hoppin and his colleagues adopted their way of seeing the world in the antebellum years, when they were young men who wanted to escape a church-centered religious community ruled by ministers preoccupied with doctrine. They then became college-based authorities on different aspects of divine meaning. Guiding readers and students through a cosmopolitan world of ideas, the scholars discriminated between true ideas leading to self-development and false ideas leading to materialism and doubt. Along the way, they won larger audiences for history, art, and literature and new respect for the authority of scholarship. Their lessons, nonetheless, could not guarantee that people coming to maturity in the last decades of the nineteenth century would continue to see mundane things as means to evangelical ends. For example, Hoppin predicted that the paintings of both Degas and Renoir would not endure because they were worthless in a New Haven sense, "for they embody but the outward, and have nothing in them more profound or spiritual." But if the paintings had more power, he feared, then they might "draw us permanently away from those deeper impressions of the imagination and spiritual life."[35] Both the crowded galleries of Impressionist paintings found in a present-day museum and the enthusiasm found at a Billy Graham meeting show that both the art Hoppin criticized and the religious faith for which he feared have endured; the New Haven perception of the link between the two has not.

9
Connections

The period of years for which publishers kept the New Haven scholars' books in print may serve as a rough indication of the time span for which their evangelical formulation of scholarly and educational ideas had relevance. (See appendix 3.) First published in the 1860s, the books went out of print between 1890 and 1915. Apparently, a new generation of college professors had no use for textbooks that affirmed divine truth and in which psychology was the science of the soul, political science was a historical subject, and history was the study of human and national development (*Bildung*). Two New Haven texts that have survived into the modern period are exceptions that prove this rule, for the modern editor of Dana's *Mineralogy* deleted his introductory references to divine truth, and Whitney's *Sanskrit Grammar* never did contain any explicit theistic statements.[1] Modern readers of current editions of these texts see merely hard data. They suspect neither the evangelical assumptions that inspired their authors nor the community of discourse that prevailed at Yale from the 1840s through the mid-1880s. During these years, New Haven scholarship reigned at the college and New Haven books had an audience. But what is more important, a unique synthesis existed that fused religious faith with scholarly vocation, teaching and writing with social action, individual with social improvement, elite education for the few with a democratic society for all.[2]

The existence of the New Haven synthesis depended upon the coming of age of a particular antebellum generation and their seeking an institutional response to problems that they perceived in Jacksonian politics, the Romantic cult of the natural genius, and doctrinal theology. Adoption of New Haven scholarship and reform of Yale College into a nurturing institution were their solutions. The home that these scholars found in New Haven and at Yale College put them at the heart of an academic and publishing world that included the British evangelical community and like-minded scholars at German universities. Because of this world, the New Haven scholars thought themselves members of a majority party to whom the future would belong. The scholars tried in the 1830s to make themselves influential in the contemporary evangelical world by choosing to advance learning instead of refining inherited doctrine and participating in the prevailing sectarian debates. The New Haven scholars sought what they defined as a "deeper" religion, that is, the essence of religious faith found in liberal Protestant sects. Their choice in the 1830s was between a religious belief divorced from the contemporary academic world and a new understanding of religion based on historical and philological scholarship. The decision was not, as it would become in the last third of the nineteenth century, between religiously informed scholarship and scholarship itself. To have their learning and faith, the New Haven scholars found the truth of religious matters in a historical Christianity and rested their faith on non-rational belief—people's supposedly innate need for God. The New Haven combination of faith, learning, and understanding the world in evangelical terms was intrinsically unstable, for even if people had faith, they still had to choose to see the world in New Haven terms.

Men graduating from college in the 1850s and 1860s chose not to continue the entire New Haven vision, perhaps because the issues that had impelled the New Haven scholars no longer had force and because these younger men had to live in a world much more complex and modern than the world of their teachers. The younger men found their opportunity in a religiously plural America by discarding for public use the religious part of the New Haven synthesis. Thus, the New Haven scholars' students took the secular part of their teachers' lessons and left the religious. To illustrate this selection, Laurence Veysey's typology of higher education is useful. He says that in the last third of the century three new educational models appeared: liberal culture, utility, and scholarly research. The college presidents whom Veysey uses as spokesmen for these types were students of the New Haven scholars—for liberal culture, Franklin Carter of Amherst; for utility, Andrew Dickson White of Cornell; and for research, Daniel Coit Gilman of Johns Hopkins. These presidents' educational careers and writings, especially White's *History of the Warfare of Science with Theology,* show their belief that religion had become a matter of not merely personal faith but also personal practice.[3]

At Yale the same process of turning religious faith into a private matter went on. In 1884 younger professors such as Sumner pressured older professors and Yale president Porter into accepting an elective system. Then between 1901 and 1903 the faculty divided the formerly unified curriculum into three divisions, so that students chose major fields and minor subjects from language and literature; mathematics and natural sciences; and mental, philosophical, and historical science. Some of the New Haven scholars' lessons remained in particular disciplines. Social scientists of the *Yale Review* tried to inform men about how to vote on matters such as civil service reform and the tariff. Lessons of historical philology lived on with professors of classics, literature, and history, who still sought to understand the character of a civilization but now suggested that this purpose was particular to their disciplines by referring to them as the "humanities." Scholars no longer recognized a generally accepted purpose for their studies other than the pursuit of their interest as scholars. The college was no longer concerned that the curriculum promote culture (*Bildung*). Students now worked, as President Arthur Twining Hadley said, "in facts, in ideas, or in affairs."[4]

The New Haven scholars were popularizers in the sense that they wrote for an educated audience whom they hoped would influence public affairs. One legacy of the New Haven men appears in the ways that academic humanists and social scientists of succeeding generations defined and addressed their publics.

Historians are used to thinking of Noah Porter and Richard Hofstadter as antagonists. By casting Porter as the enemy of academic freedom in his conflict with Sumner, Hofstadter places himself within one tradition of scholarship and Porter within another, now extinct. Admittedly, it is true that the two men drew their thinking about the college and scholarship from different cores of belief and looked forward to very different futures. Porter and his colleagues had evangelical hopes derived from Congre-

gationalism, whereas Hofstadter had entirely secular hopes, stemming from a complex of values loosely defined as liberal
cosmopolitanism. Still, neither practiced the ivory tower sort of
scholarship that Bruce Kuklick sees taking shape at Harvard in
the late nineteenth century. Then, he observes, philosophers became professionals who produced "technical specialized research
published for technically competent audiences in technical journals."[5]

Both New Haven scholars and Hofstadter saw the college as
the proper home of learning and tried to persuade educated readers of their books and articles that the lessons of scholarship were
useful. As we know, the New Haven men saw this audience as
male, and if we take as an example the title *The American Political
Tradition and the Men Who Made It* (1948), so did Hofstadter.
Both he and the New Haven men opposed the anti-intellectual
extremes of their time found in popular evangelicalism, for it
threatened, they thought, the progress of knowledge and the authority of the scholar. Hofstadter saw it leading to the irrational
reform program of populists and the unrealistic elements of Progressivism, while the New Haven men thought of individual change
and suggested that revival experiences were superficial and short-
lived, not affecting the whole man. Further, it should be noted
that both identified their reform agenda with the nation. This is
evident in the New Haven men's oft-repeated millennial hopes
and in Hofstadter's identification of an *American* reform tradition.
Nevertheless, the New Haven men and the Columbia historian
defined the usefulness of their male audience differently. With the
millennium in sight, the former saw their male leaders as useful
in a Romantic sense; they were role models and sources of ideas
for other men. Wanting society to function smoothly and equitably,
Hofstadter defined usefulness in the secular terms of practicality.
He indirectly encouraged his readers to support social scientists,
such as Charles Merriam, who supplied government with ideas
and information necessary for the management of American society.[6]

This comparison has at least two significant implications. The
hostility that the liberal Hofstadter felt toward evangelicalism shows
that liberal academe and segments of Protestant America became
estranged during the course of the twentieth century. Porter complained in 1882 of an attitude prevalent among "men of knowledge" that assumed "that Christian theism is doomed to vanish
before what is called modern science and culture." It seems that

we need to know more about the development of this attitude among men of knowledge and more about its implication for social science and its political agenda from the late nineteenth century to early twentieth.[7]

Comparison of Hofstadter and the scholars also suggests that the history of twentieth-century intellectual life is not merely the story of the rise of the isolated academic whose work interests only a small number of equally specialized scholars. Contemporary scholars with an ambition like Hofstadter's—teaching and writing for an educated audience who will influence public affairs—keep alive an older tradition that can be traced to the antebellum years of the nineteenth century and the New Haven scholars.[8] From an institutional perspective, the modern period in the history of American higher education may begin in the 1870s with the rise of the university; from the perspective of scholarship, however, the modern period has another, earlier beginning with Noah Porter and his New Haven colleagues.

In the humanities, the role of the scholar as popularizer was carried on in the 1920s and 1930s by cultural promoters such as William Lyon Phelps (Yale B.A. 1887, Ph.D. 1891). Phelps, a direct academic descendant of the New Haven scholars and professor in the Yale English department (1892–1933), was an enormously popular teacher, but he reached a far larger audience through his "As I Like It" columns for *Scribner's Magazine* and segments on radio talk shows such as the "Swift Hour." Instead of attempting to reach the educated few as his teachers had, Phelps addressed the many. In the 1920s this was a public composed of increasing numbers of high school and college graduates who, historian Joan Shelley Rubin suggests, "bought books, valued the classics, cared about the opera, liked the theater as well as the movies, and sought guidance from critics who . . . welcomed the opportunity to advise a large, literate public."[9]

Phelps retained many of his teachers' literary preferences, including distaste for unennobling "proletarian literature" and the overly symbolic, unrealistic literature of modernism. Yet his teachers had spoken for religious idealism, while he taught lessons thoroughly secular—in their content, medium, and purpose. Good literature, he believed, taught values and beliefs consistent with Christian ethics, but Phelps excluded the subject of the millennium and its coming from his public considerations altogether. As a secular commentator, he thought of culture more as an aid to personality development and less in the New Haven sense as a source of inspiration and how-to lessons on development of the whole self. It could be said that his teachers stressed a religious individualism, and Phelps a secular individuality. While estimating "the Authorised Version of the English Bible . . . the best example of English literature that the world has ever seen," he thought it useful because it could teach "more about human nature" than could "living in New York." In New Haven lessons, the cultured person drew on a religiously based value system that served as a basis for criticism of materialism. For Phelps, culture had lost this role, and materialism was no longer a subject for criticism. Whereas his teachers had used *culture* to explain the method and purpose of education, Phelps defined *culture* as a subject deserving appreciation. "To appreciate culture," Rubin explains, "was to understand that it was good for you, to pay homage to the heritage of western civilization, to acknowledge aesthetic judgments and standards, to make a limited commitment of time and energy to the improvement of personality—and then to get down to business or purchase the latest household appliances."[10] Culture became a necessary side dish to the main course of American life. Stripped of its critical power and limited in scope to literature, art, and drama, New Haven scholarship lived on with Phelps in much diluted form.

Still, it was less what Phelps said than how he said it that separated him from the New Haven scholars, who, even though popularizers, had enjoyed the respect of their college- and university-based peers. Because Phelps reached beyond an audience of fellow professionals who communicated with one another through the media of professional conference papers and journal articles, he had to forgo the respect of his more professional colleagues. The fact that Yale was the home of both Phelps and, in the post–World War II years, the New Criticism suggests the two halves into which modern academics split the New Haven ideal of scholarship.

Within academe, the next generation of professors appeared to owe no debt to the New Haven scholars. In a sense, the New Humanists—Irving Babbit, Paul Elmer More, Stuart Sherman, Norman Foerster—continued the New Haven concern with "culture." As philosophic dualists, the New Humanists formulated a vision of social wholeness based upon spiritual values. But they looked for culture narrowly, in art and literature, not broadly as the New Haven scholars had, in all subjects save the natural sciences and mathematics. The New Humanists found their apostle of culture in the agnostic Matthew Arnold, rather than in his evangelical father Thomas. And they sought to derive values from the best thought of past civilizations, especially classical Greece, never measuring their "best" against any supposedly unchanging standard, such as divine wholeness. The social position of the New Humanists within the academy also differed from that of the New Haven scholars. At the New Haven scholars' Yale, culture or self-development as the end of education dominated, whereas the New Humanists spoke for culture as a dissenting minority within the early twentieth-century academy. Their solutions to perceived problems had reform of various discipline as their basis and did not involve an entire institution. For example, when Norman Foerster wanted to recapture the spirit of interdisciplinary endeavor, he founded the American Civilization major at the University of Iowa. Because American Civilization students sought to discover the character of their country, Foerster was in effect reintroducing the purpose of philological study into historical studies. His innovation, however, was not part of a program to reshape the entire institution.[11]

In the social sciences, Progressive Era scholars discarded New Haven ways of knowing and of understanding society entirely. Despite Noah Porter's contribution to psychology and his recognition by modern historians of the discipline as someone who furthered the progress of his discipline, his work was entirely irrelevant to William James, who did not mention Porter in his famous text. Charles Beard refuted the New Haven assumption that the Constitution served the interests of all the people and argued instead that it benefited a particular economic class. Frederick Jackson Turner discarded the idea of social evolution in favor of the theory that American democracy had grown from the particular circumstances of the frontier, thus severing American life from its European intellectual heritage and making it a creation of material conditions. Vernon Parrington saw Puritanism as an ally of capitalism and characterized both as enemies of liberal values. Whereas New Haven scholars had argued that college-educated liberal men could reform society through the power of their example on friends and neighbors, Progressive reformers argued that "disinterested experts" serving on government commissions or as city managers could vanquish the power of corporations and urban bosses. Society conceived in the New Haven sense, as a collection of individuals acting on one another through face-to-face encounters, had been replaced by the impersonal world of organizations acting on one another through laws and economic force.[12]

In the New Haven scheme of things, freedom fostered self-development, a personal wholeness achieved when people realized their ultimate dependence on God and participated in the coming kingdom. Defining freedom in spiritual terms, the New Haven scholars had opposed any means to alleviate social problems that boded future spiritual enslavement. The converse also was true; freedom did not imply the absolute right to do as one wished with property. In the new age, some, such as Justice Stephen Field, argued that property was an absolute right, while others, such as Herbert Croly, would solve social problems by extending government power. From a New Haven perspective, both arguments were mistaken, for they raised either the solution of social problems or the protection of property to the status of an end.

For the New Haven scholars, traditional institutions had provided the discipline necessary for enjoyment of true freedom. In their vision New York City represented the antithesis of this freedom. "New York can do more harm in the new era than slaveholding did in that which passed away," Woolsey warned. "And the worst of it is, that the evil influences of unbridled prosperity are insidious; they paralyze and stupify; earth is made more attractive, and heavenly realities kept further off." The city's stores lured consumers toward slavery to materialism, and corporations and banking houses symbolized economic power that was dangerous because it was closed to public scrutiny.[13] In the early twentieth century a new generation of cultural critics—the supposed rebels of Greenwich Village—reversed the symbolism. Now young intellectuals sought the freedom that New York offered from traditional mores and reinterpreted small-town life as confining and the home of narrow-minded "Puritans."[14]

In the mid-nineteenth century, however, the New Haven scholars had shared their definition of truth with evangelical reformers and culture with other elite groups, although these distinctions were not always absolute. For example, the New Haven scholars knew that they and the Bostonians of the *North American Review* and the *Atlantic* were engaged in a common endeavor. All were trying to reach beyond denominational issues to educate potential leaders. Eschewing doctrinal polemics, Harvard moralists and Yale evangelicals committed themselves to developing the character of college students. Recognizing didactic power in art and literature, they saw how moral lessons could surround the individual in society. Despite this agreement, the New Haven scholars always criticized the Bostonians for narrowness and provincialism. The Boston point of view, Fisher wrote his publisher Charles Scribner in 1905, was not "a broad one, but has a decidedly provincial tinge." He defined the New Haven audience as "our larger religious communions, the journals, not of one class or sect alone, our schools of theology, and a large number of higher-minded men in our colleges." Unlike the Unitarians, Fisher and his colleagues never cut themselves off from the majority of Americans, who were marching toward an evangelical future.[15]

As nineteenth-century evangelicals, New Haven scholars thought of themselves as part of a growing movement that included other Congregationalists, as well as Baptists, Methodists, and Presbyterians.[16] Although the number of Baptist and Methodist churches was increasing faster than the number of Congregationalist churches, colleges founded by Congregationalists or staffed by Yale graduates were spreading throughout the Midwest. These colleges seemed to support the New Haven scholars' hope that educated men would belong to the evangelical host. The scholars also believed that theological schools such as Andover, Hartford, and Princeton belonged to this unity; disagreements among them were superficial and temporary. As right ideas of scholarship replaced divisive old ideas, the seminaries could not fail to realize their common cause.

New Haven research continually discovered more reasons for evangelical hope as scholarship related facts to a divine whole. Although the scholars' modification of Scottish philosophy with German idealism limited their audience to the educated, the reading of the divine from facts connected them to a far larger American public. Painters such as Thomas Cole, John Kensett, and Frederic Church used allegory and the symbolic potential of light to suggest the divine meaning inherent in nature. Dana and his fellow scientists in the American Association for the Advancement of Science found divine meaning in rock strata, fossils, and plants. Popular preachers like Henry Ward Beecher and Horace Bushnell explained how human institutions testified to a divine reality.[17]

New Haven criticism of Emerson illustrates the place of the scholars among those who found the ideal in the real. Emerson was a pantheist, the scholars contended, because he made the divine the *same* as nature, when he should have said that the divine *stood behind*. The scholars had to emphasize this distinction because of their essential agreement with Emerson that there was an overarching divine unity. If they had not emphasized Emerson's error, unsophisticated auditors at lyceum lectures might have followed the advice of "Self-Reliance" and tossed "the laws, the books, idolatries and customs out of the window." Emerson's teachings made the New Haven college of nurture sound irrelevant to the process of self-development and deprived the trained scholar of his authority.[18]

With other evangelical reformers the New Haven scholars shared the hope that people would throw off mundane dependencies and stand spiritually free, but New Haven means were gradual and emphasized the intellectual dimension of freedom. Their college would produce culture in its students and win more lasting results than would Charles Grandison Finney's anxious bench. Whereas nativists warned that sexual license could exist within the confines of a Catholic nunnery, the New Haven men worried that Jesuitical education confined the mind in unnatural ways. Temperance reformers deplored that drink made people slaves of their immediate desires, and the scholars counseled that wrong theories would bar the way to spiritual growth. Whereas women reformers stressed that women's moral power could reform society, the scholars taught that men like Luther could ensure history's evangelical progress.[19]

The New Haven scholars designed a system of education that would satisfy the intellectual and spiritual needs of men on their way to the kingdom of God. Their audience was a tiny, educated elite precisely because this was the minority whom they saw as crucial in millennial history and whose needs other evangelicals ignored. New Haven scholarship was a specialized activity within an evangelical whole, a scholarly statement of more popular conceptions of freedom and progress, and an elitist alternative to unruly antinomian tendencies of evangelicalism.

Appendix 1
Biographical Sketches of the New Haven Scholars

JAMES DWIGHT DANA (1813–95). Born Utica, N.Y., son of well-to-do parents; mother converted in revival, Utica, N.Y., 1814. Yale, 1830–33; Silliman's assistant, 1836–38; mineralogist for the Wilkes Expedition, 1838–42. Conversion experience in Utica, N.Y., 1838. Married Silliman's daughter. Professor of natural history, Yale College, 1849–64; professor of geology and mineralogy, Yale College, 1864–90. Member, and president, 1859, American Association for the Advancement of Science. From 1840, editor of Silliman's *American Journal of Science*. Original member, National Academy of Science. Fellow of the Royal Society, London. Received honorary doctor of laws degrees from Amherst College, Harvard, and the University of Edinburgh. Awarded the Copley Medal (1877) by the Council of the Royal Society of London and the Wollaston Medal of the Royal Geological Society of London (1872). Joined The Club, 1855.

TIMOTHY DWIGHT (1828–1916). Born Norwich, Conn. Grandson of Timothy Dwight. Yale, 1849; Yale Theological Department, 1850–53; Yale tutor, 1851–55; studied at Universities of Bonn and Berlin, 1856–58. Licensed to preach, 1855.

Major sources include *Dictionary of American Biography; Appleton's Nineteenth Century American Biographies;* Yale Classbooks and Obituary Records for the appropriate years; funeral sermons or obituary articles, often reprinted in the *New Englander.*

Assistant professor of sacred literature, Yale Theological Department, 1858–61; professor, 1861–86; Yale president, 1886–99. Member, American Academy of Arts and Science; member, American Committee on the Revision of the English Bible, 1873–85. Joined The Club, 1858. Associate editor of the *New Englander,* 1866–74.

GEORGE PARK FISHER (1827–1909). Born Wrentham, Mass. Conversion experience in college, 1847. Brown, 1847; Yale Theological Department, 1848; graduate, Andover Theological Seminary, 1851; studied at the University of Halle, 1852–54. Ordained, 1854. Livingston Professor of Divinity and pastor of the College Church, 1854–61. Livingston Professor of Ecclesiastical History, Yale Theological Department, 1861–78; Titus Street Professor of Ecclesiastical History, Yale Theological Department, 1878–1901; dean, Yale Divinity School, 1895–1901. Member and officer, American Society for Church History; member, and president, 1898, American Historical Association. Joined The Club, 1855. Edited the *New Englander,* 1855–57, 1866–73; from 1892, member of the *Yale Review* editorial board.

JAMES HADLEY (1821–72). Born Fairfield, N.Y., son of professor of chemistry in College of Physicians and Surgeons of the Western District of New York. Yale, 1842; Yale tutor, 1845–48. Assistant professor of Greek, Yale College, 1848–51; professor of Greek, 1851–72. Member of the American Committee for the Revision of the English Bible. President, American Oriental Society; vice-president, American Philological Association; member, National Academy of Sciences. *Essays Philological and Critical Selected from the Papers of James Hadley* edited by Whitney (1873). Joined The Club, 1861.

JAMES MASON HOPPIN (1820–1906). Descended from a prominent Rhode Island family. Yale, 1840; Harvard Law School, 1842; studied theology at Union Theological Seminary, 1842–44; studied at the University of Berlin, 1845–47. Ordained, 1850. Pastor, Crombie St. Church, Salem, Mass., 1850–59. Professor of homiletics and the pastoral charge, Yale Theological Department, 1861–79; professor of history of art, Yale School of Fine Arts, 1879–99. Member, American Oriental Society, American Historical Association, American Philosophical So-

ciety, and Victoria Philosophical Society, London. Joined The
Club, 1861.

WILLIAM AUGUSTUS LARNED (1806–62). Born Thompson,
Conn., son of a lawyer. Converted in Yale revival, 1831. Yale,
1826. Read for the law, Salisbury, N.C., 1826–28; tutor, Yale
College, 1828–31; Yale Theological Department, 1831–34.
Ordained, 1834. Pastor, Millbury, Mass., 1834; taught at the-
ological school in Troy, N.Y., until 1839. Professor of rhetoric
and English literature, Yale College, 1839–62. Founded the
Free Soil Party in Connecticut. Published *Analysis of the Sentence*
(New Haven, n.d.), which made the work of German philologist
Bekker available to a New Haven audience. Joined The Club,
1839. Edited the *New Englander,* 1854–55, and on its ongoing
editorial board from 1843.

NOAH PORTER (1811–92). Born Farmington, Conn. Father
was town's Congregationalist minister for 60 years and served
on Yale Corporation. Converted in Yale revival, 1831. Yale,
1831; Yale tutor, 1833–35; Yale Theological Department, 1833–
35. Ordained, 1836. Married daughter of Nathaniel W. Taylor.
Pastor, New Milford, Conn., 1836–43; pastor, Second Church
at Springfield, Mass., 1843–46. Clark Professor of Moral Philosophy and Metaphysics, 1847–71; Yale president, 1871–86.
Studied at the University of Berlin, 1853–54. From 1864, editor
of Noah Webster's *American Dictionary of the English Language*
and *Webster's International Dictionary of the English Language*
(1890). Received honorary doctor of laws degree from University of Edinburgh (1886) after his retirement. Joined The Club,
1847. Member of the association that edited the *New Englander*
from 1848.

EDWARD ELBRIDGE SALISBURY (1814–1901). Descended
from a wealthy Boston family and married to Woolsey's sister.
Helped endow professorships at Yale for Whitney and Dana.
Yale, 1832. Studied in Paris and Berlin, 1836–40; studied at
the University of Bonn and in Paris, 1842–43. Professor of
Arabic and Sanskrit, Yale, 1841–54; professor of Arabic, Yale,
1854–56. Founder, American Oriental Society (1842). Member, Asiatic Society, Paris, Connecticut Academy of Arts and
Science, American Academy of Arts and Science, Imperial Acad-

emy of Science and Belles Lettres, German Oriental Society, and American Antiquarian Society. Published several genealogies of his family. Joined The Club, 1840.

THOMAS A. THACHER (1815–86). Born Hartford, Conn., of an old Connecticut family. Married daughter of Jeremiah Day. Yale, 1835; Yale tutor, 1838–42. Assistant professor of Latin and Greek, 1842–43; assistant professor of Latin, 1843–51; professor of Latin language and literature, 1851–86. Studied and traveled in Germany and Italy, 1843–45. Chief fundraiser for Yale under Porter. Joined The Club, 1840.

WILLIAM DWIGHT WHITNEY (1827–94). Born Northampton, Mass. Father was a banker, and the family was distantly related to Timothy Dwight. Two of his brothers and a sister became college professors. Williams, 1845; studied with Salisbury at Yale, 1849. Studied at University of Berlin and Tübingen, 1850–53. Professor of Sanskrit, Yale, from 1854. Visiting lecturer at Johns Hopkins, 1880. Member, American Oriental Society; founder, American Philological Society and editor of its journal. Editor of the *Century Dictionary,* 1889–91. Elected to the Prussian Order of Merit in Science to fill the vacancy caused by the death of Carlyle, 1881. Joined The Club, 1855.

THEODORE DWIGHT WOOLSEY (1801–89). Born New York City to sister of Timothy Dwight, whose husband was a prosperous merchant. Yale, 1820; read law in Philadelphia; attended Princeton Theological Seminary, 1821–23; Yale tutor and student in Theological Department, 1823–25. Licensed to preach, 1825. Studied Greek in France and Germany, 1827–30. Professor of Greek, Yale College, 1831–46; Yale president, 1846–71, and teacher of the senior class in history, political science, and international law. Ordained, 1846. Member, American Social Science Association and American Committee on the Revision of the English Bible. Founder of The Club and of the *New Englander.*

Appendix 2
Biographical Sketches of Members of The Club, 1838–1880

JOHN S. C. ABBOTT (1805–77). Born Brunswick, Me., son of a gentleman. Bowdoin, 1825; Andover Theological Seminary, 1829. Ordained, 1830. First pastorate in Worcester, Mass.; pastor, Howe St. Church, New Haven, 1861–66. Author of various histories: *The Empire of Austria* (1859), *The Civil War in America* (1863, 1866), *The Romance of Spanish History* (1869), *History of Frederick the Great* (1871). Joined The Club, 1863.

LEONARD BACON (1802–81). Born Detroit, Mich., son of missionary to Ojibwa Indians. Yale, 1820; Andover Theological Seminary, 1820–23. Pastor, First Church, New Haven, 1825–81. Professor of revealed theology, Yale Theological Department, 1866–71; lecturer on ecclesiastical polity and church history, Yale Theological Department, 1871–81. Director, American Home Missionary Society, American Congregationalist Union, Society for the Promotion of Collegiate and Theological Education at the West, American Bible Society, and American Tract Society. Member, historical societies of Massachusetts, Georgia, New York, Connecticut, New Haven Colony, and Buffalo, and New England Historical and Genealogical Society. Edited the *Independent* with Richard Storrs and Joseph Parrish Thompson, 1847–63. Founder of The Club and the *New Englander*.

For major sources see note to appendix 1.

SIMEON EBEN BALDWIN (1840–1927). Son of a prominent Connecticut family. Yale, 1861; studied law at Yale and Harvard. Admitted to the bar, 1863. Faculty member, Yale Law School, 1869–1919. Founded the American Bar Association, 1878, and served as its president, 1890; president, American Social Science Association, 1897. Joined The Club, 1872.

OLIVER ELLSWORTH DAGGETT (1810–80). Born New Haven, son of a jurist. Yale, 1828; Yale Law School, 1831; Yale Theological Department, 1831–33. Pastor, South Church, Hartford, 1837–43; Congregational Church, Canandaigua, 1845–67. Yale College pastor and professor of divinity, 1867–70. Converted in 1831 Yale revival. Joined The Club, 1868.

HENRY N. DAY (1808–90). Born Connecticut, son of a prominent family, nephew of Jeremiah Day. Yale, 1828; read law with Charles Chauncey in Philadelphia. Professor of theology, Western Reserve, 1840–58; president of Ohio Female College, 1858–64. Retired in New Haven. Writer of textbooks: *The Systematic Accountant* (1861), *Introduction to the Study of English Literature* (1869), *Science of Aesthetics* (1872), *Elements of Psychology* (1876), *Elements of Mental Science* (1886). Joined The Club, 1865.

SAMUEL W. S. DUTTON (1814–66). Born Guilford, Conn. Yale, 1833; Yale Theological Department, 1836–38. Pastor, North Church, New Haven, 1838–66. Converted in 1831 Yale revival. Joined The Club, 1839. *New Englander* editor, 1843–66.

WILLIAM T. EUSTIS (1821–88). Born Boston, son of a merchant. Yale, 1841; studied theology at Yale and Andover. Pastor, Chapel St. Congregational Church, 1848–69. Joined The Club, 1849.

HENRY FARNAM (1803–83). Born into an old Connecticut family. Surveyor and shareholder in the Farmington Canal and a principal in developing Chicago as a railroad center. Joined The Club, 1870.

JOSIAH WILLARD GIBBS (1790–1861). Descended from an old New England family. Yale, 1809; Yale tutor, 1811–15.

Professor at Andover Theological Seminary, 1815–26; professor of sacred literature, Yale Theological Department, 1826–61. Published frequently in *New Englander* and *Bibliotheca Sacra,* making available the fruits of his research and the latest developments in German philological scholarship. Founder of The Club.

DANIEL COIT GILMAN (1831–1908). Descended from an old Connecticut family, son of a prosperous businessman. Yale, 1852; studied at Harvard and lived with geographer Arnold Guyot. With Yale classmate Andrew Dickson White, an attaché to the American legation at St. Petersburg, 1853–55. In the Yale Sheffield Scientific School in various capacities—librarian, secretary, fundraiser, and professor of physical and political geography, 1855–72. Then president of the University of California. First president of Johns Hopkins, 1875. From 1864, assistant editor for scientific terms of Webster's *Dictionary.* Joined The Club, 1858.

DANIEL SEELYE GREGORY (1832–1915). Born Carmel, N.Y. Princeton, 1857; Princeton Theological Seminary, 1860; tutor of belles-lettres at Princeton, 1858–60. Ordained, 1861. Pastor in New Haven, 1866–69. President of Lake Forest University. Editor with Isaac K. Funk of *The Standard Dictionary of the English Language* (1893–95). Joined The Club, 1867.

EDGAR L. HEERMANCE (1833–88). Yale, 1858; Yale Theological Department, 1858–60; graduated from Andover Theological Seminary, 1861. Married daughter of T. D. Woolsey. Held many pastorates, including one in New Haven. Joined The Club, 1871.

OLIVER P. HUBBARD (1809–1900). Son of a Connecticut merchant. Yale, 1828. Married to one of Silliman's daughters. Silliman's assistant, 1831–36. From 1836, professor of chemistry at Dartmouth. Founder, American Association for the Advancement of Science (1847) and Association of American Geologists and Naturalists (1841). Retired to New Haven and joined The Club, 1871.

CHARLES IVES (1815–80). Yale.

HENRY C. KINGSLEY (1815–86). Son of James Luce Kingsley, Yale professor of Latin and Greek. Yale, 1834. A lawyer and treasurer of the Cleveland and Pittsburgh railroads. From 1862, treasurer of Yale College. Joined The Club, 1857.

WILLIAM L. KINGSLEY (1824–96). Son of James Luce Kingsley. Yale, 1843; Yale Law School, 1843–44; Yale Theological Department, 1844–47. Traveled in Europe, 1848–49. Lived near Cleveland, Ohio, until his health failed. Proprietor of the *New Englander,* 1857–91. Active in religious, philanthropic, and literary work. Joined The Club, 1857.

CHESTER SMITH LYMAN (1814–90). Descended from an old Connecticut family. Yale, 1837; studied at Union Theological Seminary, 1839–40; graduated from Yale Theological Department, 1840–42. Ordained, 1843. Pastor, First Church, New Britain, Conn., 1843–45. Left the ministry because of ill-health. Worked on scientific terms for Webster's *Dictionary* from 1850. Professor of industrial mechanics and physics, Sheffield School, Yale, 1859–71; professor of physics and astronomy, 1871–84; professor of astronomy, 1884–90. Member and vice-president, American Association for the Advancement of Science, 1874; president, Connecticut Academy of Arts and Sciences, 1859–77. Joined The Club, 1856.

WILLIAM A. P. MARTIN (1827–1916). Son of a Presbyterian minister. Indiana University, 1846. Ordained, 1849. Went to China in 1850 as a missionary and later became involved in diplomatic work. In 1868 returned to United States to study with Woolsey. Later returned to China to teach international law. Author of works in Chinese on international law, natural science, and Christianity. Joined The Club, 1868.

FREDERICK A. NOBLE (1832–1917). Born in Maine, father a farmer and a cooper. Yale, 1858; attended Andover Theological Seminary, 1858–60; graduated from Lane Theological Seminary, 1861. Ordained, 1862. Pastor, Presbyterian Church in St. Paul, Minn., 1862–67; Third Presbyterian Church, Pittsburgh, 1867–75; First Church of Christ Congregational, New Haven, 1875–79. Joined The Club, 1877.

BIRDSEY G. NORTHROP (1817–98). Descended from an old

Connecticut family. Yale, 1841; Yale Theological Department, 1845. Ordained. Pastor, Saxonville, Mass., 1846–57. Agent for the Massachusetts Board of Education, 1857–67; secretary, Connecticut State Board of Education, 1867–83. Original trustee of Smith College; trustee of the Hampton Institute. Author of numerous books on education, village improvement, and forestry, including *Lessons from European Schools* (1877), *Tree Planting and Schools of Forestry in Europe* (1879), *Schools and Communism* (1879), and *Menticulture and Agriculture* (1881). Father of Arbor Day. Joined The Club, 1867.

TRACY PECK (1838–1921). Descended from an old Connecticut family. Yale, 1861. Studied at Berlin, Jena, and Bonn, 1861–63. Professor of Latin, Cornell, 1871–80; professor of Latin, Yale College, 1880–1908. President, American Philological Association, 1885–86. Director, American School for Classical Studies, Rome, 1898–99. Joined The Club, 1880.

PELATIAH PERIT (1786–64). Married daughter of Daniel L. Coit, prominent Connecticut man. Yale, 1802. New York businessman. Member or director of many benevolent societies, including the Bible Society and the New York Orphan Asylum. Retired to New Haven. Joined The Club, 1861.

WILLIAM H. RUSSELL (1810–85). Yale, 1833. Taught at Princeton; tutor and medical student at Yale, 1835–38. Founded New Haven Family School for Boys, 1838, which later became the Collegiate and Commercial Institute. Joined The Club, 1849.

THOMAS DAY SEYMOUR (1848–1907). Son of professor of Greek and Latin and great-nephew of Jeremiah Day. Married daughter of Western Reserve president. Western Reserve, 1870; studied for two years at Berlin and Athens. Taught at Western Reserve, 1872–80. Professor of Greek, Yale, 1880–1907. President, American Philological Association, 1888–89. Joined The Club, 1880.

JOSEPH PARRISH THOMPSON (1819–79). Born Philadelphia, son of a druggist. Yale, 1838; Yale Theological Department, 1839–40. Pastor, Chapel St. Church, New Haven, 1840–45; Broadway Tabernacle Church, N.Y.C., 1845–71. Married sister of Francis Lieber. Joined The Club, 1841. Founder of the *New Englander.*

HENRY A. TOMLINSON (1806–40). Yale, 1828. Studied medicine at Yale, 1828–32. Practiced medicine in New Haven. Original member of The Club.

ALEXANDER C. TWINING (1801–84). Son of Yale treasurer; sister married James Hadley. Close friend of Woolsey's. Yale, 1820; Andover Theological Seminary, 1822–23; student of mathematics and Yale tutor, 1823–24; completed studies in engineering at West Point. Railroad engineer and consultant, 1834–39. Professor of mathematics and natural philosophy at Middlebury College, 1839–49. After 1849, an engineer, with his home in New Haven. Joined The Club, 1849.

FRANCIS AMASA WALKER (1840–97). Amherst, 1860. Studied law. Taught at Williston Academy and wrote editorials for the *Springfield Daily Republican.* Professor of political economy, Sheffield Scientific School, Yale, 1873–81. Then president of M.I.T. Joined The Club, 1872.

FRANCIS WAYLAND (1826–1904). Descended from an old New England family and married into a prominent New Haven family. Brown, 1846; graduated from Harvard Law School. Probate court judge, 1864–65; lieutenant governor of Connecticut, 1869. Instructor, Yale Law School, 1871; professor, 1872; dean, 1873. President, American Social Science Association, then vice-president and chairman of its jurisprudence department, 1876–1902. Joined The Club, 1867.

JOHN FERGUSON WEIR (1841–1926). Educated by private tutors. Studied art in Europe, 1868–69. Director and professor of painting and design, Yale School of Fine Arts, 1870–1913. A sculptor and artist whose more important works include a statue of Benjamin Silliman, 1884; *Forging the Shaft*; *The Gun Foundry*; *Tapping the Furnace*; and various landscapes, including *Niagara Falls, The Rainbow,* and *Venice: Grand Canal.* Published a biography of John Trumbull (1901) and *The Way: The Nature and the Means of Revelation* (1889). Joined The Club, 1876.

HENRY WHITE (1803–80). Descended from an important

Connecticut family. Yale, 1821; Yale tutor and law student, 1823–25. New Haven lawyer. First president, New Haven County Historical Society; deacon of the Center Church. Original member of The Club.

S. WELLS WILLIAMS (1812–84). Born Utica, N.Y. Descended from an old New England family. Sinologist. Honorary professor of Chinese language and literature, Yale College, 1877–84. Author of a standard reference work on China, *The Middle Kingdom* (1848). Joined The Club, 1877.

Appendix 3
Publishing History of Selected Books by the New Haven Scholars

Author, Title	U.S. Editions	Foreign Editions	Last Edition	Last Date
A. James Dwight Dana				
System of Mineralogy[*]	New Haven: Durrie & Peck, 1837			
	New York: Wiley & Putnam, 1844	London, 1844	11th ed., 1890	1909
Rev. ed., various authors	New York: J. Wiley & Sons, 1892			1951– 52
Manual of Mineralogy	New Haven: Durrie, 1849	London, 1860	12th ed., 1894	1909
Rev. ed., various authors	New York: J. Wiley & Sons, 1913		19th ed., 1977	
Manual of Geology	Philadelphia: T. Bliss, 1863	London, 1863	4th ed., 1894	1896
Geological Story	New York: Ivison, Blakeman, Taylor, 1875			1903
B. George Park Fisher				
Essays on the Supernatural Origin of Christianity[a]	New York: C. Scribner & Co., 1865		Enlarged ed., 1870	1901
The Reformation[*][b]	New York: Scribner, Armstrong & Co., 1873	London, 1873	3d ed., 1906	1920

Appendix 3 *Continued*

Author, Title	U.S. Editions	Foreign Editions	Last Edition	Last Date
Beginnings of Christianity	New York: Scribner, Armstrong & Co., 1877	Edinburgh, 1877		1916
Christian Religion^c	New York: C. Scribner's Sons, 1882 New York: Chautauqua Press, 1885		2d ed., 1886	1899 1888
Faith and Rationalism	New York: C. Scribner's Sons, 1879		New ed., 1885	1890
Outline of Universal History	New York: American Book Co., 1885		New ed., 1904	1904
*History of the Christian Church***	New York: C. Scribner's Sons, 1887	London, 1890		1928
Manual of Christian Evidences	New York: C. Scribner's Sons, 1888 Meadville, Pa: Flood & Vincent, 1892^d	Japan, 1891	New ed., 1892	1919
Colonial Era	New York: C. Scribner's Sons, 1892	London, 1892		1920
C. James Hadley *Greek Grammar* Rev. ed., F. D. Allen	New York: D. Appleton & Co., 1860 New York: American Book Co., 1884			1883 1912
Introduction to Roman Law With preface by A. R. Bellinger*	New York: D. Appleton & Co. New Haven: Yale University Press, 1931	London, 1931		1911 1931
D. James Mason Hoppin *Old England*	New York: Hurd & Houghton, 1867		12th ed., 1893	1900
Office and Work of the Christian Ministry Reissued in 2 vols.	New York: Sheldon & Co., 1869		3d ed., 1879	
Homiletics	New York: Dodd, Mead & Co., 1882		4th ed., 1893	
Pastoral Theology	NewYork: Funk & Wagnalls, 1884	London, 1884	5th ed., 1901	

Appendix 3 *Continued*

Author, Title	U.S. Editions	Foreign Editions	Last Edition	Last Date
Early Renaissance*ᵉ	Boston: Houghton, Mifflin & Co., 1892		1895	
Great Epochs in Art History	Boston: Houghton, Mifflin & Co., 1901		2d ed., 1903	
E. Noah Porter				
Human Intellect	New York: C. Scribner & Co., 1868	London, 1872	4th ed., 1869	1899
American Colleges and the American Public	New Haven: C. C. Chatfield & Co., 1870 New York: C. Scribner's Sons, 1878			1890
Books and Reading*	New York: C. Scribner & Co., 1871		5th ed., 1881	1901
Elements of Intellectual Science	New York: C. Scribner's Sons, 1871	London, 1872		1891
Elements of Moral Science	New York: C. Scribner's Sons, 1885	London, 1885		1903
F. William Dwight Whitney				
Language and the Study of Language*	New York: C. Scribner & Co., 1867	Munich, 1874; London, 1870, 1880; Haarlam, 1877–81	6th ed., 1895	1904
Compendious German Grammar	New York: H. Holt & Co., 1870	London, 1879, 1882, 1900	6th ed., 1888	1901
Oriental and Linguistic Studies*	New York: C. Scribner & Co., 1872–74			1893
Life and Growth of Language*	New York: D. Appleton & Co., 1875	London, 1875; Leipzig, 1876; Paris, 1876		1911
Essentials of English Grammar*	Boston: Ginn & Heath, 1877			1903

Appendix 3 *Continued*

Author, Title	U.S. Editions	Foreign Editions	Last Edition	Last Date
Sanskrit Grammar	2d ed., Boston: Ginn & Co., 1889 Cambridge: Harvard University Press, 1921	Leipzig, 1879		1984
G. Theodore Dwight Woolsey				
Introduction to the Study of International Law	Boston: J. Munroe & Co., 1860; New York: C. Scribner, 1864	London, 1879 Japan, 1873–5	6th ed., 1889	1908
Divorce and Divorce Legislation	New York: C. Scribner, 1869		Rev. ed., 1882	
Political Science; or The State	New York: C. Scribner's Sons, 1877			1905
Communism and Socialism	New York: C. Scribner's Sons, 1880	London, 1879		1894

[1]Woolsey's son Theodore Salisbury Woolsey edited the text after his father's death in 1889.

Source: The National Union Catalogue: Pre-1966 Imprints, 1980 ed.

Note: Titles followed by an asterisk (*) are currently available in a reprint edition.

[a]Several chapters were previously published in *New Englander* 23 (1864).
[b]From the Lowell Lectures, 1871.
[c]Reprinted from the *North American Review* 134 (1882). The Chautauqua Press edition was in the Chautauqua Home Reading Series.
[d]For the Chautauqua Reading Circle Series.
[e]Several of the essays in this volume were previously published in either the *New Englander* for 1866, 1877, and 1890, the *Church Review* for 1887, or the *Forum* for 1887.

Appendix 4
Subjects of *New Englander* Articles, 1843–1861

Subject	Number (Total = 663)	Percentage of Total
Religious Topics		
Popular aspects: hymns, service, church architecture, missionary work	55	
Congregationalism and the ministry	33	
Criticism and analysis of other denominations	51	
Theological and Biblical study	47	
Theological reviews and biographies	92	
Total	278	42%
Current events		
United States	110	
Non–United States	30	
The slave problem, or the South	31	
Obituaries of national figures	6	
Total	177	27
Cultural topics		
Literature	40	
Manners: art, architecture, fashion and taste, gentlemanliness	21	
Reading	3	
Education	4	
Obituaries	37	
Total	105	16
Scholarly developments		
Natural science	41	
Biblical criticism or history	10	

Appendix 4 Continued

Subject	Number (Total = 663)	Percentage of Total
Higher education	13	
Women's education	1	
The scholar	3	
Greek grammar	3	
German	9	
Philosophy	9	
Philology	11	
Political science	3	
Total	103	16

Source: "Index to the *New Englander*, Volumes I to XIX," *New Englander* 20 (1862). This index includes articles, not shorter book notices.

Appendix 5
The New Haven Scholars Popularize
German Philosophy and Scholarship

The *New Englander* introduced its readers to German philosophy and scholarship, especially in philology. See, for instance, the following articles in the *New Englander*: [Theodore Dwight Woolsey,] "Noehden's German Grammar," 1 (1843): 141 ff., "Classical Studies," 5 (1847): 183 ff., "Rise of Universities," 10 (1852): 21 ff., "The Study of Words," 10 (1852): 438 ff.; [Edward Elbridge Salisbury,] "Sketch of the Life of Neander," 2 (1844): 267 ff.; [William Augustus Larned,] "Sketch of the Life and Letters of Niebuhr," 10 (1852): 526 ff., "Constitutional History of Athenian Democracy," 18 (1860): 651 ff.; [Noah Porter,] "The American Student in Germany," 15 (1857): 574 ff.; [James Hadley,] "Notice of Dwight's *Modern Philology*," 18 (1860): 1089 ff.

Other *New Englander* writers and Club members joined in this effort. See "Memoirs of Augustus William Schlegel," 2 (1844): 185 ff.; [F. H. Hedge,] "Prose Writers of Germany," 13 (1855): 483 ff.; [D. H. Hamilton,] "The Kantian Philosophy," 5 (1847): 61 ff.; and [D. C. Gilman,] "Humboldt, Ritter, and the New Geography," 18 (1860): 754 ff. Josiah Willard Gibbs, the Biblical scholar, drew upon his knowledge of German Biblical criticism and published the resulting articles in vols. 1 (1843), 10–11 (1852–53), and 15–18 (1857–60). The *New Englander* also published in its brief "Notices of Books" short reviews of German historians' and theologians' works that were important to the scholars, such as the Biblical commentaries of Augustus Tholuck and the church histories of John C. L. Gieseler.

The scholars reached a larger audience through their publications in other periodicals. From its founding in 1849, the *Journal of the American Oriental Society* carried Salisbury's and Whitney's articles on philology. Whitney's and Hadley's pieces also appeared regularly in the *Transactions of the American Philological Association* from its founding in 1869.

Besides the texts discussed in the previous pages, the scholars' other books also disseminated the methods of German scholarship. Larned published *The Analysis of the Sentence* (New Haven, n.d.), which made the work of German philologist Bekker available to a New Haven audience. Fisher's *Essays on the Supernatural Origin of Christianity* (1865) criticized the Biblical criticism of Renan, Strauss, and the Tübingen School and used German methods of historical criticism to affirm the essential truths of the Bible. Porter wrote a supplement to Friedrich Ueberweg's *History of Philosophy* (1874) and a critical essay, *Kant's Ethics* (1886). He also lectured at the Concord School of Philosophy in 1882, presumably on some aspect of German philosophy. Hoppin wrote a nonscholarly volume, *Notes of a Theological Student* (1854), which treated Germany as the home of Romanticism and scholarship, not unbelief. Whitney aided American students wishing to learn the German language with the publication of *A Compendious German Grammar* (1869) and *A German Reader* (1870).

Notes

CHAPTER ONE. INTRODUCTION

1. See Faust, *Sacred Circle;* Howe, *Unitarian Conscience;* Hutchison, *Modernist Impulse;* idem, *Transcendentalist Ministers;* Marsden, *Evangelical Mind;* idem, *Fundamentalism;* Meyer, *Instructed Conscience;* and Smith, *Professors.* See also Daniel Walker Howe, "Victorian Culture in America," in Howe, *Victorian America,* 3–28.

2. Fisher, *Grounds of Theistic and Christian Belief,* 41.

3. Leonard Bacon, "Sermon," in *Discourses and Addresses at the Ordination of the Reverend Theodore Dwight Woolsey, LL.D. to the Ministry of the Gospel and His Inauguration as President of Yale College, October 21, 1846* (New Haven, 1846), 28. On truth see Bozeman, *Protestants,* 55–60.

4. Williams, *Culture and Society,* 263–64; idem, *Keywords,* 55–60.

5. Houghton, *Victorian Frame of Mind,* 221, 14. In his *Genteel Endeavor,* 8, John Tomsich says that despair characterized his group of Victorian editors. Compare the scholars' optimism with the pessimism of the Boston Brahmins (Fredrickson, *Inner Civil War,* 29–35).

6. See, for example, Daniel Walker Howe, "The Social Science of Horace Bushnell," *Journal of American History* 70 (1983): 305–23.

7. Fredrickson, *Inner Civil War,* 23 and chap. 2.

8. See Howe, *American Whigs,* 1–42; Richard Jensen, *Illinois,* (New York: W. W. Norton and Co., 1979), chaps. 2 and 3; idem, *The Winning of the Midwest* (Chicago: University of Chicago Press, 1971); and Ronald E. Formisano, *The Birth of Mass Political Parties* (Princeton: Princeton University Press, 1971).

9. Howe, "Bushnell"; J. David Hoeveler, Jr., "Personality and Progressivism: E. A. Ross and American Sociology" (Paper delivered at the annual

meeting of the Organization of American Historians, 1983); idem, "Religion and the New University: From Moral Philosophy to the Social Sciences" (Paper delivered at the spring meeting of the American Society of Church History, 1983).

10. Cockshut, *Truth to Life,* 70.

11. On choice see Berger, *Heretical Imperative,* chap. 1; on secularization see idem, *Sacred Canopy,* 107, 113–51. See also idem, *Facing Up to Modernity,* esp. chap. 14; and Berger, Berger, and Kellner, *Homeless Mind,* esp. chap. 3.

12. Berger, *Sacred Canopy,,* 158; Berger, Berger, and Kellner, *Homeless Mind,* 79.

13. Noah Porter, *An Historical Discourse Delivered at the Celebration of . . . the Congregational Church in Farmington, Connecticut* (Hartford, 1873), 24, 20, 43; idem, *A Historical Discourse . . . in Commemoration of the Original Settlement of the Ancient Town,* 37, 9; Fisher, *Colonial Era,* 85, 99, 167–69.

14. See Brown, *Modernization;* and idem, "Modernization: A Victorian Climax," in Howe, *Victorian America,* 29–44. My discussion draws upon the following works: Mary Ryan, *Cradle of the Middle Class: The Family in Oneida County, New York, 1790–1865* (New York: Cambridge University Press, 1981); Bledstein, *Culture of Professionalism;* Lipson, *Free Masonry in Federalist Connecticut;* Marzio, *Democratic Art;* and Scott, *From Office to Profession.*

15. Berger observes that opponents of total modernization often use some of the effects of modernization to cure its defects (Berger, *Sacred Canopy,* 41–42).

16. See esp. George Santayana, "The Genteel Tradition in American Philosophy," in his *Genteel Tradition;* Brooks, *America's Coming of Age;* and Mencken, *Book of Prefaces.* For the "mush" comment see ibid., 221. See also Douglas, *Feminization of American Culture.*

17. Cf. Brooks, *America's Coming of Age,* 13–14; and Fisher, *Colonial Era,* 319–20.

18. White, *Social Thought in America,* esp. chaps. 1–3; Veysey, *American University,* chap. 1. Porter also appears as a spokesman for the old-time college in Walter P. Metzger, "The Age of the University," vol. 2 of Hofstadter and Metzger, *Development of Academic Freedom,* 279. When discussing Woolsey, Porter, Fisher, et al., historians usually assume an apologetic stance and blame them for preventing Yale from becoming a university (see Kelley, *Yale,* 253, 270–72; and Pierson, *Yale,* 57–65). For a more appreciative perspective see Bainton, *Yale and the Ministry;* and Gabriel, *Religion and Learning at Yale.* They discuss how German Biblical criticism reformed religious teaching at Yale but do not notice how the lessons of Biblical criticism carried over into other subjects.

19. See n. 9 above and Crunden, *Ministers of Reform.* See also Hoeveler, *McCosh;* Bozeman, *Protestants;* Hovenkamp, *Science and Religion;* Bledstein, *Culture of Professionalism,* 136–46; and McLachlan, "Transmission of Culture." Revisions under way are summarized in idem, "The American College in the Nineteenth Century: Towards a Reappraisal," *Teachers College Record* 80 (1978):

287–306; and most recently Martin Finkelstein, "From Tutor to Specialized Scholar: Academic Professionalization in Eighteenth and Nineteenth Century America," *History of Higher Education Annual* 3 (1983): 123–44.

20. Hutchison, *Modernist Impulse,* 2; see his chaps. 1 and 2 for the roots of modernism. The most recent instance of this focus on Bushnell appears in Turner, *Without God, Without Creed,* 107.

21. See Hofstadter, *Progressive Historians,* 27.

22. I am referring to Douglas, *Feminization of American Culture.* The classic discussion of the cult is Barbara Welter, "The Cult of True Womanhood, 1820–1860," *American Quarterly* 18 (1966): 151–74.

23. This paragraph reformulates Edmund Morgan's statement of the "Puritan Dilemma" (Morgan, *The Puritan Dilemma: The Story of John Winthrop* [Boston: Little, Brown and Co., 1958], xii). When considering the relationship between individualism and community, politically liberal academics are more likely to agree with Sacvan Bercovitch's indictment rather than George Gilder's celebration of the American tendency to identify individual and national interest (cf. Bercovitch, *American Jeremiad;* and George Gilder, *Wealth and Poverty* [New York: Basic Books, 1981]).

CHAPTER TWO. THE NEW HAVEN MILIEU

1. Noah Porter, Sr., "Charge," in *Discourses and Addresses at the Ordination of Woolsey,* 49. Descriptions of the ceremonies appear on pp. 3–4.

2. "The Present State of Metaphysics," *Quarterly Christian Spectator* 6 (1834): 609. Other examples are "Preaching on Ability," ibid. 7 (1835): 223–57 and "German Literature," ibid., 13–31. For a discussion of the Taylorite attitude see Gura, *Wisdom of Words,* 56.

3. Woolsey, "Inaugural Discourse," 4.

4. Ibid., 6, 7.

5. "Introduction," in *Addresses at the Inauguration of Noah Porter, D.D., LL.D., as President of Yale College, Wednesday, October 11, 1871* (New York, 1871), 3–7; Theodore Dwight Woolsey, "Address of Induction," in ibid., 13; Porter, "Inaugural Address," 30–34.

6. The Yale Report is reprinted in Richard Hofstadter and Wilson Smith, eds., *American Higher Education: A Documentary History,* 2 vols. (Chicago: University of Chicago Press, 1961), 1:274–91.

7. Noah Porter to William Graham Sumner, 12 June 1879, in Starr, *Sumner,* 346. Chapter 15 of Starr's biography was the definitive statement of the controversy. More recently, Burton Bledstein called for new appreciation of Porter's position (Bledstein, "Noah Porter versus William Graham Sumner," *Church History* 43 [1974]: 340–49). Donald C. Bellomy now offers the definitive account, and he gives each perspective a full and fair hearing in his "Molding of an Iconoclast," chap. 12.

8. In 1843 the older Yale professors were Jeremiah Day, mathematics;

James Luce Kingsley, Greek and Latin; and Benjamin Silliman and Denison Olmsted, who split the natural sciences between them. In the Theological Department the professors were Nathaniel William Taylor, Josiah Willard Gibbs, Elizur T. Fitch, and Chauncey Goodrich. Goodrich and Taylor were the principals behind the *Quarterly Christian Spectator.*

9. Mead, *Taylor,* 112; and see chap. 3 on Taylor's moral-government theory. For a clear, brief summary of the Scottish philosophy see Marsden, *Fundamentalism,* 14–17.

10. Marsden, *The Evangelical Mind,* 56–58; Sandeen, *Roots of Fundamentalism,* chap. 5; Noah Porter, Sr., to Noah Porter, Jr., 21 January 1833, Miss Porter's School Archives, Leila Dilworth Jones Memorial Library, Miss Porter's School, Farmington, Conn. A new book on Princeton, which only recently came to my attention, offers a fresh perspective on Old School theologians (see Mark A. Noll, ed., *The Princeton Theology, 1812–1921: Scripture, Science and Theological Method from Archibald Alexander to Benjamin Breckenridge Warfield* [Grand Rapids, Mich.: Baker Book House, 1983]).

11. David Allmendinger argues that mid-nineteenth-century college presidents found the college revival disruptive of college discipline, searched for a new source of college order, and then initiated a new form of relationship between students and professors (Allmendinger, *Paupers and Scholars,* 119–21). This questioning of Taylor's theology appears in the letters between Charles Loring Brace, a student at Yale College (1842–46) and then in the Yale Theological Department (1847–48), and his close friend Frederick Law Olmsted (see Emma Brace, ed., *The Life of Charles Loring Brace* [New York: C. Scribner's Sons, 1894], 8–18). An example is Olmsted to Charles Loring Brace, 25 March 1848, in Frederick Law Olmsted, *The Formative Years,* vol. 1 of *The Papers of Frederick Law Olmsted,* ed. Charles Capen McLaughlin et al. (Baltimore: Johns Hopkins University Press, 1977), 315–17. Olmsted wrote his friend Frederick Kingsbury, "I am beginning to have a horror of ministers. They are such a set of conceited, dogmatical, narrow minded, misanthropic, petty mind tyrants" (22 August 1846, in ibid., 275–76).

12. Christopher M. Jedrey, *The World of John Cleaveland: Family and Community in Eighteenth-Century New England* (New York: W. W. Norton Co., 1979), 22–42.

13. Marsden, *Fundamentalism,* 15–17.

14. Hadley, *Diary,* 97.

15. Fisher contrasted the two generations of scholarship in his "Address," in *Memorial of Nathaniel W. Taylor, D.D.* (New Haven, 1858), 32; and he discussed the controversies that Taylorism inspired in "Historical Address," in *The Semi-Centennial Anniversary of the Divinity School of Yale College* (New Haven, 1872), 3–30.

16. Dwight, *Whitney and Dana,* 21.

17. Mary Taylor Porter, "Temple Street Forty Years Ago," *New Haven Palladium,* 24 February 1869, in Mary Taylor Porter Scrapbook, Yale University Library; Hadley, *Diary,* 60, 100, 140; and various newspaper clippings

in the Mary Taylor Porter Scrapbook. The other pallbearers were Porter's former student and close friend historian Franklin Bowditch Dexter and John Ferguson Weir.

18. No historian of Yale but Daniel Coit Gilman discussess The Club (see Gilman, *Dana,* 164–65). Information about The Club is drawn from Witherspoon, *The Club,* including Franklin Bowditch Dexter's "Historical Sketch," on pp. 8–17. See also Hadley, *Diary;* Gilman, *Dana,* 182–83; and Weir, *Recollections,* 83–84 and passim. Among educated elites discussion groups were prevalent in the mid-nineteenth century. Bostonians had first the Anthology Society and later the Saturday Club, and New York was the home of various groups of Knickerbocker writers and artists and then the Century Club. These groups often sponsored or were informally connected with a magazine or journal (see Faust, *Sacred Circle,* 6; Callow, *Kindred Spirits,* chap. 1; Lewis P. Simpson, ed., *The Federalist Literary Mind* [Baton Rouge: Louisiana State University Press, 1969], 10–11; and Howe, *Unitarian Conscience,* 176–77).

19. Weir, *Recollections,* 83–84. For biographical information see appendixes 1 and 2. For a list of Club members and when they joined see Witherspoon, *The Club,* 51–53.

20. On the later hostility to Spencer see Kelley, *Yale,* 270–71; and Pierson, *Yale,* 75. This change occurred slowly. The list of topics and speakers in Witherspoon, *The Club,* (57–75), suggests that when religious topics were discussed, the speakers were members of the New Haven scholars' generation or new members who were ministers. See below, chapter 3.

21. For the list of topics see Witherspoon, *The Club,* 57–75. The ritual of Club meetings appears in ibid., 8–17. No copies of these papers survive, but some were reprinted in the *New Englander* (see the appropriate years). Sumner's stance on Spencer might have made The Club an uncongenial place for him. However, given the facts that Woolsey and he agreed on many political and economic matters and that the Spencer controversy did not erupt until 1879, Sumner's not belonging is less explicable, unless his habitual cigar smoking excluded him (see Starr, *Sumner,* 127–28, on his smoking; and Bellomy, "Molding of an Iconoclast," chap. 2, p. 13, for his agreement with Woolsey).

22. Merriam, *Noah Porter,* 61, 78, 179, and passim. Writing to Woolsey about a ministerial council in Boston, Porter first conceded that the meeting was given to "clap trap" but then said that his younger colleagues Dwight and Fisher should see "the absolute necessity of connecting themselves with such gatherings, if they desire to have any influence or friendship with the clergy" (Porter to Woolsey, 20 June 1865, Woolsey Family Papers, Yale University Library, Yale University, New Haven, Conn.). Unless otherwise noted, all correspondence cited below appears in Woolsey Family Papers, and all manuscript collections are located at the Yale University Library.

Between Fisher and Porter little love was lost. Porter advised that Woolsey should ignore the recommendation of Edwards Amasa Park and doubted whether "any body who could suit Dr. T[aylor] and Prof. G[oodrich] would please me—our practical views are so different" (Porter to Woolsey, 13 December 1853, 16 April 1854). Although Fisher's writings show no animosity, in a memorial article he said that Porter wrote "in behalf of the New Haven doctrines, and of the mitigated form of Calvinism which brought upon the New Haven divines so large an amount of odium. . . . One of the obnoxious points in Dr. Taylor's system was his ethical theory. This theory was warmly espoused by Dr. Porter and was maintained long after he assumed the Chair of Philosophy at Yale" (Fisher, "Theological Opinions," in Merriam, *Noah Porter,* 103–4).

23. See Sally Gregory Kohlstedt, "Savants and Professionals: The American Association for the Advancement of Science, 1848–1860," in Oleson and Brown, *Pursuit of Knowledge,* 299–325; and A. Hunter Dupree, "The National Pattern of American Learned Societies," in ibid., 21–32. For an example of an interchange of ideas see George Park Fisher's references to Asa Gray in Fisher, *Faith and Rationalism,* 108–9. On the literary societies see Kelley, *Yale,* 78, 107–8, 222–23. For accounts of philology meetings see Hadley, *Diary.* The American Oriental Society attracted ministers and missionaries, as well as college professors. The regular members of the Philological Society were Porter, Hadley, Woolsey, Larned, Thacher, Whitney, and Gibbs.

24. See appendixes 1 and 3 and the selected bibliography. Woolsey's Phi Beta Kappa address is *Relations of Honor to Political Life;* Fisher's talks are "Function of the Historian" and *The Historical Method in Theology;* Whitney's definition appears in *Encyclopaedia Britannica,* 11th ed. See correspondence between Noah Porter and Charles and George Merriam filed under *American Dictionary of the English Language,* 1864 ed., in the as yet unprocessed G. and C. Merriam Company Papers, Beinecke Rare Book and Manuscript Library, Yale University, New Haven, Conn. The quotation given in the text is from Porter to G. and C. Merriam, June 1857.

25. On the *Independent* see Louis Filler, "Liberalism, Anti-Slavery, and the Founders of the *Independent,*" *New England Quarterly* 27 (1954): 291–306. See also Noah Porter, "The Late Dr. Bacon," *Independent,* 12 January 1882, clipping in Miscellaneous Manuscripts of Noah Porter, Yale University Library; and [Noah Porter,] "Bushnell on Christian Nurture," *New Englander* 6 (1848): 121–47. This pattern of connections is one of many. Patterns stemmed from family, faith, institutional membership, and intellectual interests. Thompson married the sister of political scientist Francis Lieber, whose political theories had much in common with Woolsey's and who served with Woolsey on the American Social Science Association. Friendships, as in the case of Bushnell, often predated Yale and existed between families. New Haven ideas also penetrated families through the education of children. Fisher and Whitney sent their daughters to Noah Porter's sister's school in Farmington, Connecticut. Sarah Porter adapted her brother's educational ideas for her women students (see Stevenson, "Sarah Porter Educates Useful La-

dies"). The similarity between the political theory held by Thompson and that held by Bushnell is noted by Fredrickson in his *Inner Civil War*, 23–28, but he does not suspect the institutional basis.

26. Gilman, *Dana*, 182–83.

27. Ahlstrom, *Religious History*, 462–63; Marsden, *The Evangelical Mind*, 58; Sandeen, *Roots of Fundamentalism*, chap. 5. For Harvard see Howe, *Unitarian Conscience*. For typical New Haven views on the Unitarians see Joseph Parrish Thompson, "Unitarians in New York," *New Englander* 5 (1847): 22; and [Noah Porter,] "Theodore Parker and Liberal Christianity," ibid. 2 (1844): 528–59. The Parker-Porter correspondence is described in Merriam, *Noah Porter*, 121–22; the quote is from p. 122. Porter relates Parker's opinion in Porter to Woolsey, 30 January 1846.

28. Porter to McCosh, 3 November 1868, and McCosh to Porter, 30 January 1886, both in James McCosh Collection, Princeton University Library, Princeton, N.J.; Hoeveler, *McCosh*, 308; and on Harvard, Howe, *Unitarian Conscience*, 112–23. The *Boston Lectures* were published in 1870, 1871, and 1872. They had the subtitle *Christianity and Scepticism*.

29. Kelley, *Yale*, 285.

30. Hawkins, *Pioneer*, 68.

CHAPTER THREE. NEW HAVEN SCHOLARSHIP

1. For Whitney's higher education see Diehl, *Americans and German Scholarship*, 120–30, 141–43. For Dana see Hovenkamp, *Science and Religion*, 125–29; and Daniels, *American Science*, 205. For the other scholars see appendix 1.

2. Diehl, *Americans and German Scholarship*, 73. Diehl points out that previous historians referred uncritically to these Bostonians as "scholars" because they paid little attention to the content and method of their work.

3. For a college revival and the college president's involvement see Reuben Aldridge Guild, "Account of the Revival in Brown University," Reuben Aldridge Guild Collection, John Hay Library, Brown University, Providence, R.I. Fisher was converted at this revival. For Yale see Chauncey A. Goodrich, "Narrative of Revivals of Religion in Yale College," *American Quarterly Register* 10 (1838): 295–365.

4. For Taylor's contention against Episcopalians and Tyler's opposition to New Haven theology see Mead, *Taylor*, 93–94, 139; and on the Taylor-Tyler dispute see Ahlstrom, *Religious History*, 420–421. Silliman's opposition to scientific discoveries in disagreement with the Bible is found in Hovenkamp, *Science and Religion*, 125–29; and Daniels, *American Science*, 223. For a more general discussion of the ministry see Scott, *From Office to Profession*, 64–65.

5. W. W. Andrews, "Student at Yale," in Merriam, *Noah Porter*, 17–23;

Gura, *Wisdom of Words,* 55. Gura's chap. 2 contains a helpful discussion of Coleridge's impact on Marsh and Bushnell.

6. James Marsh, "Preliminary Essay," in Coleridge, *Aids to Reflection,* 11; Porter, "Coleridge," 163, 144, 133. Forty years later, when Porter became president of Yale, Bushnell reminded his friend of the importance of language. "There is nothing so fruitful in the real culture of mind," he wrote, "as the practical drill of language and linguistic criticism. Would that every human soul could know how much and what there is for it in language" (Bushnell to Porter, quoted in Merriam, *Noah Porter,* 184). Philip Gura considers Porter's review of *The Aids to Reflection* as "still one of the best introductions to Marsh's thought" (Gura, *Wisdom of Words,* 176 n. 31). Though discussing Marsh's and Bushnell's responses to Coleridge, Gura nonetheless overlooks Bushnell's circle of friends at Yale, who were just as intent as Marsh and Bushnell to save Congregationalism from the rationalism of the New Haven theology. For the impact of Coleridge on Congregational liberals see Marsden, *Evangelical Mind,* 152–53; and Ahlstrom, *Religious History,* 594–95. Older works such as Pochmann, *German Culture in America,* and Riley, *American Philosophy,* 34–36, create the impression that German philosophy reached New Haven via the transcendentalists.

7. Andrews, "Student at Yale," 14–15. See also Goodrich, "Narrative of Revivals of Religion"; and for the experience of Porter's friend W. A. Larned see *Biographical Sketch of the Class of 1826* (Utica, N.Y., 1866), 34–35. From 1830 to 1846 the curriculum in Yale College did not change (see *Catalogue of Officers and Students in Yale College* [New Haven, 1830–46]). Thus, all the scholars had identical college educations. Porter's acceptance of German philosophy may have followed the same course as Bushnell's. Porter says that Bushnell had read Edwards, Butler, Locke, Reid, and Stewart. Then he reacted to his extracurricular reading of German philosophy as if it were "half repulsive and half attractive, but ever challenging curiosity and compelling investigation" (Noah Porter, "Horace Bushnell," *New Englander* 36 [1877]: 166). Bushnell also read Kant and Carlyle, but he reached "theological conviction" only after reading Schleiermacher and Neander. For Porter's comment on college preaching see Porter to Woolsey, 28 November 1845.

8. Noah Porter, Sr., to Noah Porter, Jr., 21 January 1833, Miss Porter's School Archives.

9. [Porter,] "Edmund Burke"; idem, "Wordsworth"; Noah Porter, "The Characteristics of English Literature," *American Biblical Repository* 2 (1839): 329–52; idem, "Transcendentalism"; [Noah Porter,] "Theodore Parker," *New Englander* 2 (1844): 371–96; idem, "Theodore Parker and Liberal Christianity," 528–59; Porter to Woolsey, 26 September 1845.

10. Porter, "Youth of the Scholar," 96–97.

11. Ralph Waldo Emerson, "The American Scholar," in *Selected Writings of Ralph Waldo Emerson,* ed. W. H. Gilman (New York: New American Library, 1965), 233–34.

12. Porter "Youth of the Scholar," 97; [Noah Porter,] "Dr. Thomas Arnold," *New Englander* 5 (1847): 371; idem, "On Moral Science," 570, 572.

13. Porter, "Youth of the Scholar," 97.

14. Porter to Woolsey, 28 July 1846. See also Porter to Woolsey, 5 February and 16 April 1854.

15. Pfeiffer, *Classical Scholarship*, 171. For the University of Berlin see Herbst, *German Historical School*, 16–18.

16. Mention of philology club meetings appears in Hadley, *Diary;* for the reading of these men see Records of the New Haven Book Club, Hillhouse Family Papers, Yale University Library; and the index to the *New Englander.* Willis B. Glover discusses the significance of these British journals for philology in his *Evangelical Nonconformists,* 41, 42. Fisher learned about Biblical criticism at Andover from his teacher Moses Stuart (Brown, *Biblical Criticism,* 45–59).

17. Porter to Woolsey, 22 February 1854, 13 December 1853. For the reaction of the other New Haven scholars to study in Germany see Fisher, "Record of Student Days in Germany," Miscellaneous Personal Papers of George Park Fisher, Yale Divinity School Library, Yale University, New Haven, Conn.; Hoppin, *Notes of a Theological Student,* esp. 1–27; and appropriate years in the Woolsey and Whitney Family Papers. While in Berlin, Porter lived with a German family and, after classes at the university, attended concerts, operas, and the theater. He became a close friend of Trendelenburg's and conversed with Schelling, Humboldt, and Ritter (Merriam, *Noah Porter,* 94–95; and correspondence with Woolsey). At other universities, the New Haven men found an equally congenial life. Fisher tells of his experiences at Halle, conversations with Tholuck, and attendance at various parties where he amused the ladies with discussions of *Uncle Tom's Cabin* and American woman's rights conventions (Fisher, "Record of Student Days in Germany," 16 November and 12 December 1852). Carl Diehl describes Woolsey's and Whitney's experiences in *Americans and German Scholarship,* 92–94, 120–30.

18. [Noah Porter,] "The American Student in Germany," *New Englander* 15 (1857): 578, 581, 586, 583, 584; Porter to Woolsey, 13 December 1853.

19. Porter to Woolsey, 12 July 1858.

20. Porter to Woolsey, 27 March 1859.

21. Porter, *Human Intellect,* 5.

22. Ibid.; Fisher, *Universal History,* v–vii; Tracy Peck, "Lecture Notes," Yale Lectures; Whitney, *Language and the Study of Language.*

23. Salisbury, *Inaugural Discourse,* 44, 50; James Dwight Dana to Francis Wayland, 25 July 1850, as quoted in Stanley M. Guralnick, "The American Scientist in Higher Education, 1820–1910," in *The Sciences in the American Context: New Perspectives,* ed. Nathan Reingold (Washington, D.C.: Smithsonian Institution Press, 1979), 116; Fisher to Charles Scribner, 14 October and 24 January 1878, Charles Scribner's Sons Papers, Princeton University Library.

24. Fisher, *Universal History,* 6–7; David Nelson Beach, "Lecture Notes on Church History," Yale Divinity School Library; Fisher, *The Reformation,* v–viii; Porter, *Human Intellect,* 7. See also [Noah Porter,] "Recent Works in Psychology," *New Englander* 13 (1853): 133–34.

25. Peck, "Lecture Notes"; Whitney, *Language and the Study of Language,* 10.

26. Maurice Mandelbaum associates the Scottish philosophy with this theory of social change (Mandelbaum, *History, Man, and Reason,* 143).

27. [Porter,] "On Moral Science," 578, 575. For Woolsey's theory of elites see his "Leading Elements in Civilization," lecture notes, 1865, p. 30, Woolsey Family Papers. Thomas Bender compares Henry Ward Beecher's idea that a minister must preach to both the few and the many with Henry Tappan's advocacy of an urban university (Bender, "Erosion of Public Culture," 91–95). James Mason Hoppin wrote that Beecher best expounded "that new style of preaching providentially adapted to . . . reach the great masses of the people fast falling away from the old unsympathetic methods of teaching" ("Henry Ward Beecher," *New Englander* 29 [1870]: 437–38).

28. Woolsey, *International Law,* x; Porter, *Human Intellect,* v. Silliman's *Journal* was founded in 1818, and the *Journal of the American Oriental Society* in 1849.

29. See Fisher, *Bibliographies.*

30. Hoppin, *Homiletics* (New York: Dodd, Mead and Co., 1882), 428. See also, [Noah Porter,] "Congregationalism in New England," *New Englander* 1 (1843): 576. On the usefulness of books and articles see David D. Hall, "The Victorian Connection," in Howe, *Victorian America,* 91.

31. See n. 14 above. Harvard offered Whitney a position that paid more and required less teaching. Yale raised enough money to retain Whitney (see Thomas Thacher to Edward Salisbury, 2 October 1869, Salisbury Family Papers, Yale University Library). It should be stressed, however, that even Harvard salaries were inadequate to support a family; professors often sought means to supplement their income, including the tutoring of young women (Horowitz, *Alma Mater,* 102). My analysis of the New Haven scholars' relationship to their audience draws into question Robert A. McCaughey's contention that if Whitney had been paid more, he "almost certainly would have abandoned his popular audience in favor of one made up exclusively of his fellow academic specialists" (McCaughey, *International Studies and Academic Enterprise,* 45). The idea that scholars should write only for other scholars appeared in the early twentieth century. Then "the order of the day was technical specialized research published for technically competent audiences in technical journals, with popularizations in all areas of speculation frequently relegated to hacks, incompetents, and has-beens" (Kuklick, *Rise of American Philosophy,* 565).

32. Mott, *American Magazines,* 2:312–15; advertisement, *New Englander* 38 (1879): 91.

33. Prospectus, *New Englander* 1 (1843): 2; Publisher's Note, ibid. 16

(1858); Leonard Bacon to Alexander Twining, 26 March 1843, Bacon Family Papers, Yale University Library.

34. Prospectus, *New Englander* 2; Editor's Note, ibid. 29 (1870); advertisement, ibid. 38 (1879): 91.

35. [George Park Fisher,] "Review of Mrs. Stowe's *Dred,*" ibid. 14 (1856): 515–26; George Park Fisher, "Of the Distinction between Natural and Political Rights," ibid. 23 (1864): 1–27; [Noah Porter,] *"Thorndale;* or, the Conflict of Opinions," ibid. 17 (1859): 652–86.

36. Fisher's essays were reprinted in Fisher, *Supernatural Origin;* and Hoppin's were reprinted in Hoppin, *"The Early Renaissance".* Cf. [William Dwight Whitney,] "China and the West," *New Englander* 19 (1861): 1–31; and idem, "On the Nature and Designation of the Accent in Sanskrit," *Transactions of the American Philological Association for 1869–1870,* 1871, 20–45.

37. Editors' Note, *New Englander* 15 (1857).

38. Mott, *American Magazines,* 1:310. For example, "Goldsmith and His Writing," *Quarterly Christian Spectator* 10 (1838): 18–36; and "Theatrical Amusements," ibid., 557–72.

39. Editors' Statement, *Yale Review* 1 (1893).

40. Noah Porter, manuscript of James Luce Kingsley's death, Miscellaneous Manuscripts of Noah Porter; Philip Schaff to Leonard Bacon, 28 August 1849, Bacon Family Papers; Ahlstrom, *Religious History,* 420–21; Fisher, *The Reformation,* vii, 6–7; Williston Walker, "Why Did Not Massachusetts Have a Saybrook Platform?" *Yale Review* 1 (1893): 68–86; idem, "A Study of a New England Town," ibid., 368–80.

41. Peter L. Berger's description of secularization parallels the process of change from the *Quarterly Christian Spectator* through the *Yale Review* (see his *Sacred Canopy,* 107, 113–51; and idem, *Facing Up to Modernity*).

42. On Merriam see Karl, *Merriam.* Yale president Timothy Dwight argued in 1892 that Yale graduate programs should admit women, who would receive specialized training in preparation for careers specificallly suited to their nature (see his "Education for Women at Yale," *Forum* 13 [1892]: 451–63). Thus it is improper to see *scholar* and *scholarship* including only men after this date, even though both terms had a special meaning when applied to women.

43. For example, Fisher compares Woolsey to Niebuhr (Fisher, "Academic Career of President Woolsey," 716); and Porter invoked the example of Arnold in his "Inaugural Address," 51.

44. Porter, "Youth of the Scholar," 96, 99, 97; idem, "American Student," 585. Porter is at his most pessimistic in *Human Intellect,* viii. Fisher, "Academic Career of President Woolsey," 716.

45. Porter dedicated his *American Colleges* to Woolsey, and Fisher asked Woolsey to read his manuscripts before publication (Woolsey to Fisher, n.d., Miscellaneous Personal Papers of George Park Fisher, Yale Divinity School Library); see also Fisher, "Academic Career of President Woolsey," 716.

46. See, for instance, Porter, *Human Intellect,* 512–26, and the various

essays in his *"Science and Sentiment";* Fisher, *Supernatural Origin;* idem, *History of the Christian Church,* 625–26; Whitney, *Language and the Study of Language,* 429, 52, 421, 441; idem, "On Darwinism and Language," 88; and idem, "The Value of Linguistic Science to Ethnology," *New Englander* 26 (1867): 30–52. For an example of how Whitney's ideas were used see Charles Mellen Tyler, *Bases of Religious Belief: Historic and Ideal* (New York: G. P. Putnam's Sons, 1893).

47. [Noah Porter,] "The New Infidelity," *New Englander* 11 (1853): 277–95; George Park Fisher, "The Conflict with Scepticism and Unbelief," ibid. 23 (1864): 115, 116.

CHAPTER FOUR. THE COLLEGE, THE SCHOLAR, AND THE LIBERAL MAN

Epigraph to Porter's *American Colleges and the American Public.*

1. Porter, "Inaugural Address," 40. Historians focus on Porter's *American Colleges* as the most important expression of his views on collegiate education. Porter's complete opus on education and scholarship suggests that his "Inaugural Address" and speeches (*The Christian College* and "The Ideal Scholar" [see n. 9 below]) represent mature thought on subjects of lifelong concern).

2. Porter, "Inaugural Address," 46. On the relationship between nineteenth-century colleges and reform see Bledstein, *Culture of Professionalism,* esp. 136–46; McLachlan, "Transmission of Culture," 184–206; and Peterson, *New England College,* chap. 2. New Haven definitions of *culture, liberal,* and *independent* appear in Porter and Goodrich, *An American Dictionary of the English Language;* and Porter, *Webster's International Dictionary of the English Language.*

3. Porter, "Inaugural Address," 45–46. The standard works on Porter's opposition to college reform are Veysey, *American University* (see chap. 1); and Metzger, "Age of the University" (see pp. 279 and 335–38). These historians generally pair Porter with James McCosh of Princeton and label both "conservative." Porter explained his differences with Eliot, Angell, Gilman, and White in his *American Colleges,* chap. 1. David Hoeveler's recent biography of James McCosh revises previous interpretations of McCosh but continues to type Porter as a conservative opposed to all change (*McCosh,* esp. 235).

4. Hawkins, *Between Harvard and America,* chap. 4 and 133–38; idem, *Pioneer,* 68–69; Porter, *The Christian College,* 21–22.

5. Arnold, *Culture and Anarchy,* 109, 130.

6. See Fisher, "Elements of Puritanism"; Julian Monson Sturtevant, "The Antagonism of Religion and Culture," *New Englander* 31 (1872): 200–218; and review of *Culture and Anarchy* in ibid. 28 (1870): 182–85.

7. Porter, *Christian College,* 14, 15, 19–21.

8. Ibid., 20.

9. Ibid., 9–11; and see idem, "The Ideal Scholar," in *Lectures Delivered*

before the Students of Phillips Exeter Academy, 1885–1886 (Boston, 1887), 145–79.

10. Porter, *Christian College,* 12.

11. Brooks, *America's Coming of Age,* 24.

12. See, for example, Turner, *Ritual Process;* and idem, *Forest of Symbols,* esp. chaps. 4 and 7.

13. See *Catalogue of the Officers and Students of Yale College,* issues for 1831–86 (New Haven, various dates); and Pierson, *Yale,* 69–73.

14. Porter, *American Colleges,* 293.

15. Ibid., 167–70, 173.

16. See ibid., 218–37; and idem, *Christian College,* 17–30.

17. Porter, *American Colleges,* 182. During the Great Yale revival of 1831, Bushnell was a tutor and Porter was a student (see Porter, "The Late Dr. Bacon"). Porter reviewed *Christian Nurture* favorably and criticized American society for its materialism and worship of Mammon ([Porter,] "Bushnell on Christian Nurture"). Even after the publication of Bushnell's more controversial works, Porter supported his friend (see idem, "Nature and the Supernatural," *New Englander* 17 [1859]: 224–58). In contrast to Porter and his colleagues, Princeton's McCosh continued to encourage revivals (Hoeveler, *McCosh,* 255–62). Porter's comment that college preaching should be more adapted "to [the students'] hearts and feelings" shows his organic conception of religion and education (Porter to Woolsey, 28 November 1845).

18. Allmendinger, *Paupers and Scholars,* 121–22. The shift to college nurture was no reaction to the town-gown riots of the 1850s, for the New Haven scholars' criticism of the college of mental discipline and commitment to change antedated them. On the riots see Kelley, *Yale,* 216–20.

19. See Pierson, *Yale,* 73–94; and Kelley, *Yale,* 271–72, 235–66.

20. Woolsey, "Inaugural Discourse," 4–5.

21. Pfeiffer, *Classical Scholarship,* 181; Holger Pederson, *The Discovery of Language,* trans. John Webster Spargo (1931; reprint, Bloomington: Indiana University Press, 1962), 79–80.

22. Ringer, *German Mandarins,* 19, 86–87; Sorkin, "Wilhelm Von Humboldt," 60, 64, 65, 66–67.

23. Fisher, "Study of Greek," 117; [Theodore Dwight Woolsey,] "Guizot's *History of Civilization,*" *New Englander* 19 (1861): 413, 415.

24. A recent example of the assumption that the research-oriented university destroyed the unity of the college curriculum is Rudolph, *Curriculum,* 150.

25. Ringer, *German Mandarins,* 18–19; Fisher, "Study of Greek," 118; Porter, *American Colleges,* 51.

26. Porter, *American Colleges,* 48–59.

27. Hawkins, *Between Harvard and America,* 95–101, 173–75, as quoted in Paul Gamble, "Westminster College: Pioneer in Co-education and Participant in the 1850–1900 Curriculum Revolution" (Paper presented at the Duquesne History Forum, 21 October 1983). I am thankful to Mr. Gamble

for describing this incident in some detail in a recent letter (letter to author, 24 April 1985).

28. Porter to Henry Barnard, 28 March 1845, Henry Barnard Papers, Fale Library, New York University, New York, N.Y. Sheldon Rothblatt discusses Arnold's influence in *Revolution of the Dons,* 180–89, 246; and he presents the models of the saintly and Socratic professors in his *Tradition and Change,* 176–80. Porter, *Christian College,* 12.

29. Rothblatt, *Tradition and Change,* 177–80; Porter, *American Colleges,* 119–33, esp. 126–28.

30. Porter, "Inaugural Address," 30, 31, 28, 37, 46.

31. In 1856, Porter told Woolsey, "All this year I have felt on the verge of some dreadful brain attack, paralysis, or apoplexy" (Porter to Woolsey, 17 July 1856; see also Porter to Woolsey, 16 April 1854).

32. Porter, "Inaugural Address," 31, 32, 33–36, 41. Even before he knew that he was to be the next president, Porter said that there should be reform; he wanted "a more efficient system than we have and one that shall excite more enthusiasm in the students." But he feared that "the college has before it not the most uninterrupted career of harmony. . . . The next president will have a hard time" (Porter to Salisbury, 12 March 1871, Salisbury Family Papers). After learning of his appointment, he wrote Woolsey that he had read his old friend's inaugural address and saw "nothing for [him] to do but to go forward, without misgiving and with no sanguine hopes" (Porter to Woolsey, 13 September 1871).

33. See May, *Enlightenment,* pt. 4, and esp. chap. 2. See also Smith, *Professors*; and Meyer, *Instructed Conscience.* Meyer and Smith group older professors, such as Francis Wayland, with younger professors, such as the New Haven scholars, who modified the Scottish philosophy.

34. Dwight, *Whitney and Dana,* 8, 11. Dwight also noted the new form of discipline, which he said was motivated by the force of love (see his *Memories of Yale Life and Men,* 33–35, 381, 464–73). Gilman, *Dana,* 154; Kingsley, *Yale College,* 1:148; White, *Autobiography,* 1:27, 29; Parker to Porter, 15 July 1859, quoted in Merriam, *Noah Porter,* 122; Porter, *American Colleges,* 348; and Julian Monson Sturtevant as quoted in Hofstadter and Smith, *American Higher Education,* 1:275.

35. Yale *College Courant,* 23 July 1870, quoted in Starr, *Sumner,* 82–83; Holt, *"Garrulities,"* 36, 34.

36. Bellomy, "Molding of an Iconoclast," chap. 2, p. 3; Holt, *"Garrulities,"* 80; Tobias, *Old Dartmouth on Trial,* 9–13). With the rise of its New York alumni and their stand against a religion-centered college, Dartmouth appears to have experienced tensions similar to Yale's, though at a later date.

37. William Graham Sumner, "Review of the Month," *The Living Church* 1 (November 1869): 98 (Donald Bellomy drew this article to my attention, and I thank him for the loan of his copy); idem, *The Forgotten Man,* 418–19.

38. For example, Kelley, *Yale,* 241. An exception is Donald Bellomy, who

says that "even Porter was committed to transforming Yale into what he conceived of as a university" (Bellomy, "Molding of an Iconoclast," chap. 5, p. 3). For current revisions see above, chap. 1, n. 19. For negative evaluations see above n. 3; Pierson, *Yale,* 1:57–65; and Kelley, *Yale,* 236–53, 271–72. In his *American University,* chap. 1, Veysey uses Porter as a spokesman for mental discipline. Both Veysey and Rothblatt use the terms *teacher* and *researcher* as alternate models (Veysey, *American University,* 221–33; Rothblatt, *Tradition and Change,* 177–80). Veysey's notes to his chap. 3, "Research," also support this generalization. Pierson finds Porter to be the lone spokesman for the value of classical education and insists that Dana and Whitney disagreed. While there is disagreement on means, there is agreement on ends. All New Haven scholars thought that the purpose of education was self-development and that college professors should be scholars (see Whitney, "Aim and Object of This Department of Yale College," esp. 15, 16, 18; and Dana, *New Haven University,* 7–8).

39. Hugh Hawkins refines our understanding of the new research-oriented universities. In the first years, university presidents valued teaching highly. Their emphasis on research was not an exclusive concern (Hawkins, "University Identity: The Teaching and Research Functions," in Oleson and Voss, *Organization of Knowledge,* 286–87).

40. Hawkins, *Between Harvard and America,* 86–96.

41. Porter, *Christian College,* 17.

CHAPTER FIVE. SCIENCE: OBSERVING A FACT, KNOWING THE DIVINE

1. For New Haven definitions see Webster's *American Dictionary of the English Language,* 1864 ed.; and *Webster's International Dictionary of the English Language,* 1890 ed. The definition of *science* as a physical science first appeared as the third meaning in the latter. Woolsey's definition appears in his "Leading Elements in Civilization," 36, 44.

2. On Biblical criticism see esp. Brown, *Biblical Criticism,* 48. William Irvine discusses popularization of Darwin's theories in his *Apes, Angels, and Victorians.*

3. Conrad Cherry, in his *Nature and Religious Imagination,* 113–31, makes evident the relationship between the Scottish philosophy and Taylor's moral didacticism. For Taylor's rejection of natural science see above, chap. 2, nn. 13, 14; and for Silliman's modification of facts see Hovenkamp, *Science and Religion,* 126.

4. Fisher, *Grounds of Theistic and Christian Belief,* 456–57; Dana, "Thoughts on Species," 871; Porter, "Inaugural Address," 53; George Park Fisher, "The Folly of Atheism," *New Englander* 36 (1877): 88.

5. Porter's discussion of German idealism is the earliest among the scholars (see his *Human Intellect,* 519–26). It appears that Fisher was a slow convert

to the idea of dependence. He supports the moral argument for God and disputes Schleiermacher in *Supernatural Origin,* 569–72.

6. Porter, *Human Intellect,* 662.

7. Ibid., 5. For the new use of *psychology* among English scientists see the *Oxford English Dictionary.* [Porter], "Recent Works on Psychology," 133–34, shows Porter's early use of the new word and his disagreement with Wayland. W. T. James says that the influence of Trendelenburg was crucial in helping Porter synthesize these two schools of thought (see his "Noah Porter," 179). Apparently, Porter was unaware that Friedrich Augustus Rauch had introduced Hegelianism to American in 1840. Rauch's work, however, was not scholarly in the New Haven sense. He included no footnotes, did not acknowledge authorities in footnotes, and consulted no facts (see Rauch, *Psychology; or A View of the Human Soul: Including Anthropology, Being the Substance of a Course of Lectures, Delivered to the Junior Class, Marshall College, Pennsylvania* [New York: M. W. Dodd, 1840], 1–5).

8. Porter, *Human Intellect,* 15, vii–viii, 59. For Mill and his school, I use the modern terms *associationist* and *associationism,* but Porter used *associationalist* and *associationalism.*

9. Ibid., 16, 26–28, 53–60.

10. Ibid., 113.

11. Ibid., 55, 25, 26. For a discussion of the relationship between the theories of phrenologist Gall and those of scientist Bain see Young, *Mind, Brain, and Adaptation,* 1–8 and chaps. 2 and 3. Herbert Hovenkamp explains that idealists "saw connections between objects as part of the structure of the universal mind" (Hovenkamp, *Science and Religion,* 107–10).

12. Porter, *"Science and Sentiment,"* 36–37.

13. Porter, *Human Intellect,* 662.

14. Ibid., 482–86.

15. Gilman, *Dana,* 161; Hovenkamp, *Science and Religion,* 125–29; Daniels, *American Science,* 205; Irvine, *Apes, Angels, and Victorians,* 16.

16. For the various editions of Dana's text see appendix 3. The most current is *Manual of Mineralogy after J. D. Dana,* ed. Cornelius S. Hurlbut, Jr., and Cornelis S. Klein, 19th ed. (New York: John Wiley and Sons, 1977).

17. Thomas L. Haskell discusses "the Lazzaroni" in *Professional Social Science,* 70. The Dana-Darwin correspondence appears in the James Dwight Dana Scientific Papers (hereafter Dana Papers), Yale University Library. Darwin wrote Dana that he expected Dana to be "liberal and philosophic" in his criticism of the *Origins.* Dana, he expected, would give a better response than his own countrymen (30 July 1861, Dana Papers).

18. Dana, *Address before the American Association for the Advancement of Science,* 2, 4.

19. Dana, "Science and the Bible," 632. The Dana-Lewis controversy is discussed by most historians of antebellum science and in Gilman, *Dana,* 183–87. Benjamin Peirce, the Harvard mathematician, wrote Dana that he was delighted with his stand in this controversy. "Upon your points of the

mutual adaptation of the human mind and God's physical creation, I have myself delivered to my class a course of lectures last winter, . . . I have looked at the matter, exclusively and designedly, from the geometric standpoint, and think that you would be surprised and pleased at some of my conclusions" (Peirce to Dana, 11 July 1856, in ibid., 186).

20. Silliman as quoted in Fisher, *Silliman,* 2:23; Daniels, *American Science,* 63–66; Hovenkamp, *Science and Religion,* 23–24; Bozeman, *Protestants,* 21, 79. See also Margaret W. Rossiter, "Benjamin Silliman and the Lowell Institute: The Popularization of Science in Nineteenth-Century America," *New England Quarterly* 44 (1971): 602–26.

21. Hovenkamp, *Science and Religion,* 125–29; Daniels, *American Science,* 223; Fisher, *Silliman,* 324–26, 352.

22. Hovenkamp, *Science and Religion,* 113–17; Dana, *Manual of Mineralogy,* 95.

23. For a discussion of Romantic science see Hovenkamp, *Science and Religion,* 97–117. Noah Porter condemned pantheism among transcendentalists in "Theodore Parker and the Boston Association," *New Englander* 3 (1845): 450–68, and "Transcendentalism."

24. Dana, "Thoughts on Species," 855.

25. See ibid., 854–74; and Hovenkamp, *Science and Religion,* 113–17.

26. On Agassiz see Dupree, *Gray,* 227. Dupree explains that Agassiz lent his scientific theories to the cause of proslavery southerners. Dana, however, did not support racial equality. He said that blacks and whites were one species, and he foresaw all "savage" peoples "sink[ing] into the ground before the power and energy of higher intelligence" ("Thoughts on Species," 866).

27. Dana, "Thoughts on Species," 855; Hovenkamp, *Science and Religion,* 115; James, "Noah Porter," 180.

28. James Dwight Dana, "Lectures on Evolution," lecture 1, Dana Papers. See Porter, *Human Intellect,* 634; Fisher, *Faith and Rationalism,* 105–6; and idem, *Manual of Natural Theology,* 37–39, 46. See also William Rice, "The Darwinian Theory of the Origin of the Species," *New Englander* 26 (1867): 603–25; and James B. Tighe, "Evolutionism in Natural History as Related to Christianity," ibid. 30 (1871): 463–70.

29. Sanford, "Dana and Darwinism," 531–32. Edward J. Pfeiffer dates Dana's conversion to Darwinism earlier, 1874, and makes Dana seem a strong opponent of evolution before 1859 (see his essay "United States" in *The Comparative Reception of Darwin,* ed. Thomas F. Glick [Austin: University of Texas Press, 1972], 168–206). Pfeiffer does not account for Darwin's favorable estimation of how Dana would receive the *Origins* (see above, n. 17). Dana also supported Asa Gray in his argument with Agassiz on species and evolution (see Dupree, *Gray,* 224, 230–31, 256–57). In correspondence with Sir Archibald Geikie of the Edinburgh Geological Society, Dana reveals that he supported Darwin and opposed Agassiz even after publication of the *Descent of Man.* Dana's research in the South Sea Islands confirmed Darwin's theories and suggested that "Agassiz's conclusions are wholly assumptions . . .

not based on any facts mentioned by him or others" (Dana to Geikie, 17 December 1884, 18 April 1890, General File, Letters to Sir Archibald Geikie, Edinburgh University Library, Edinburgh, Scotland).

30. Sanford, "Dana and Darwinism," 540; Dana, "Lectures on Evolution," lectures 4 and 5.

31. For the discussion in this and the preceding paragraphs see Sanford, "Dana and Darwinism," 533; and Dana, "Lectures on Evolution," lectures 5 – 8. Asa Gray questioned Dana's reading of the word *struggle,* which Dana thought of as a conscious and willful effort (Gray to Dana, 22 June 187?, Dana Papers).

32. Porter, *"Science and Sentiment,"* 14.

33. Ibid., 28–29.

34. See Porter, *Human Intellect,* 519–26; and idem, *"Science and Sentiment,"* 49–69, a succinct statement of the essential New Haven position.

35. Fisher, *Discussions in History and Theology,* 482; Porter, *Evolution,* 30; idem, "What We Mean by Christian Philosophy," 47.

36. Fisher, *Grounds of Theistic and Christian Belief,* 459–69; Porter, *"Science and Sentiment,"* 379; Whitney, "On Darwinism and Language." Whitney said, "Darwinian theory belongs in the hands of biologists" (88).

37. For a discussion of Bain's importance to the history of psychology see Young, *Mind, Brain, and Adaptation,* chap. 3. For Porter's comments on Comte, Mill, Bain, and Spencer see his *"Science and Sentiment,"* 53, 60–61, 224–26, 378–411. The comment on men of knowledge appears on p. 455 in a chapter entitled "The Collapse of Faith," which affirms Porter's belief that regardless of learned men's skepticism, common people will discern the truth.

38. Woolsey, *"Eros,"* 6–8.

39. For Porter see the discussion in chap. 4 above.

40. See B. N. Martin, "Professor Porter's Work on the Human Intellect," *New Englander* 28 (1869): 114–36. Richard T. Ely, *Ground under Our Feet: An Autobiography* (New York: Macmillan Co., 1938), 36, 38. Porter advised Ely to see H. Ulrici, who by the 1870s had retired. Earlier, Ulrici had introduced George Sylvester Morris, who later introduced John Dewey "to a full-fledged idealism" (Bruce Kuklick, *Churchmen and Philosophers, from Jonathan Edwards to John Dewey* [New Haven: Yale University Press, 1985], 231). Donald Bellomy's dissertation brought this incident to my attention (Bellomy, "Molding of an Iconoclast," chap. 2, p. 25).

41. Williams, *Keywords,* 233–35; the quote is from 234.

42. Mills, *Ladd,* 106. On the new psychology see Ross, *Hall,* chaps. 3–6.

43. James, *Psychology,* 1:vi, 1; 2:677; Flower and Murphey, *Philosophy in America,* 2:640–57.

44. See James, "Noah Porter," 184.

45. For Porter's comments see Porter, *"Science and Sentiment,"* 28–29. James's not mentioning or referring to Porter or *The Human Intellect* in his *Psychology* is even less explicable when we realize that the two men had met

by chance in the late 1870s while on separate hikes in the Adirondack Mountains. Porter's companion noted "how quickly, as by common impulse, the two fell into psychological discourse" (Merriam, *Noah Porter,* 159).

46. Sumner, *"The Challenge of Facts,"* 401, 425, and see 415–25 and 15–52; idem, *Essays,* 1:44, 46.

CHAPTER SIX HISTORY: FROM FACT TO PROVIDENCE

1. Tillotson, *Victorian Literature,* 1; Woolsey, *International Law,* x; Whitney, *Life and Growth of Language,* 312; Noah Porter, "The New Criticism," *New Englander* 29 (1870): 306.

2. George Park Fisher, "Address to the Professors," in *Addresses at the Inauguration of the Professors* . . . (New Haven, 1861), 12.

3. Mandelbaum, "Historicism." The difference between Enlightenment and nineteenth-century history is discussed in Iggers, *German Conception of History,* 31–32; Ringer, *German Mandarins,* 96, 98–102; and Becker, *Heavenly City,* 96–105.

4. Owen Chadwick, *From Bossuet to Newman,* 100–101.

5. Helpful discussions of Romantic and scientific historians and their different methods appear in Chadwick, *Secularization,* chap. 8; Higham, Krieger, and Gilbert, *History,* 92–97; Jordy, *Henry Adams,* chap. 1. esp. pp. 1–5 and 22; and Levin, *History as Romantic Art.*

6. Porter to Woolsey, 16 July 1858; [Porter,] "Arnold," 371–72; Fisher, *Colonial Era,* 325. See also [T. H. Stone,] "Realism Revived," *New Englander* 13 (1855): 529.

7. [Woolsey,] "Guizot's *History of Civilization,*" 413, 415. Fisher discusses materialist and antitheistic historians at greater length in his *Grounds of Theistic and Christian Belief,* 457–69.

8. Fisher, "Function of the Historian," 16, 22–26, 33.

9. Iggers, *German Conception,* 65–66; and Merz, *European Thought,* 1:138–39, are the most important sources. For the relationship of history and philology see Diehl, *German Scholarship,* x, 21–26; and Herbst, *German Historical School,* 181–82. Consult table 1 (in chap. 3 above) for the New Haven scholars' direct contact with the historical school and appendix 4 for the transmission of the school's ideas through the *New Englander.* Hans Aarsleff explains the importance of the *British Quarterly Review* (Aarsleff, *Language in England,* 192–94). See also above chap. 3, n. 16. Fisher made his comment in "Study of Greek," 24. Salisbury traced the line of influence from philology to history in *Inaugural Discourse,* 42.

10. For method see Herbst, *German School,* 55; White, *Metahistory,* 15, 16, 188; Iggers, *German Conception,* 66–76; Krieger, *Ranke,* 16; and Ranke to Heinrich Ranke, March 1820, quoted in ibid., 361 n. 13.

11. For a helpful discussion of the secular nature of historicism see Ross, "Historical Consciousness"; the quote is from p. 910.

12. Comparison between historical and scientific method is informed by George M. Marsden's description of the relationship between Baconian science, postmillennialism, and evangelical culture in his *Fundamentalism*, 48–62.

13. Fisher, *Universal History*, 4. For application to Garrison and Webster see idem, *The Reformation*, 2, and "Function of the Historian," 16, 33. For the role of the individual in Ranke's history see Tonsor, "History," 240–41. For Arnold see Gooch, *History and Historians*, 18, 299.

14. Krieger, *Ranke*, 25.

15. Fisher, *Universal History*, 633.

16. See Chadwick, *Secularization*, chap. 1, for a discussion of the implications of liberalism.

17. Bercovitch, *American Jeremiad*, 23 and chap. 6; idem, *Puritan Origins*, 145, 185.

18. Fisher, *Universal History*, 2.

19. Ibid., 72, 71, 232.

20. Hoppin, *"The Early Renaissance,"* 130; see also 129–42.

21. Fisher, *Colonial Era*, 318, 320.

22. Fisher, *The Reformation*, 551, 552.

23. Hoppin, *"The Early Renaissance,"* 54, 51.

24. Fisher, *Universal History*, 94.

25. Hoppin, *Greek Art on Greek Soil*, 144, 224; idem, "Athletic Games," 21.

26. Fisher, *Universal History*, 101; Hoppin, "Athletic Games," 21.

27. Woolsey, *International Law*, 22.

28. Theodore Dwight Woolsey, "Destiny: Remarks on the Idea in History," lecture, in Woolsey Family Papers; Edward Elbridge Salisbury, "Principles of Domestic Taste," *New Englander* 36 (1877): 322; Fisher, *Beginnings of Christianity*, 93, 155, 167, 189–90, 220.

29. Two recent books describe British Victorians' use of the Greek image to construct ideal men and civilizations: Jenkyns, *Victorians and Ancient Greece;* and Turner, *Greek Heritage.*

30. Fisher, *The Reformation*, vii; idem, "Historical Address," 24, 21. Leonard Bacon, Fisher's friend and Taylor's successor to his New Haven pulpit, said Taylor's theology addressed "forgotten issues" of a past era. He found himself by the 1850s unwilling "to confide in any man's theory of Christianity, made up of philosophical deductions and logical inferences" (as quoted in Wayland, "The Theological Department," 414, 411).

31. Fisher, *Beginnings of Christianity*, 405.

32. Fisher rebutted Strauss and Renan in *Supernatural Origin*, chaps. 4–8 and chap. 10, respectively; see also v–ix, 4–6, and chap. 11 is especially crucial for an understanding of the miracles issue.

33. Ibid., vii–viii and 4–6, and more generally chap. 1 for a discussion of infidelity in the present age.

34. Fisher, *Grounds of Theistic and Christian Belief*, chap. 17; idem, *Beginnings of Christianity*, 30–31 and see chap. 1. Another source for Fisher's

idea of development probably was Philip Schaff's *What Is Church History? A Vindication of the Idea of Historical Development* (1846). Schaff and Fisher were good friends, and both studied under Tholuck at Halle. Their collaboration was instrumental to the founding of the American Society of Church History (1888) (Ahlstrom, *Religious History,* 618).

35. Barbara Welter and Ann Douglas have seen the new emphasis on Christ as evidence of feminization of religion (Douglas, *Feminization of American Culture,* chaps. 4–5; Welter, "The Feminization of American Religion," in *Clio's Consciousness Raised,* ed. Mary Hartmann and Lois W. Banner [New York: Harper Torchbooks, 1974], 137–57).

36. Holmes to Porter, 13 December 1879, Miscellaneous Manuscripts of Noah Porter). *New Englander* proprietor William L. Kingsley remarked that the dedication of a monument at Plymouth Rock "called out a surprising number of attacks and sneers at our New England ideas, most of which are founded on total ignorance" (Kingsley to Salisbury, 23 August 1888 [1889?], Salisbury Family Papers). See also Louis C. Schaedler, "Whittier's Attitude towards Colonial Puritanism," *New England Quarterly* 21 (1948): 356–68.

37. See Fisher's discussion of Luther and Calvin in *The Reformation,* 85–135, 192–241; quotes are from 98–99, 203, 204, 221, and 199. Fisher effectively reveals his apologetic posture when he says, "Lecky, in common with other writers at the present day, makes persecution the necessary result of undoubting convictions on the subject of religion, coupled with a belief that moral obliquity is involved in holding opposite views. These writers would make scepticism essential to the exercise of toleration" (ibid., 225 n. 15).

CHAPTER SEVEN. POLITICAL SCIENCE: THE STATE AS MEANS TO SELF-DEVELOPMENT

1. Woolsey's political science lectures are in Box 46, Woolsey Family Papers (all lectures referred to may be found at this location); his text *Political Science* repeats most of the points made in the lectures. This chapter discusses only Woolsey's theories; they were general, however, among *New Englander* authors and the New Haven scholars (see Fisher, "Of the Distinction between Natural and Political Rights"; [Samuel Harris,] "The Dependence of Popular Progress upon Christianity," ibid. 5 [1847]: 433–51; and [W. W. Andrews,] "National Unity," ibid. 6 [1848]: 577–90).

2. John Witherspoon, *Lectures on Moral Philosophy,* quoted in Fiering, "President Samuel Johnson," 234.

3. Porter, *Moral Science,* discusses the more private duties; see his table of contents for topics.

4. The relationship of Scottish philosophy to moral science and to the social sciences is discussed in Bryson, *Man and Society,* 171–72; Schneider, *Scottish Moralists,* xxix–xlvii; and Dorothy Ross, "The Development of the

Social Sciences in Modern America," in Oleson and Voss, *Organization of Knowledge,* 107–38. Woolsey, "Leading Elements in Civilization," 36; idem, *Political Science,* 1:4; idem, "Rights," lectures 1 and 2, 1853 or 1858.

5. On the ASSA see Haskell, *Professional Social Science,* 101, 103, 104.

6. Freidel, *Lieber,* 189; Smith, *Professors,* 101; Diggins, *Bard of Savagery,* 36. My reading of Sumner's published essays, esp. "Politics in America, 1776–1876" and "The Administration of Andrew Jackson," in *"The Forgotten Man,"* serves as the basis for this generalization about the similarity between student's and teacher's thought. Donald Bellomy, who has read extensively in Sumner's published and unpublished writing, confirms their agreement (see Bellomy, "Molding of an Iconoclast," esp. chap. 6, pp. 9–10).

7. May, *Enlightenment,* 342, 358; Silverman, *Dwight,* 95; Dennis, "Federalist Persuasion," chap. 3.

8. The notes in *Political Science* show that Woolsey was influenced by European scholars such as Abicht, Rotteck, Zachariae, Röder, Ahrens, and Stahl (see 1:131–36; see also Woolsey "Political Philosophy since Grotius," lectures). The German emigré Francis Lieber may have influenced Woolsey (see Freidel, *Lieber,* 265–66; and King, *Woolsey,* 48 and passim). King and Freidel argue that Woolsey did not come into contact with Lieber until he reviewed Lieber's *On Civil Liberty and Self-Government* in *New Englander* 14 (1856): 329–44. Woolsey's mention of Lieber in an earlier article suggests that he had read Lieber's *Manual of Political Ethics* (1838) (see [Theodore Dwight Woolsey,] "The True Gentleman," *New Englander* 5 [1847]: 485). If so, Lieber's early influence may have activated Woolsey's interest in German Romantic political theory and philosophy. On their impact on Lieber see Brown, *American Conservatives,* 7–18, 171–72.

9. On Rousseau see Woolsey, *Political Science,* 1:172–82; and idem, "Political Philosophy since Grotius." Woolsey discusses limitations on state power in *Political Science,* 1:232, and see 2:422–38. For Sumner's critique of Rousseauistic liberty see Bellomy's chapter "The Independent Commentator, 1886–1891," 29–31, from his biography of Sumner in progress.

10. Woolsey's discussion is in his lectures "Rights," "Political Philosophy since Grotius," and "Political Theory." Sumner also criticized majority rule and likened its sovereignty to that of a "despot" (Sumner, *"The Forgotten Man,"* 290–91).

11. See Woolsey's discussion in his lectures "Particular Rights," and "The Social Compact" (1851); and idem, *Political Science,* vol. 1, chaps. 1 and 2.

12. See Theodore Dwight Woolsey, "Attributes of the State," lecture 5; and idem, *Political Science,* 1:193, 192–98.

13. See Woolsey, "Attributes of the State"; and the discussion in idem, *Political Science,* vol. 1, chap. 2.

14. See Woolsey, *Political Science,* 1:217, 220–23, and the general discussion in chap. 4; see also 2:397–404.

15. Ibid., 1:226–30.

16. Ibid., 226–27.

17. Ibid., 230.

18. See the discussion in ibid., 2:406–10. President of the University of Illinois, Yale graduate, and friend of the New Haven scholars Julian Monson Sturtevant argued similarly in his "Denominational Colleges," *New Englander* 18 (1860): 60–89. Woolsey also opposed establishment of a national university (Woolsey to E. L. Godkin, 2 January 1874, Woolsey Family Papers).

19. Woolsey, *Political Science,* 1:232, and see 2:422–38.

20. Ibid., 2:420–21, 1:234. Commitment to science among ASSA members sometimes fed into support for scientific, eugenicist solutions to social problems (Donald K. Pickens, *Eugenics and the Progressives* [Nashville: Vanderbilt University Press, 1968], 41).

21. Iggers compares English and German liberalism in *German Conception,* 93–95. On Mill see Woolsey, *Political Science,* 1:249–61; the quote is from 261.

22. Sumner also deplored the democratic theories of Jacksonianism, which meant that "the laws and Constitution may give way to what shall seem, although not constitutionally expressed, the will of the people" (Sumner, *"The Forgotten Man,"* 349). Woolsey, *Relations of Honor to Political Life,* 27–28.

23. Woolsey, *Political Science,* 2:115, and see chap. 6. Sumner disagreed with Woolsey here and thoroughly criticized Federalists and Jeffersonian Republicans (Sumner, *"The Forgotten Man,"* 292–302).

24. Woolsey, "Experiment of the Union," 274.

25. Woolsey discusses the suffrage in *Political Science,* 1:299–302, and "Experiment of the Union," 273. See also Fisher, "Of the Distinction between Natural and Political Rights." Here Fisher repeats Woolsey's arguments and applies them to suffrage for women and freed slaves. For Woolsey on woman suffrage, which he opposed, see "Rights" and *Political Science,* 1:300–301.

26. Woolsey, *Political Science,* 2:144.

27. Woolsey, "Experiment of the Union," 277–78; idem, *Political Science,* 1:322; [Theodore Dwight Woolsey,] "Relation of Christianity to the Doctrine of Natural Rights," *New Englander* 15 (1857): 631; and the discussion in "Practical Politics," lecture.

28. Woolsey, *Relations of Honor to Political Life,* 27; idem, "Experiment of the Union," 273.

29. Woolsey, *Political Science,* 2:522, 523–26; see also his "The True Gentleman." Idem, "Leading Elements in Civilization," 30.

30. Woolsey, *Political Science,* 2:548, 565–67; idem, *Relations of Honor to Political Life,* 27, 26, 21–28. Sumner, too, deplored political parties and the retreat of honorable men from public life (Sumner, *"The Forgotten Man,"* 327–30).

31. Woolsey, "Attributes of the State"; idem, *Political Science,* 1:320, 322; idem, *Communism and Socialism,* 237, 266–67.

32. Woolsey, *Political Science,* 2:601. Porter and Fisher were optimists (see Fisher, "American Civil War"; and Porter, "The United States since the War," *British Quarterly Review* 45 [1867]: 178–214).

33. Woolsey, *Political Science*, 2:606. On millennialism and republicanism see Ross, "Liberal Tradition Revisited," 116–31, esp. 121.

34. For the context of evangelical reform see Thomas, "Romantic Reform"; and Ronald G. Walters, "The Erotic South: Civilization and Sexuality in American Abolitionism," *American Quarterly* 25 (1973): 177–201. For Whig political and social thought see Foner, *Free Soil, Free Labor, Free Men,* esp. chap. 1; Major L. Wilson, "The Concept of Time and the Political Dialogue in the United States, 1828–48," *American Quarterly* 19 (1967): 619–44; and Howe, *American Whigs*, chaps. 1 and 2 and his conclusion. Howe also notes the connection between self-control and social control and calls the Whig vision "broadly humanistic in a structured way" (300–301).

Historians of other groups of nineteenth-century academics note that they also developed distinct value systems and reform agendas. In a general sense these often resembled those of the New Haven scholars. James McLachlan, through analysis of college presidents' speeches and a statistical analysis of participants in liberal Republican politics, attempts to establish a causal connection between college attendance and reform political activity (McLachlan, "Transmission of Culture," 184–206). Because he considers college presidents as a unified group, he incorrectly includes Noah Porter in his sample. While the New Haven scholars thought that college-educated men could help reform American society, they never called upon them to act politically. German professors, whom Fritz K. Ringer calls mandarins, criticized both the old German aristocracy and the new bourgeoisie. Ringer says that the mandarins' claim to moral authority implied a claim to rule in the new industrial world (*German Mandarins,* 123). In the United States, Thomas L. Haskell sees the Pendleton Act as the culmination of a broad cultural reform movement that included "the creation of the modern American university and a system of professional and quasi-professional functional elites built upon it" (Haskell, *Professional Social Science,* 64, 120).

35. Woolsey, *International Law,* x; Hawkins, *Between Harvard and America,* chaps. 4 and 5.

36. Woolsey, "Experiment of the Union," 272, 275–76; Noah Porter quoted in a clipping dated 29 December 1876 in Mary Taylor Porter Scrapbook.

37. Historians are revising previous views of the transition in social thought that occurred from the Gilded Age to the Progressive Era. In the work of Morton White, we find the latter period to be unique, because its thinkers revolted against formalism in favor of an active state. By casting Sumner as a social Darwinist, Richard Hofstadter obfuscated Sumner's actual social thought and did much to establish the postbellum years as a sort of *ancien régime* in need of drastic reform. Robert M. Crunden argues that Progressive achievements had roots in the Republican–Free Soil–Whig beliefs of the families of Progressive reformers. An older Whig emphasis on moral development was, Crunden argues, a precondition for Progressivism. Cf. White, *Social Thought in America,* chap. 2; and Crunden, *Ministers of Reform,* esp. chap. 1.

See also Howe, *American Whigs,* 303–4; David Hoeveler's two papers, "Personality and Progressivism" and "Religion and the New University"; Ross, "Socialism and American Liberalism," 33; and Haskell, *Professional Social Science,* 140. Whoever is tempted to use the term social Darwinist to describe Sumner's thought should first consult a recent article by Donald Bellomy, "Social Darwinism' Revisited," esp. 28– 38, which reveals the insufficiencies of Hofstadter's *Social Darwinism in American Thought* and questions Bannister's *Social Darwinism.*

CHAPTER EIGHT. FROM WHOLE MAN TO WHOLE SOCIETY

1. Theodore Dwight Woolsey, *The Christian Student* (New Haven, 1866), 4; idem, *Religion of the Present and of the Future,* 223; [Porter,] "Edmund Burke," 245; idem, "What We Mean by Christian Philosophy," 39; Fisher, *Christian Principle,* 6–7; idem, *Baccalaureate Sermon, July 22, 1860* (New Haven, 1860), 10.

2. Fisher, *Christian Principle,* 6–7; Woolsey, *Political Science,* 1:26; idem, "Rights."

3. Woolsey, *Political Science,* 1:6, 23.

4. See Fisher, *Universal History,* 634–37; idem, *The Reformation,* chap. 15; and idem, *History of the Christian Church,* 646–58.

5. Woolsey, "Experiment of the Union," 274; Porter, *Educational Systems of the Puritans and Jesuits,* 62, 16, 44–45.

6. For the discussion in this and the previous paragraph see [Leonard Bacon,] "The Southern Apostasy," *New Englander* 12 (1854): 627–62; [A. P. Marvin,] "The South-Side View of Slavery," ibid. 13 (1855): 61–90; [S. W. S. Dutton,] "Slavery—Its Effect on Property, Intelligence, and Morals of the Whites," ibid. 14 (1856): 264–95; [J. P. Thompson,] "The Test-Hour of Popular Liberty and Republican Government," ibid. 21 (1862): 222–47; W. Eustis, "The Reformation of the South," ibid. 25 (1866): 359–64; and Theodore Dwight Woolsey, "A Letter to Southern Gentlemen," *Independent,* 186?, clipping in Woolsey Family Papers.

7. See [Timothy Dwight,] "England and the United States—Agriculture, Manufactures, and Rail Roads," *New Englander* 6 (1848): 281–92; see also Samuel Harris, "The Christian Doctrine of Labor," ibid. 24 (1865): 244.

8. *The Gun Foundry* is discussed in Kasson, *Civilizing the Machine,* 168– 70; and Patricia Hills discusses Weir in *The Painters' America: Rural and Urban Life, 1810–1910* (New York: Praeger, 1974), 123, 153. Barbara Novak discusses this use of light in landscape painting in her *Nature and Culture,* 40–43.

9. Woolsey, *Communism and Socialism,* 205.

10. [Porter,] *"Thorndale,"* 655.

11. On social reforms see [J. P. Thompson,] "Social Reforms," *New Englander* 8 (1850): 452–70; [S. W. S. Dutton,] "'New Themes' Controversy:

The Relationship of Christianity to Poverty," ibid. 4 (1846): 56–72; and [Harris,] "Christian Doctrine," 247–72.

12. Porter, *"Thorndale,"* 654, 655.

13. In Porter's funeral sermon, Munger said that Porter had defended him and other liberal Congregationalists against conservative ministers, who opposed the liberal movement for greater toleration among Protestants. Liberals refused "to pronounce dogmatically on the fate of the heathen who had never heard of the gospel" and would not "avow an eternity of conscious misery for any soul" (Merriam, *Noah Porter,* 126–27 and n. 1). For discussion of the Social Gospel in this and the preceding paragraph see Ahlstrom, *Religious History,* 613 and chap. 47. Porter, *Moral Science,* 411. Henry F. May notes Porter's attitude toward private property and Woolsey's toward socialism. Not inquiring further, he labels both conservative (May, *Protestant Churches,* 195, 151). Woolsey, *Political Science,* 1:64. For Porter's attitude see above, chap. 5, nn. 32, 33; and idem, *"Science and Sentiment,"* 411. Albert Bolles, "The Conflict between Labor and Capital," *New Englander* 35 (1876): 593–94. And for state regulation, Leonard Bacon, "Railways and the State," ibid. 30 (1871): 713–38. For discussion of the various routes to socialism in the late nineteenth century see Ross, "Socialism and American Liberalism," esp. 33 and 37; and Haskell, *Professional Social Science,* 140. Between 1877 and 1882, the *New Englander* published a series of articles by John Bates Clark in which he found correspondence between the moral laws of nature and theories of classical political economy. These articles were later republished as *The Philosophy of Wealth* (1886), in which he praised "the beautiful law" governing the marketplace (Ross, "Socialism and American Liberalism," 37).

14. For consideration of the "usefulness" of education see Eva T. H. Brann, *Paradoxes of Education in a Republic* (Chicago: University of Chicago Press, 1979), chap. 1.

15. Fisher, *Baccalaureate Sermon,* 10; Leonard Bacon, *American Literature: Address before the Phi Beta Kappa Society of Dartmouth College, July 30, 1845* (Hanover, N.H., 1845), 6, 9, 20.

16. [Horace Bushnell,] "Taste and Fashion," *New Englander* 1 (1843): 153–68, quote from 163; [Mrs. Sarah Allen,] "Manners and Society," ibid., 372, 373; [Donald G. Mitchell,] "The Fashionable Monthlies," ibid. 2 (1844): 96–105.

17. [Theodore Dwight Woolsey,] "Cemeteries and Rural Monuments," ibid. 7 (1849): 495, 498.

18. Bushnell, "Taste," 157, 166, 168; "Landscape Gardening and Rural Architecture," *New Englander* 1 (1843): 208–9. See also Salisbury, "Principles of Domestic Taste," 310–28.

19. Porter, *Books and Reading,* 9; [Noah Porter,] *"The Atlantic Monthly* and the Professor at the Breakfast Table," *New Englander* 7 (1859): 774; idem, "The New Infidelity," 287–88; Porter, *"Thorndale,"* 685. By 1879 Holmes and Porter could banter. Writing Porter after a New Haven visit,

the "Autocrat" thanked Porter for "giving me a good character with my orthodox friends, who will be glad to learn I am so much of a Calvinist" (Holmes to Porter, 13 December 1879, Miscellaneous Manuscripts of Noah Porter).

20. Porter, *"Thorndale,"* 665; idem, "The Ideal Scholar," 173; Hall, "World of Print," 171–72 and esp. 173–75.

21. On Eliot and Norton see Hall, "The Victorian Connection," 89–90; on reading see Bledstein, *Culture of Professionalism,* 77–79. A *New Englander* reviewer hailed publication of the Household Library series in England and hoped that people would buy them for "railroad reading" or to stock seaside houses ("Notices of Books," *New Englander* 17 [1859]: 821).

22. Porter, *Books and Reading,* 33, 36 50, 231, 222.

23. Ibid., 162, 223, 163, 138–39, 190–91, 66–69, 243, 257, 263.

24. [S. W. S. Dutton,] "Nathaniel Hawthorne," *New Englander* 5 (1847): 56–58, 66–68; [William O. Bourne,] "Missionary Operations in Polynesia," ibid. 6 (1848): 42–58; "Notices of New Books," ibid. 4 (1846): 449; [Leonard Bacon,] "The Minister's Wooing from the Dr. Dryasdust Point of View," ibid. 18 (1860): 47; "Review of Longfellow's *Evangeline,*" ibid. 6 (1848): 556; [J. P. Thompson,] "Dickens' Notes on America," ibid. 1 (1843): 66, 84, 81.

25. Porter, "The New Criticism," 303, 306, 299.

26. Hoppin, *Notes of a Theological Student,* 244–55. See his biography in appendix 1; and Stein, *John Ruskin,* 234–41.

27. Scottish aesthetic theory received its fullest espression in Archibald Allison's *Essays on the Nature and Principles of Taste* (1790, American editions through 1870). Yale courses on mental and moral philosophy, which used the texts of Dugald Stewart and Thomas Brown, communicated Allison's theories to the scholars (Hersey, *High Victorian Gothic,* 30, 10). Hoppin, *Greek Art on Greek Soil,* 247.

28. Hoppin explains his criticism of idealism and realism in his "Tendencies of Modern Art," *New Englander* 46 (1887): 467–68; idem, *"The Early Renaissance,"* 61–67, 197; idem, "Philosophy of Art," 16, 18; idem, *Greek Art on Greek Soil,* 225–31; and "Principles of Art," *New Englander* 24 (1865): 685.

29. James Mason Hoppin, "The Relations of Art to Education," *New Englander* 25 (1866): 603, 607, 606, 611–12; idem, *"The Early Renaissance,"* 186–87; idem, "Art in Popular Education," 333.

30. Hoppin, *Greek Art on Greek Soil,* 247; idem, *"The Early Renaissance,"* 235–54.

31. Samuels, *Berenson,* 28–31, 53, 86, 152.

32. Hoppin, "Tendencies," 464, 467; idem, "Some Criticisms of French Landscape Painting," *New Englander* 52 (1890): 324–25.

33. On multiplication of art forms see John F. Weir, "Some Suggestions and Points of Contact between Science and Art," ibid. 32 (1874): 173–84; "Yeast, a Problem by Charles Kingsley," ibid. 10 (1852): 177–97; Porter,

Books and Reading, 91–92; James Mason Hoppin, "The Nude in Art," clipping from the *New Haven Leader,* 1900.

34. Hoppin, *Methods of Art Education,* 17–19; idem, *"The Early Renaissance,"* 172–75.

35. Hoppin, *"The Early Renaissance,"* 94.

CHAPTER NINE. CONNECTIONS

1. Cf. Dana, *Manual of Mineralogy,* and Hurlbut and Klein, *Manual of Mineralogy after J. D. Dana;* William Dwight Whitney, *A Sanskrit Grammar* (Leipzig, 1879), vii.

2. Historians have discussed the relationship between philology and history, but as far as I know, no historian has discussed the common method of scholars in liberal arts, social sciences, and natural sciences in the mid-nineteenth century. Jurgen Herbst discusses the philological roots of historical criticism but focuses on the development of the social sciences (see Herbst, *German Historical School,* chaps. 2 and 5). More recently, Dorothy Ross explores the meaning of *social science* in the last third of the nineteenth century, while Laurence Veysey discusses the organizational development of the humanities (see Ross, "Social Sciences"; and Laurence Veysey, "The Plural Organized World of the Humanities," in Oleson and Voss, *Organization of Knowledge,* 51–106).

3. Veysey, *American University,* 12; White, *History of the Warfare of Science with Theology.* Although Carter did not graduate from Yale College, he attended from 1859 to 1861 and taught there from 1873 to 1880.

4. Pierson, *Yale,* 167–69, Hadley quote on 307; Kelley, *Yale,* 240–41, 270.

5. Hofstadter, *Social Darwinism in American Thought,* 20–21; Kuklick, *Rise of American Philosophy,* 565.

6. A close rereading of Hofstadter's *The Age of Reform: Bryan to F.D.R.* (New York: Alfred A. Knopf, 1955) and *Anti-Intellectualism in American Life,* esp. pts. 2 and 3, yields this view.

7. Porter, *"Science and Sentiment,"* 455.

8. In his *Intellectual Life in America: A History* (New York: Franklin Watts, 1984), Lewis Perry continues the tradition of making knowledge useful to educated college students, but ironically, he sees the history of education in the twentieth century as limited to the rise of specialized scholarship that isolates the academic in a world of "sterile discourse" (see xiv, 453–54, 291, 440; and my review in *Intellectual History Newsletter,* 7 [April 1985]: 8–13).

9. The discussion in this paragraph is based on Joan Shelley Rubin's extremely useful article "'Information, Please!': Culture and Expertise in the Interwar Period," *American Quarterly* 35 (1983): 499–517; the quote is from 500. See also idem, "Swift's Premium Ham: William Lyon Phelps and the

Redefinition of Culture," in *Mass Media between the Wars: Perceptions of Cultural Tensions, 1918–1940*, ed. Catherine L. Covert and John D. Stevens (Syracuse: Syracuse University Press, 1984), 3–19.

10. William Lyon Phelps, *Human Nature in the Bible* (New York: Charles Scribner's Sons, 1923), ix, x; Rubin, "'Information, Please!'" 502, 507–8. See also William Lyon Phelps, *As I Like It* (New York: Charles Scribner's Sons, 1923), which reprints the *Scribner's Magazine* columns.

11. Hoeveler, *The New Humanism*.

12. For opposing evaluations of Progressive history see Hofstadter, *Progressive Historians;* and Tonsor, "History," 237–38.

13. Woolsey, "The New Era," *New Englander* 25 (1866): 199.

14. See Leslie Fishbein, *Rebels in Bohemia: The Radicals of the Masses, 1911–1917* (Chapel Hill: University of North Carolina Press, 1982); and May, *End of American Innocence*.

15. Fisher to Charles Scribner, 16 March 1905, Charles Scribner's Sons Papers. For an earlier expression of this feeling see [Joseph Parrish Thompson,] "The Dilemma of Unitarianism," *New Englander* 4 (1846): 494–506.

16. See above; see also Porter to Woolsey, 22 February 1854. For the relative growth of different denominations see Gaustad, *Historical Atlas of Religion in America,* 43–44, figs. 31–33.

17. See Novak, *Nature and Culture,* 3–17; Hovenkamp, *Science and Religion;* Cherry, *Nature and Religious Imagination;* and McLoughlin, *The Meaning of Henry Ward Beecher*.

18. Emerson, *Selected Writings,* 273.

19. The idea for this comparison comes from Thomas, "Romantic Reform in America," although he emphasizes the relationship between Emerson and antinomian strains in evangelicalism.

Bibliography

Primary Sources

Manuscript Collections

Beinecke Rare Book and Manuscript Library, Yale University, New Haven, Conn.
    G. and C. Merriam Company Papers.
Fale Library, New York University, New York, N.Y.
    Henry Barnard Papers.
John Hay Library, Brown University, Providence, R.I.
    Reuben Aldridge Guild Collection.
Leila Dilworth Jones Memorial Library, Miss Porter's School, Farmington, Conn.
    Miss Porter's School Archives.
Princeton University Library, Princeton, N.J.
    Alexander Family Papers.
    James McCosh Collection.
    Charles Scribner's Sons Papers.
Yale Divinity School Library, Yale University, New Haven, Conn.
    Miscellaneous Personal Papers of George Park Fisher.
    Miscellaneous Personal Papers of James Mason Hoppin.
Yale University Library, Yale University, New Haven, Conn.
    Bacon Family Papers.
    James Dwight Dana Scientific Papers.
    Miscellaneous Personal Papers of George Park Fisher.
    Hillhouse Family Papers.
    Miscellaneous Manuscripts of Noah Porter.
    Salisbury Family Papers.
    Whitney Family Papers.

Woolsey Family Papers.

Yale Lectures.

Published Works

Arnold, Matthew. *Culture and Anarchy: An Essay in Political and Social Criticism.* Edited by Ian Gregor. Indianapolis: Bobbs Merrill, 1971.

Bacon, Leonard. *A Discourse before the Literary Societies of Hamilton College.* Utica, N.Y., 1847.

——. *The Genesis of the New England Churches.* New York: Harper and Brothers, 1874.

——. *Oration before the Phi Beta Kappa Society of Dartmouth College.* Hanover, N.H., 1845.

Bushnell, Horace. *Christian Nurture.* 1847. 3d. ed. New York: C. Scribner and Co., 1861.

Coleridge, Samuel Taylor. *Aids to Reflection.* 1840. Reprint of the 4th ed. Port Washington, N.Y.: Kennikat Press, 1971.

Dana, James Dwight. *Address before the American Association for the Advancement of Science, August, 1855.* Cambridge, Mass., 1855.

——. *Manual of Geology.* Philadelphia: T. Bliss and Co., 1863.

——. *Manual of Mineralogy.* 1848. 2d ed. New Haven: H. H. Peck, 1867.

——. *New Haven University.* New Haven, 1871.

——. "Science and the Bible." *Bibliotheca Sacra* 13 (1856): 80–129, 631–56; 14 (1857): 388–413, 461–525.

——. "Thoughts on Species." *Bibliotheca Sacra* 14l (1857): 854–74.

Dwight, Timothy. *Travels in New England and New York.* 4 vols. London, 1823.

Dwight, Timothy. "Education in Boyhood." *Forum* 9 (1890): 133–49.

——. "Formative Influences." *Forum* 10 (1891): 497–507.

——. *Memories of Yale Life and Men, 1845–1899.* New York: Dodd, Mead and Co., 1903.

——. *Professors William Dwight Whitney and James Dwight Dana.* New Haven, 1895.

——. "The True Purpose of the Higher Education." *Forum* 13 (1892): 311–24.

——. *What a Yale Student Ought to Be.* New Haven, 1887.

Dwight, Timothy, et al. *Leonard Bacon: Pastor of the First Church of New Haven.* New Haven, 1882.

Fisher, George Park. "The Academic Career of President Woolsey." *Century Magazine* 24 (1882): 709–17.

——. "The American Civil War." *British Quarterly Review* 55 (1872): 381–412.

——. *The Beginnings of Christianity with a View of the State of the Roman World at the Birth of Christ.* New York: Scribner, Armstrong and Co., 1877.

————. *The Christian Principle of Self-Devotion.* New Haven, 1855.

————. "The Christian Religion." *North American Review* 134 (1882): 170–219.

————. *The Colonial Era.* New York: C. Scribner's Sons, 1892.

————. "The Decline of Clerical Authority." *North American Review* 135 (1882): 564–79.

————. *Discussions in History and Theology.* New York: C. Scribner's Sons, 1880.

————. "The Elements of Puritanism." *North American Review* 133 (1881): 326–37.

————. *Essays on the Supernatural Origin of Christianity with Special Reference to the Theories of Renan, Strauss, and the Tübingen School.* New York: C. Scribner and Co., 1865.

————. *Faith and Rationalism with Short Supplementary Essays on Related Topics.* New York: C. Scribner's Sons, 1879.

————. "The Function of the Historian as a Judge of Historic Persons." In *Annual Report of the American Historical Association for the Year 1898,* 13–33. Washington, D.C., 1899.

————. *The Grounds of Theistic and Christian Belief.* New York: C. Scribner's Sons, 1883.

————. *The Historical Method in Theology: A Paper Read before the International Congregational Council at Boston, September 21, 1899.* New Haven, 1899.

————. *History of the Christian Church.* New York: C. Scribner's Sons, 1887.

————. "How the New Testament Came Down to Us." *Scribner's Monthly Magazine* 21 (1881): 611–20.

————. "Jefferson and the Social Compact Theory." In *Annual Report of the American Historical Association for the Year 1893,* 163–77. Washington, D.C., 1894.

————. *The Life of Benjamin Silliman.* 2 vols. New York: C. Scribner and Co., 1865.

————. *Manual of Christian Evidences.* New York: C. Scribner's Sons, 1888.

————. *Manual of Natural Theology.* New York: C. Scribner's Sons, 1893.

————. "Martin Luther after Four Hundred Years." *Century Magazine* 26 (1883): 860–69.

————. "Miracles and Their Place in Christian Evidence." *Journal of Christian Philosophy* 2 (April 1883): 270–82.

————. *Outlines of Universal History.* New York: American Book Co., 1885.

————. *The Reformation.* New York: Scribner, Armstrong and Co., 1873.

————. "The Revised New Testament." *Century* 22 (1881): 293–301.

————. "The Study of Greek." *Princeton Review* 60 (March 1884): 111–26.

Fisher, Irving, ed. *Bibliographies of the Present Officers of Yale University.* New Haven: Tuttle, Morehouse & Taylor, 1893.

Gilman, Daniel Coit. *Life of James Dwight Dana.* New York: Harper and Brothers, 1899.

Hadley, James. "A Brief History of the English Language." In *Webster's In-*

ternational Dictionary of the English Language, edited by Noah Porter, xxix–xliv. 1890 ed.

———. *Diary (1843–1852) of James Hadley*. Edited by Laura Hadley Moseley. New Haven: Yale University Press, 1951.

———. *Essays Philological and Critical*. Edited by William Dwight Whitney. New York: Holt and Williams, 1873.

Hoppin, James Mason. "Art in Popular Education." *Forum* 7 (1887): 331–38.

———. *The Athletic Games and Their Effect on Greek Sculpture*. New Haven, 1893.

———. *"The Early Renaissance," and Other Essays on Art Subjects*. Boston: Houghton, Mifflin and Co., 1892.

———. *Great Epochs in Art History*. Boston: Houghton, Mifflin and Co., 1901.

———. *Greek Art on Greek Soil*. Boston: Houghton, Mifflin and Co., 1897.

———. *Methods of Art Education* . . . . New Haven, 1893.

———. *Notes of a Theological Student*. New York: D. Appleton and Co., 1854.

———. *Office and Work of the Christian Ministry*. New York: Sheldon and Co., 1869.

———. *Old England; its Scenery, Art, and People*. Boston: Houghton, Mifflin and Co., 1867.

———. "The Philosophy of Art." Paper read at the One Hundred Fiftieth Anniversary of the American Philosophical Society, Philadelphia, 25 March 1893. Reprinted in *Proceedings of the American Philosophical Society* 32 (1893): 1–20.

———. *Sermons on Faith, Hope and Love*. New York: Dodd, Mead and Co., 1891.

James, William. *The Principles of Psychology*. 2 vols. New York: H. Holt and Co., 1890.

Kingsley, William L., ed. *Yale College: A Sketch of Its History*. 2 vols. New York: H. Holt and Co., 1879.

Merriam, George S., ed. *Noah Porter: A Memorial by Friends*. New York: C. Scribner's Sons, 1893.

Mill, John Stuart. *Auguste Comte and Positivism*. 1871. Reprint. Ann Arbor, Mich.: University of Michigan Press, Ann Arbor Paperback, 1961.

New Englander, 1843–92.

Porter, Noah. *The American Colleges and the American Public, with Afterthoughts on College and School Education*. 1870. 2d ed. New York: C. Scribner's Sons, 1878.

———. *Books and Reading; or, What Books Shall I Read, and How Shall I Read Them?* 1871. 4th ed. New York: C. Scribner's Sons, 1875.

[———.] "The Character and Writings of Edmund Burke." *Quarterly Christian Spectator* 6 (1834): 226–50.

———. *The Christian College. An Address Delivered at Wellesley College, May 27, 1880* . . . . Boston, 1880.

————. "Coleridge and His American Disciples." *Bibliotheca Sacra* 4 (1847): 117–71.

————. *The Educational Systems of the Puritans and Jesuits Compared . . . .* New York, 1851.

————. *The Elements of Intellectual Science.* New York: C. Scribner's Sons, 1871.

————. *The Elements of Moral Science, Theoretical and Practical.* New York: C. Scribner's Sons, 1885.

————. *Evolution. A Lecture Read before the Nineteenth Century Club in the City of New York, May 25, 1886.* New York, 1886.

————. *Fifteen Years in the Chapel of Yale College, 1871–1886.* New York: C. Scribner's Sons, 1888.

————. "Froude's History of England." *Hours at Home* 3 (1866): 426–32.

————. "Greek and a Liberal Education." *Princeton Review* 60 (1884): 195–218.

————. *A Historical Discourse . . . in Commemoration of the Original Settlement of the Ancient Town, in 1640.* Hartford, 1841.

————. *The Human Intellect: With an Introduction upon Psychology and the Soul.* New York: C. Scribner and Co., 1868.

————. "Inaugural Address." In *Addresses at the Inauguration of Noah Porter, D.D., LL.D., as President of Yale College, Wednesday, October 11, 1871.* New York, 1871.

————. "John Stuart Mill." *International Review* 1 (1874): 385–406.

[————.] "Mr. Herbert Spencer's New Work." *Round Table* 1 (1864): 277–79.

[————.] "On Moral Science, as a Branch of Academical Education." *Quarterly Christian Spectator* 6 (1834): 226–50.

————. "Recent English Works on Logic and Metaphysics." *Bibliotheca Sacra* 6 (1849): 596–602.

————. *"Science and Sentiment," with Other Papers, Chiefly Philosophical.* New York: C. Scribner's Sons, 1882.

————. "Transcendentalism." *American Biblical Repository* 8 (1842): 195–218.

————. "What We Mean by Christian Philosophy." *Christian Thought Monthly* 2 (1881): 33–48. 1

[————.] "Wordsworth and His Poetry." *Quarterly Christian Spectator* 8 (1836): 127–51.

————. "The Youth of the Scholar." *Bibliotheca Sacra* 3 (1846): 95–121.

————, ed. *Webster's International Dictionary of the English Language.* 1890 ed.

Porter, Noah, and Chauncey Goodrich, eds. *An American Dictionary of the English Language.* 1864 ed.

Salisbury, Edward Elbridge. *An Inaugural Discourse on Arabic and Sanskrit Literature delivered in New Haven, Wednesday, August 16, 1843.* New Haven, 1843.

Sumner, William Graham. *"The Challenge of Facts" and Other Essays.* Edited by Albert Galloway Keller. New Haven: Yale University Press, 1914.

———. *Essays of William Graham Sumner.* Edited by Albert Galloway Keller and Maurice R. Davie. 2 vols. New Haven: Yale University Press, 1934.

———. *"The Forgotten Man" and Other Essays.* Edited by Albert Galloway Keller. New Haven: Yale University Press, 1918.

Taylor, Nathaniel William. *Lectures on the Moral Government of God.* Edited by Noah Porter. New York: Clark, Austin and Smith, 1859.

Webster, Noah. *An American Dictionary of the English Language.* 1841 ed.

Weir, John Ferguson. "American Art, Its Progress and Prospects." *Princeton Review* 54 (1878): 815–29.

———. "Popular Art Education." *North American Review* 132 (1881): 64–78.

———. *The Recollections of John Ferguson Weir.* Edited by Theodore Sizer. New York and New Haven: New-York Historical Society and the Associates in Fine Arts at Yale University, 1957.

White, Andrew Dickson. *Autobiography of Andrew Dickson White.* 2 vols. New York: Century Co., 1905.

———. *History of the Warfare of Science with Theology.* 2 vols. New York: D. Appleton and Co., 1896.

Whitney, William Dwight. "The Aim and Object of This Department in Yale College." In *Third Annual Report of the Sheffield Scientific School, 1867–1868,* 9–21. New Haven, 1867.

———. "Language and Education." *North American Review* 113 (1871): 343–74.

———. *Language and the Study of Language: Twelve Lectures on the Principles of Linguistic Science.* New York: C. Scribner and Co., 1867.

———. *The Life and Growth of Language: An Outline of Linguistic Science.* New York: D. Appleton and Co., 1875.

———. "On Darwinism and Language." *North American Review* 119 (1874): 61–88.

———. *Oriental and Linguistic Studies: The Veda; the Avesta, the Science of Language.* New York: C. Scribner and Co., 1872–74.

———. "Philology." In *Encyclopaedia Britannica.* 11th ed. 1911.

Woolsey, Theodore Dwight. *Addresses.* 2 vols. New Haven, 1864–82.

———. *Communism and Socialism in Their History and Theory.* New York: C. Scribner's Sons, 1880.

———. *Divorce and Divorce Legislation, especially in the United States.* 1869. 2d ed. New York: C. Scribner's Sons, 1882.

———. *"Eros" and Other Poems.* New Haven: Tuttle, Morehouse, and Taylor, 1880.

———. "The Experiment of the Union, with Its Preparations." In Theodore Dwight Woolsey et al., *The First Century of the Republic: A Review of American Progress,* 260–78. New York: Harper and Brothers, 1876.

———. "Inaugural Discourse." In *Discourses and Addresses at the Ordination of the Reverend Theodore Dwight Woolsey, LL.D. to the Ministry of the Gospel and His Inauguration as President of Yale College, October 21, 1846.* New Haven, 1846.

———. *An Introduction to the Study of International Law.* 1860. 4th ed. New York: Scribner, Armstrong and Co., 1874.

———. *Political Science or the State Theoretically and Practically Considered.* 2 vols. 1877. New York: Scribner, Armstrong and Co., 1878.

———. *The Relations of Honor to Political Life: A Phi Beta Kappa Address to Harvard College . . . .* New Haven, 1875.

———. *The Religion of the Present and of the Future.* New York: C. Scribner and Co., 1871.

———, et al. *Christianity and Scepticism: The Boston Lectures for 1870.* Boston: Congregational Publishing Society, 1870.

SELECTED SECONDARY WORKS

Aarsleff, Hans. *The Study of Language in England, 1780–1860.* Princeton: Princeton University Press, 1967.

Ahlstrom, Sydney E. *A Religious History of the American People.* New Haven: Yale University Press, 1972.

———. "The Scottish Philosophy and American Theology." *Church History* 24 (1955): 257–72.

Allmendinger, David. *Paupers and Scholars: The Transformation of Student Life in Nineteenth-Century New England.* New York: St. Martin's Press, 1975.

Andrew, John A., III. *Rebuilding the Christian Commonwealth: New England Congregationalists and Foreign Missions, 1800–1830.* Lexington: University Press of Kentucky, 1976.

Annan, Noel G. "The Intellectual Aristocracy." In *Studies in Social History: A Tribute to G. M. Trevelyan,* edited by J. H. Plumb, 241–87. London: Longmans, Green, 1955.

———. *Leslie Stephen: His Thought and Character in Relation to His Time.* London: MacGibbon and Kee, 1951.

Bainton, Roland. *Christian Unity and Religion in New England.* London: Hodder and Stoughton, 1964.

———. *Yale and the Ministry: A History of Education for the Christian Ministry at Yale from the Founding to 1701.* New York: Harper and Brothers, 1957.

Bannister, Robert C. *Social Darwinism: Science and Myth in Anglo-American Social Thought.* Philadelphia: Temple University Press, 1979.

Barrow, J. W. *Evolution and Society: A Study in Victorian Social Theory.* Cambridge: Cambridge University Press, 1966.

Becker, Carl L. *The Heavenly City of the Eighteenth-Century Philosophers.* 1932. Reprint. New Haven: Yale University Press, 1968.

Bellomy, Donald C. "The Molding of an Iconoclast: William Graham Sumner, 1840–1885." Ph.D. diss., Harvard University, 1980.

————. " 'Social Darwinism' Revisited." *Perspectives in American History*, n.s. 1 (1984): 1–129.

Bender, Thomas. "The Erosion of Public Culture: Cities, Discourses, and Professional Disciplines." In *The Authority of Experts in History and Theory*, edited by Thomas L. Haskell, 84–106. Bloomington: Indiana University Press, 1984.

Bercovitch, Sacvan. *The American Jeremiad*. Madison: University of Wisconsin Press, 1978.

————. *The Puritan Origins of the American Self*. New Haven: Yale University Press, 1975.

Berger, Peter L. *Facing Up to Modernity: Excursions in Society, Politics, and Religion*. New York: Basic Books, 1977.

————. *The Heretical Imperative: Contemporary Possibilities of Religious Affirmation*. Garden City, N.Y.: Anchor Books, 1979.

————. *The Sacred Canopy: Elements of a Sociological Theory of Religion*. Garden City, N.Y.: Doubleday and Co., 1967.

Berger, Peter L., Brigitte Berger, and Hansfried Kellner. *The Homeless Mind: Modernization and Consciousness*. New York: Random House, 1973.

Berk, Stephen E. *Calvinism versus Democracy: Timothy Dwight and the Origins of American Evangelical Orthodoxy*. Hamden, Conn.: Archon Books, 1974.

Blau, Joseph L. *Men and Movements in American Philosophy*. New York: Prentice-Hall, 1952.

Bledstein, Burton J. *The Culture of Professionalism: The Middle Class and the Development of Higher Education in America*. New York: W. W. Norton and Co., 1976.

Boller, Paul F., Jr. *American Thought in Transition: The Impact of Evolutionary Naturalism, 1865–1900*. Chicago: Rand McNally, 1969.

————. *American Transcendentalism, 1830–1860: An Intellectual Inquiry*. New York: G. P. Putnam's Sons, 1974.

Bozeman, Theodore Dwight. *Protestants in an Age of Science: The Baconian Ideal and Antebellum Religious Thought*. Chapel Hill: University of North Carolina Press, 1977.

Brooks, Van Wyck. *America's Coming of Age*. 1915. Reprint. New York: Octagon Books, 1975.

————. *The Flowering of New England, 1815–1865*. New York: E. P. Dutton and Co., 1936.

————. *New England: Indian Summer, 1865–1915*. New York: E. P. Dutton and Co., 1940.

Brown, Bernard Edward. *American Conservatives: The Political Thought of Francis Lieber and John W. Burgess*. New York: Columbia University Press, 1951.

Brown, Ford K. *Fathers of the Victorians: The Age of Wilberforce*. Cambridge: Cambridge University Press, 1961.

Brown, Jerry Wayne. *The Rise of Biblical Criticism in America, 1800–1870:*

The New England Scholars. Middletown, Conn.: Wesleyan University Press, 1969.

Brown, Richard D. *Modernization: The Transformation of American Life, 1600–1865*. New York: Hill and Wang, 1976.

Bryson, Gladys. *Man and Society: The Scottish Inquiry of the Eighteenth Century*. Princeton: Princeton University Press, 1945.

Bushman, Richard L. *From Puritan to Yankee: Character and the Social Order in Connecticut, 1690–1765*. Cambridge: Harvard University Press, 1967.

Calhoun, Daniel H. *Professional Lives in America: Structure and Aspiration, 1750–1850*. Cambridge: Harvard University Press, 1965.

Callcott, George H. "Historians in Early Nineteenth-Century America." *New England Quarterly* 32 (1959): 496–520.

Callow, James T. *Kindred Spirits: Knickerbocker Writers and American Artists, 1807–1855*. Chapel Hill: University of North Carolina Press, 1967.

Carter, Paul A. *The Spiritual Crisis of the Gilded Age*. DeKalb: Northern Illinois University Press, 1971.

Cawelti, John G. *Apostles of the Self-Made Man*. Chicago: University of Chicago Press, 1965.

Chadwick, Owen. *From Bossuet to Newman: The Idea of Doctrinal Development*. Cambridge: Cambridge University Press, 1957.

———. *The Secularization of the European Mind in the Nineteenth Century*. Cambridge: Cambridge University Press, 1975.

Cherry, Conrad. *Nature and Religious Imagination: From Edwards to Bushnell*. Philadelphia: Fortress Press, 1980.

Church, Robert L. "The Development of the Social Sciences as Academic Disciplines at Harvard University, 1869–1900." Ph.D. diss., Harvard University, 1965.

Clark, Clifford E., Jr. *Henry Ward Beecher: Spokesman for a Middle-Class America*. Urbana: University of Illinois Press, 1978.

Cockshut, A. O. J. *Truth to Life: The Art of Biography in the Nineteenth Century*. New York: Harcourt Brace Jovanovich, 1974.

Cross, Barbara M. *Horace Bushnell: Minister to a Changing America*. Chicago: University of Chicago Press, 1958.

Crunden, Robert M. *Ministers of Reform: The Progressives' Achievement in American Civilization, 1889–1920*. New York: Basic Books, 1982.

Daniels, George H. *American Science in the Age of Jackson*. New York: Columbia University Press, 1968.

Dennis, William Cullen, II. "A Federalist Persuasion: The American Ideal of Connecticut Federalists." Ph.D. diss., Yale University, 1971.

Diehl, Carl. *Americans and German Scholarship, 1770–1870*. New Haven: Yale University Press, 1978.

Diggins, John P. *The Bard of Savagery: Thorstein Veblen and Modern Social Theory*. New York: Seabury Press, 1978.

Douglas, Ann. *The Feminization of American Culture*. New York: Alfred A. Knopf, 1977.

Dupree, A. Hunter. *Asa Gray, 1810–1888.* Cambridge: Harvard University Press, Belknap Press, 1959.

Engel, Arthur. "The Emerging Concept of the Academic Profession at Oxford, 1800–1854." In *The University in Society.* Vol. 1 of *Oxford and Cambridge from the Fourteenth to the Early Nineteenth Century,* edited by Lawrence Stone, 305–51. Princeton: Princeton University Press, 1974.

Faust, Drew Gilpin. *A Sacred Circle: The Dilemma of the Intellectual in the Old South, 1840–1860.* Baltimore: Johns Hopkins University Press, 1977.

Fiering, Norman S. "President Samuel Johnson and the Circle of Knowledge." *William and Mary Quarterly,* 3d ser., 28 (1971): 199–236.

Fiske, John. *"A Century of Science" and Other Essays.* Boston: Houghton, Mifflin and Co., 1900.

Flower, Elizabeth, and Murray G. Murphey. *A History of Philosophy in America.* 2 vols. New York: G. P. Putnam's Sons, 1977.

Foner, Eric. *Free Soil, Free Labor, Free Men: The Ideology of the Republican Party before the Civil War.* New York: Oxford University Press, 1970.

Foster, Charles I. *An Errand of Mercy: The Evangelical United Front, 1790–1837.* Chapel Hill: University of North Carolina Press, 1960.

Foster, Frank Hugh. *A Genetic History of the New England Theology.* Chicago: University of Chicago Press, 1907.

Fredrickson, George M. *The Inner Civil War: Northern Intellectuals and the Crisis of the Union.* New York: Harper and Row, 1965.

Freidel, Frank. *Francis Lieber: Nineteenth Century Liberal.* Baton Rouge: Louisiana State University Press, 1947.

Furner, Mary O. *Advocacy and Objectivity: A Crisis in the Professionalization of American Social Science, 1865–1905.* Lexington: University Press of Kentucky, 1975.

Gabriel, Ralph Henry. *The Course of American Democratic Thought.* New York: Ronald Press, 1940.

———. *Religion and Learning at Yale: The Church of Christ in the College and University, 1757–1957.* New Haven: Yale University Press, 1958.

Garland, Martha McMackin. *Cambridge before Darwin: The Ideal of a Liberal Education, 1800–1860.* New York: Cambridge University Press, 1980.

Gaustad, Edwin Scott. *Historical Atlas of Religion in America.* Rev. ed. New York: Harper and Row, 1976.

Glover, Willis B. *Evangelical Nonconformists and Higher Criticism in the Nineteenth Century.* London: Independent Press, 1955.

Gooch, G. P. *History and Historians in the Nineteenth Century.* 2d ed. 1913. Reprint. London: Longmans, Green and Co., 1967.

Grave, S. A. *The Scottish Philosophy of Common Sense.* New York: Oxford University Press, 1960.

Green, V. H. *Religion at Oxford and Cambridge.* London: SCM Press, 1964.

Grimsted, David. *Melodrama Unveiled: American Theater and Culture, 1800–1850.* Chicago: University of Chicago Press, 1968.

Gross, John J. *The Rise and Fall of the Man of Letters: Aspects of English Literary Life since 1800.* London: Weidenfield and Nicolson, 1969.

Gura, Philip F. *The Wisdom of Words: Language, Theology, and Literature in the New England Renaissance.* Middletown, Conn.: Wesleyan University Press, 1981.

Guttmann, Allen. *The Conservative Tradition in America.* New York: Oxford University Press, 1967.

Hall, David D. "The World of Print and Collective Mentality in Seventeenth-Century New England." In *New Directions in American Intellectual History,* edited by John Higham and Paul K. Conkin, 166–80. Baltimore: Johns Hopkins Press, 1979.

Haroutunian, Joseph. *Piety versus Moralism: The Passing of the New England Theology.* New York: H. Holt and Co., 1932.

Haskell, Thomas L. *The Emergence of Professional Social Science: The American Social Science Association and the Nineteenth-Century Crisis of Authority.* Urbana: University of Illinois Press, 1977.

Hawkins, Hugh. *Between Harvard and America: The Educational Leadership of Charles W. Eliot.* New York: Oxford University Press, 1971.

———. *Pioneer: A History of Johns Hopkins University, 1874–1889.* Ithaca: Cornell University Press, 1960.

Hawkins, Richmond Lauren. *Auguste Comte and the United States, 1816–1853.* Cambridge: Harvard University Press, 1936.

Herbst, Jurgen. *The German Historical School in American Scholarship: A Study in the Transfer of Culture.* Ithaca: Cornell University Press, 1965.

Hersey, George L. *High Victorian Gothic: A Study in Associationism.* Baltimore: Johns Hopkins University Press, 1972.

Higham, John, with Leonard Krieger and Felix Gilbert. *History: The Development of Historical Studies in the United States.* Englewood Cliffs, N.J.: Prentice-Hall, 1965.

Himmelfarb, Gertrude. *On Liberty and Liberalism: The Case of John Stuart Mill.* New York: Alfred A. Knopf, 1974.

———. *Victorian Minds.* London: Weidenfeld and Nicolson, 1968.

Hoeveler, J. David, Jr. *James McCosh and the Scottish Intellectual Tradition: From Glasgow to Princeton.* Princeton: Princeton University Press, 1981.

———. *The New Humanism: A Critique of Modern America, 1900–1940.* Charlottesville: University of Virginia Press, 1977.

Hofstadter, Richard. *Anti-Intellectualism in American Life.* New York: Alfred A. Knopf, 1963.

———. *The Progressive Historians: Turner, Beard, Parrington.* New York: Alfred A. Knopf, 1968.

———. *Social Darwinism in American Thought.* Rev. ed. Boston: Beacon Press, 1955.

Hofstadter, Richard, and Walter P. Metzger. *The Development of Academic Freedom in the United States.* 2 vols. New York: Columbia University Press, 1955.

Holt, Henry. *"Garrulities of an Octogenarian Editor,"* with Other Essays Somewhat Biographical and Autobiographical. Boston: Houghton Mifflin Co., 1923.

Horowitz, Helen Lefkowitz. *Alma Mater: Design and Experience in the Women's Colleges from Their Nineteenth-Century Beginnings to the 1930s.* New York: Alfred A. Knopf, 1984.

Houghton, Walter E. *The Victorian Frame of Mind, 1830–1870.* New Haven: Yale University Press, 1959.

Hovenkamp, Herbert. *Science and Religion in America, 1800–1860.* Philadelphia: University of Pennsylvania Press, 1978.

Howe, Daniel Walker. *The Political Culture of the American Whigs.* Chicago: University of Chicago Press, 1979.

————. *The Unitarian Conscience: Harvard Moral Philosophy, 1805–1861.* Cambridge: Harvard University Press, 1970.

————, ed. *Victorian America.* Philadelphia: University of Pennsylvania Press, 1976.

Hutchison, William R. *The Modernist Impulse in American Protestantism.* Cambridge: Harvard University Press, 1976.

————. *The Transcendentalist Ministers: Church Reform in the New England Renaissance.* New Haven: Yale University Press, 1959.

Iggers, Georg G. *The German Conception of History: The National Tradition of Historical Thought from Herder to the Present.* Middletown, Conn.: Wesleyan University Press, 1968.

Irvine, William. *Apes, Angels, and Victorians: The Story of Darwin, Huxley, and Evolution.* New York: Time, 1963.

James, Walter T. "The Philosophy of Noah Porter, 1811–1892." Ph.D. diss., Columbia University, 1951.

Jenkyns, Richard. *The Victorians and Ancient Greece.* Cambridge: Harvard University Press, 1980.

Jordy, William H. *Henry Adams: Scientific Historian.* New Haven: Yale University Press, 1952.

Joyce, Walter E. "Noah Porter as President of Yale, 1871–1886: A Conservative Response in a Time of Transition." Ph.D. diss., New York University, 1972.

Karl, Barry D. *Charles E. Merriam and the Study of Politics.* Chicago: University of Chicago Press, 1974.

Kasson, John F. *Civilizing the Machine: Technology and Republican Values in America, 1776–1900.* New York: Grossman Publishers, 1976.

Kelley, Brooks Mather. *Yale: A History.* New Haven: Yale University Press, 1974.

Kelley, Robert Lloyd. *The Transatlantic Persuasion: The Liberal-Democratic Mind in the Age of Gladstone.* New York: Alfred A. Knopf, 1969.

Kent, Christopher. "Higher Journalism and the Mid-Victorian Clerisy." *Victorian Studies* 13 (1969): 181–98.

King, George A. *Theodore Dwight Woolsey: His Political and Social Ideas.* Chicago: Loyola University Press, 1956.

Knoff, Gerald Everett. "The Yale Divinity School, 1858–1899." Ph.D. diss., Yale University, 1936.

Kohlstedt, Sally Gregory. *The Formation of the American Scientific Community: The American Association for the Advancement of Science, 1848–1860.* Urbana: University of Illinois Press, 1976.

Kraus, Michael. *A History of American History.* New York: Farrar and Rinehart, 1937.

Krieger, Leonard. *Ranke: The Meaning of History.* Chicago: University of Chicago Press, 1975.

Kuklick, Bruce. *The Rise of American Philosophy.* New Haven: Yale University Press, 1977.

Levin, David. *History as Romantic Art: Prescott, Bancroft, Motley, and Parkman.* Stanford: Stanford University Press, 1959.

Lipson, Dorothy Ann. *Free Masonry in Federalist Connecticut.* Princeton: Princeton University Press, 1977.

McCaughey, Robert A. *International Studies and Academic Enterprise: A Chapter in the Enclosure of American Learning.* New York: Columbia University Press, 1984.

———. *Josiah Quincy, 1772–1864: The Last Federalist.* Cambridge: Harvard University Press, 1974.

———. "The Transformation of American Academic Life: Harvard University, 1821–1892." *Perspectives in American History* 8 (1974): 239–332.

McLachlan, James. *American Boarding Schools: A Historical Study.* New York: Charles Scribner's Sons, 1970.

———. "American Colleges and the Transmission of Culture: The Case of the Mugwumps." In *The Hofstadter Aegis: A Memorial,* edited by Stanley Elkins and Eric McKitrick, 184–206. New York: Alfred A. Knopf, 1974.

McLoughlin, William G. *The Baptists and the Separation of Church and State.* Vol. 2 of McLoughlin, *New England Dissent, 1630–1883.* Cambridge: Harvard University Press, 1971.

———. *The Meaning of Henry Ward Beecher: An Essay on the Shifting Values of Mid-Victorian America.* New York: Alfred A. Knopf, 1970.

Mandelbaum, Maurice. "Historicism." In *Encyclopedia of Philosophy.* 1967 ed.

———. *History, Man, and Reason: A Study in Nineteenth-Century Intellectual Thought.* Baltimore: Johns Hopkins Press, 1971.

Marsden, George M. *The Evangelical Mind and the New School Presbyterian Experience: A Case Study of Thought and Theology in Nineteenth-Century America.* New Haven: Yale University Press, 1970.

———. *Fundamentalism and American Culture: The Shaping of Twentieth Century Evangelicalism, 1870–1925.* New York: Oxford University Press, 1980.

Martin, Terence. *The Instructed Vision: Scottish Common Sense Philosophy and the*

212

Origins of American Fiction. Bloomington: University of Indiana Press, 1961.
Marwick, Arthur. *The Nature of History*. London: Macmillan, 1970.
Marzio, Peter C. *The Democratic Art: Chromolithography, 1840–1900, Pictures for a Nineteenth-Century America*. Boston: David R. Godine, 1979.
May, Henry F. *The End of American Innocence: A Study of the First Years of Our Own Time, 1912–1917*. New York: Alfred A. Knopf, 1959.
———. *The Enlightenment in America*. New York: Oxford University Press, 1976.
———. *Protestant Churches and Industrial America*. New York: Octagon Books, 1963.
Mead, Sidney Earl. *The Lively Experiment: The Shaping of Christianity in America*. New York: Harper and Row, 1963.
———. *Nathaniel William Taylor, 1786–1858: A Connecticut Liberal*. Chicago: University of Chicago Press, 1942.
Mencken, H. L. *A Book of Prefaces*. Garden City, N.Y.: Doubleday and Co., 1917.
Merriam, Charles E. *American Political Ideas*. New York: Macmillan Co., 1920.
———. *A History of American Political Theories*. 1903. Reprint. New York: Macmillan Co., 1928.
Merz, John Theodore. *A History of European Thought in the Nineteenth Century*. 4 vols. 1904–12. Reprint. New York: Dover Publications, 1965.
Meyer, D. H. *The Instructed Conscience: The Shaping of the American National Ethic*. Philadelphia: University of Pennsylvania Press, 1972.
Miller, Perry. *The Life of the Mind in America, from the Revolution to the Civil War*. New York: Harcourt, Brace and World, 1965.
Mills, Eugene S. *George Trumbull Ladd: Pioneer American Psychologist*. Cleveland: Case Western Reserve University Press, 1969.
Morse, Jarvis Means. *A Neglected Period of Connecticut's History, 1818–1850*. New Haven: Yale University Press, 1933.
Mott, Frank Luther. *A History of American Magazines*. 5 vols. Cambridge: Harvard University Press, Belknap Press, 1938–68.
Nichols, James Hastings. *Romanticism in American Theology: Nevin and Schaff at Mercersburg*. Chicago: University of Chicago Press, 1961.
Niebuhr, H. Richard. *The Kingdom of God in America*. 1937. Reprint. New York: Harper and Brothers, 1957.
Novak, Barbara. *Nature and Culture: American Landscape and Painting, 1825–1875*. New York: Oxford University Press, 1980.
Oleson, Alexandra, and Sanborn C. Brown, eds. *The Pursuit of Knowledge in the Early American Republic: American Scientific and Learned Societies from Colonial Times to the Civil War*. Baltimore: Johns Hopkins University Press, 1976.
Oleson, Alexandra, and John Voss, eds. *The Organization of Knowledge in Modern America, 1860–1920*. Baltimore: Johns Hopkins University Press, 1979.

Osterweis, Rollin G. *Three Centuries of New Haven, 1638–1938*. New Haven: Yale University Press, 1953.

Peckham, Morse, ed. *Romanticism: The Culture of the Nineteenth Century*. New York: George Braziller, 1965.

Pederson, Holger. *The Discovery of Language: Linguistic Science in the Nineteenth Century*. Translated by John Webster Spargo. 1931. Reprint. Bloomington: Indiana University Press, 1962.

Peel, J. D. Y. *Herbert Spencer: The Evolution of a Sociologist*. London: Heinemann Educational, 1971.

Persons, Stow. *The Decline of American Gentility*. New York: Columbia University Press, 1973.

Pessen, Edward. *Riches, Class, and Power before the Civil War*. Lexington, Mass.: D. C. Heath and Co., 1973.

Peterson, George E. *The New England College in the Age of the University*. Amherst, Mass.: Amherst College Press, 1964.

Pfeiffer, Rudolf. *A History of Classical Scholarship from 1300 to 1850*. Oxford: Clarendon Press, 1976.

Pierson, George W. *Yale College: An Educational History, 1871–1921*. Vol. 1 of Pierson, *Yale: College and University, 1871–1937*. New Haven: Yale University Press, 1952.

Pochmann, Henry A. *German Culture in America: Philosophical and Literary Influences, 1600–1900*. Madison: University of Wisconsin Press, 1957.

Purcell, Edward A., Jr. *The Crisis of Democratic Theory: Scientific Naturalism and the Problem of Value*. Lexington: University Press of Kentucky, 1973.

Riley, I. Woodbridge. *American Philosophy: The Early Schools*. 1907. Reprint. New York: Russell and Russell, 1958.

Ringer, Fritz K. *The Decline of the German Mandarins: The German Academic Community, 1890–1923*. Cambridge: Harvard University Press, 1969.

Rodgers, Daniel T. *The Work Ethic in Industrial America, 1850–1920*. Chicago: University of Chicago Press, 1978.

Rosenberg, Rosalind. *Beyond Separate Spheres: Intellectual Roots of Modern Feminism*. New Haven: Yale University Press, 1982.

Ross, Dorothy. *G. Stanley Hall: The Psychologist as Prophet*. Chicago: University of Chicago Press, 1972.

———. "Historical Consciousness in Nineteenth-Century America." *American Historical Review* 89 (1984): 909–28.

———. "The Liberal Tradition Revisited and the Republican Tradition Addressed." In *New Directions in American Intellectual History,* edited by John Higham and Paul K. Conkin, 116–31. Baltimore: Johns Hopkins University Press, 1979.

———. "Socialism and American Liberalism: Academic Social Thought in the 1880's." *Perspectives in American History* 11 (1977–78): 5–79.

Rothblatt, Sheldon. *The Revolution of the Dons: Cambridge and Society in Victorian England*. London: Faber and Faber, 1968.

————. *Tradition and Change in English Liberal Education: An Essay in History and Culture*. London: Faber and Faber, 1976.

Rudolph, Frederick. *The American College and University: A History*. New York: Alfred A. Knopf, 1962.

————. *Curriculum: A History of the American Undergraduate Course of Study*. San Francisco: Jossey-Bass, Publisher, 1977.

Russett, Cynthia Eagle. *Darwin in America: The Intellectual Response, 1865–1912*. San Francisco: W. H. Freeman and Co., 1976.

Samuels, Ernest. *Bernard Berenson: The Making of a Connoisseur*. Cambridge: Harvard University Press, Belknap Press, 1979.

Sandeen, Ernest R. *The Roots of Fundamentalism: British and American Millenarianism, 1800–1930*. 1970. Reprint. Grand Rapids, Mich.: Baker Book House, 1978.

Sanford, William F., Jr. "Dana and Darwinism." *Journal of the History of Ideas* 26 (1965): 531–46.

Santayana, George. *The Genteel Tradition: Nine Essays*. Edited by Douglas L. Wilson. Cambridge: Harvard University Press, 1967.

Schmidt, George P. *The Liberal Arts College: A Chapter in American Cultural History*. New Brunswick, N.J.: Rutgers University Press, 1957.

————. *The Old Time College President*. New York: Columbia University Press, 1930.

Schneider, Herbert W. *A History of American Philosophy*. New York: Columbia University Press, 1946.

Schneider, Louis, ed. *The Scottish Moralists on Human Nature and Society: Selected Papers*. Chicago: University of Chicago Press, 1967.

Scott, Donald M. *From Office to Profession: The New England Ministry, 1750–1850*. Philadelphia: University of Pennsylvania Press, 1978.

Silverman, Kenneth. *Timothy Dwight*. New York: Twayne Publishers, 1969.

Simpson, Lewis P., ed. *The Man of Letters in New England and the South: Essays on the History of the Literary Vocation in America*. Baton Rouge: Louisiana State University Press, 1973.

Sklar, Kathryn Kish. *Catherine Beecher: A Study in American Domesticity*. New Haven: Yale University Press, 1973.

Sloan, Douglas. *The Scottish Enlightenment and the American College Ideal*. New York: Columbia Teachers' College Press, 1971.

Smith, Wilson. *Professors and Public Ethics: Studies of Northern Moral Philosophers before the Civil War*. Ithaca: Cornell University Press, 1956.

Sorkin, David. "Wilhelm Von Humboldt: The Theory and Practice of Self-Formation (Bildung), 1791–1810." *Journal of the History of Ideas* 44 (1983): 55–73.

Starr, Harris E. *William Graham Sumner*. New York: H. Holt and Co., 1925.

Stein, Roger B. *John Ruskin and Aesthetic Thought in America, 1840–1900*. Cambridge: Harvard University Press, 1967.

Stern, Fritz, ed. *The Varieties of History: From Voltaire to the Present*. New York: Meridian Books, 1956.

Stevenson, Louise L. "Sarah Porter Educates Useful Ladies, 1847–1900." *Winterthur Portfolio* 18, no. 1 (Spring 1983): 39–59.

Stokes, Anson Phelps. *Memorials of Eminent Yale Men: A Biographical Study of Student Life and University Influences during the Eighteenth and Nineteenth Centuries.* 2 vols. New Haven: Yale University Press, 1915.

Struik, Dirk J. *The Origins of Science (New England).* New York: Cameron Books, 1948.

Sweet, William Warren. *Religion in the Development of American Culture, 1765–1840.* New York: Charles Scribner's Sons, 1952.

Taylor, William R. *Cavalier and Yankee: The Old South and American National Character.* New York: Harper and Row, 1961.

Tewksbury, Donald G. *The Founding of American Colleges and Universities before the Civil War with Particular Reference to the Religious Influences Bearing upon the College Movement.* New York: Columbia Teachers' College Press, 1932.

Thistlethwaite, Frank. *The Anglo-American Connection in the Early Nineteenth Century.* Philadelphia: University of Pennsylvania Press, 1959.

Thomas, John L. "Romantic Reform in America, 1815–1865." *American Quarterly* 17 (1965): 656–81.

Thwing, Charles F. *The American and the German University: One Hundred Years of History.* New York: Macmillan Co., 1928.

Tillotson, Geoffrey. *A View of Victorian Literature.* Oxford: Clarendon Press, 1978.

Tobias, Marilyn. *Old Dartmouth on Trial: The Transformation of the Academic Community in Nineteenth-Century America.* New York: New York University Press, 1981.

Tomsich, John. *A Genteel Endeavor: American Culture and Politics in the Gilded Age.* Stanford: Stanford University Press, 1971.

Tonsor, Stephen J. "History, a Revolutionary or Conservative Discipline?" *Intercollegiate Review* 2 (1966): 235–43.

Turner, Frank M. *The Greek Heritage in Victorian Britain.* New Haven: Yale University Press, 1981.

Turner, James. *Without God, Without Creed: The Origins of Unbelief in America.* Baltimore: Johns Hopkins University Press, 1985.

Turner, Victor. *The Forest of Symbols: Aspects of Ndembu Ritual.* Ithaca: Cornell University Press, 1967.

———. *The Ritual Process: Structure and Anti-Structure.* Chicago: Aldine Publishing, 1969.

Tyack, David. *George Ticknor and the Boston Brahmins.* Cambridge: Harvard University Press, 1967.

Vanderbilt, Kermit. *Charles Eliot Norton: Apostle of Culture in a Democracy.* Cambridge: Harvard University Press, Belknap Press, 1959.

Van Tassel, David D. *Recording America's Past: An Interpretation of the Development of Historical Studies in America, 1607–1884.* Chicago: University of Chicago Press, 1960.

Veblen, Thorstein. *The Theory of the Leisure Class*. 1899. Reprint. New York: A. M. Kelley, 1965.

Veysey, Laurence R. *The Emergence of the American University*. Chicago: University of Chicago Press, 1965.

Warch, Richard. *School of the Prophets: Yale College, 1701–1740*. New Haven: Yale University Press, 1973.

Wayland, James T. "The Theological Department in Yale College." Ph.D. diss., Yale University, 1933.

Webb, R. K. *Harriet Martineau: A Radical Victorian*. New York: Columbia University Press, 1960.

White, Hayden. *Metahistory: The Historical Imagination in Nineteenth Century Europe*. Baltimore: Johns Hopkins University Press, 1973.

White, Morton. *Science and Sentiment in America: Philosophical Thought from Jonathan Edwards to John Dewey*. New York: Oxford University Press, 1972.

———. *Social Thought in America: The Revolt against Formalism*. Boston: Beacon Press, 1970.

Wiebe, Robert H. *The Search for Order, 1877–1920*. New York: Hill and Wang, 1967.

Williams, Raymond. *Culture and Society, 1780–1950*. New York: Harper and Row, Harper Torchbooks, 1966.

———. *Keywords: A Vocabulary of Culture and Society*. New York: Oxford University Press, 1976.

Williamson, Eugene L. *The Liberalism of Thomas Arnold: A Study of His Religious and Political Writings*. University: University of Alabama Press, 1964.

Witherspoon, Alexander. *The Club: The Story of Its First One Hundred and Twenty-Five Years*. New Haven: privately printed, 1964.

Wright, Benjamin Fletcher. *American Interpretations of Natural Law: A Study in the History of Political Thought*. Cambridge: Harvard University Press, 1931.

Wyllie, Irvin G. *The Self-Made Man in America*. New York: Free Press, 1966.

Wymer, Norman. *Dr. Arnold of Rugby*. London: R. Hale, 1953.

Young, G. M. *Victorian England: Portrait of an Age*. 2d ed. London: Oxford University Press, 1953.

Young, Robert M. *Mind, Brain and Adaptation in the Nineteenth Century: Cerebral Localization and Its Biological Context from Gall to Ferrier*. Oxford: Clarendon Press, 1970.

Index

Agassiz, Louis, 20, 24, 77, 185nn. 26, 29
Alexander, Archibald, 19, 27
American Dictionary of the English Language. See Porter, Noah
American Social Science Association, 25, 103–4
Antebellum reform, 25–26, 114–15, 147. *See also* Whiggery
Arnold, Matthew, 42, 52, 144
Arnold, Thomas, 46, 60, 66, 90, 92, 130, 144
Associationism, 70–71, 132. *See also* Bain, Alexander; Dana, James Dwight; New Haven scholars; Porter, Noah

Bacon, Leonard, 3, 22, 26
Bain, Alexander, 71, 80, 81–82
Bancroft, George, 4, 88, 89, 130
Barnard, Henry, 60
Beecher, Henry Ward, 178n. 27
Beecher, Lyman, 20, 49
Bellamy, Edward, 113–14
Bellomy, Donald C., xi, 171n. 7, 182–83n. 38, 190n. 6, 193n. 37
Bercovitch, Sacvan, 93–94, 170n. 18
Berenson, Bernard, 133, 134
Berger, Peter L., theory of, 7–9, 170n. 15, 179n. 41

Biblical criticism, 31, 47, 68, 98–99, 124. *See also* Fisher, George Park; Taylor, Nathaniel William
Bildung, 58, 93, 94, 95, 100, 109, 118–19, 138, 140. *See also* Culture; New Haven scholars
Boeckh, August, 35, 58, 62, 90
Brooks, Van Wyck, 5, 9, 54, 94
Buckle, Henry Thomas, 81, 89
Bushnell, Horace, 5, 26, 32, 35, 124, 146, 181n. 17; and German influence 176nn. 6, 7; social and cultural criticism, 56–57, 124, 127–28

Carter, Franklin, 29, 140, 196n. 3
Coleridge, Samuel Taylor, 20, 68, 71, 73; impact of *Aids to Reflection*, 26, 31–32, 176n. 6
College of New Jersey. *See* Princeton University
Colleges, 28–29, 62–63, 103, 146, 181n. 24; as agencies of reform, 50–51, 192n. 34; antebellum northern, 6, 17–18, 27–28, 57, 172n. 11, 181n. 18. *See also* Historiography; Porter, Noah
Comte, Auguste, 80, 83, 89
Congregationalism. *See* Bushnell, Horace; Porter, Noah; Taylor, Nathaniel William; Yale College

Culture: as educational ideal, 4, 15, 16, 52–53, 140; feminization of, 13, 99–100, 189n. 35; as method of self-development, 142–44. *See also Bildung; names of individual scholars;* New Haven scholars
Curtis, George William, 33

Dana, James Dwight, 1, 2, 27, 63, 119, 146; on conflict between science and religion, 69, 74–75, 81; Darwin, response to, 77–79, 184n. 17, 185–86n. 29, 186n. 31; education, definition of, 73–74, 75; publishing, 74, 138; on races, 185n. 26; as Romantic scientist, 75–77; scholarship, definition of, 38; scientist, role of, 74, 81
Darwin, Charles, 48, 53, 68, 73; New Haven response to, 77–79, 184n. 17
Day, Jeremiah, 16
Dexter, Franklin Bowditch, 16, 173n. 17
Dwight, Timothy (the elder), 19, 48, 104–5
Dwight, Timothy (the younger), 21, 25, 63, 179n. 42

Eliot, Charles W., 50, 51, 60, 66, 115, 129
Ely, Richard T., 84
Emerson, Ralph Waldo, 5, 20, 42, 93, 130, 146–47; scholar, definition of, 34–35, 48–49, 62

Fisher, George Park, 2, 3, 7, 21, 42, 115, 119, 146; on biblical criticism, 98–99; career of, 37–38; on conflict between science and religion, 69; education of, 37, 177n. 17; on historical progress, 92–93; on historical progress as self-development (*Bildung*), 94–95, 100–101; on historical progress in colonial New England, 94–95; on history, 87–88, 89; on idealism, 68, 184n. 5; Porter, relationship with, 24, 173–74n. 22; on positivism, 80; on Protestant Reformation, 100–101; on the

scholar's usefulness, 46; stance as historian, 45, 97–98, 189n. 37; on Tubingen school, 47
Fitch, Elizur T., 32–33

George, Henry, 113–14
German historical school, 58, 90–93, 109, 124. *See also* Fisher, George Park
Gibbs, Josiah Willard, 35
Gilder, Richard Watson, 26
Gilman, Daniel Coit, 29, 51, 63, 65, 140
Godkin, E. L., 26
Goodrich, Chauncey, 32
Gray, Asa, 24, 186n. 31
Guizot, F.P.G., 4, 67, 81, 93, 94
Gura, Philip, 32, 176n. 6

Hadley, Arthur Twining, 29, 140
Hadley, James, 2, 20, 22, 25, 29; and philology, 35; as teacher, 63
Harris, William Torrey, 29
Harvard College. *See* Eliot, Charles W.; Harvard moralists
Harvard moralists, 6, 28, 145–46
Hawthorne, Nathaniel, 130–31
Historiography: of German thought, 176n. 7; of higher education, 5, 10, 62–63, 139–42, 181n. 24, 182–83nn. 38, 39, 192n. 34, 196nn. 2, 8; of Progressivism, 192–93n. 37; of Puritan tradition, 9–10, 93–94, 100–101, 144–45; of religious modernism, 11; of Victorian America, 10. *See also* May, Henry
History: development as discipline, 87–88, 196n. 2; and idea of development in, 98
Hodge, Charles, 19, 27, 36
Hofstadter, Richard, 12, 140–42
Holmes, Oliver Wendell, 100, 128
Holt, Henry, 24, 64, 65–66
Hoppin, James Mason, 2, 42; art criticism, 132–37; career, 131–32; on history of Greece, 95–96; idealism of, 69, 132–34; on preaching, 41, 178n. 27
Houghton, Walter, *Victorian Frame of Mind*, 4, 81–82

Idealism, German, 4, 20, 36, 69, 146. *See also* Bushnell, Horace; Marsh, James; Porter, Noah
Independent, 26

James, William, 71, 84–85, 134, 144, 186–87n. 45

Kelley, Brooks Mather, 57
Kingsley, William L., 63, 189n. 36
Kuklick, Bruce, 141, 178n. 31

Ladd, George Trumbull, 84
Larned, William Augustus, 32
Lewis, Tayler, 74
Lieber, Francis, 103, 190n. 8
Literary societies, 173n. 18. *See also* The Club
Lloyd, Henry Demarest, 113–14

McCosh, James, 15, 28, 50, 181n. 17
Marsh, James, 31–32, 33
May, Henry, 5, 63, 194n. 13
Melville, Herman, 131
Mencken, H. L., 9
Mental discipline. *See* Yale Report of 1828
Merriam, Charles, 25, 45, 47, 141
Mill, John Stuart, 23, 42, 53, 67, 80, 81, 82, 93; associationism of, 70, 71; on history, 88–89
Ministry, 7; appeal as profession, 31
Modernism, religious, 11, 171n. 20
Modernization, theory of, 6–9, 170n. 15
Munger, Theodore Thornton, 124, 194n. 13

New Englander, 26, 41–45; writers in, 121, 125, 130
New Haven, Conn., 21–22, 24, 27
New Haven scholars: assessments of, 57–58, 170n. 18; audience of, 4, 27, 40–41, 49, 98–99, 115, 141, 145–46, 174n. 25; as authors, 24, 27, 40–43, 48, 138, 140–41; careers of, 30, 54, 138–39; cosmopolitanism and provincialism of, 2–3, 27, 84; cultural criticism of, 118–19, 127–29, 135–37; and culture,
3–4, 15, 16, 54, 58, 118–20, 142–44; and Darwinism, 77–79; description, 1, 2–3, 11–13, 17–18, 21–24, 137, 138–39, 140–41, 147; discussion groups among, 24–25, 28–29, 173n. 21, 174n. 23; evangelicalism of, 3, 48, 57, 66, 73, 97, 101, 140–41, 145–47; German studies of, 17, 20, 35, 125; and Greek history and literature, 59–60, 95–97; historicism of, 88–89; history, definition of, 90–91; idealism of, 3, 36, 48–49, 68–69, 76, 101, 122, 134, 146; legacy of, 29, 139–40, 143–45; mediating role of, 4–5, 60, 66, 69–70, 76, 77, 83, 84, 88, 89–90, 109, 133–34, 146–47; as modernizers, 8–9, 114; New Haven community of, 21–22, 28; optimism of, 4, 83–84, 112, 119–20, 146–47, 169n. 5, 191n. 32; and political liberalism, 93–94, 109, 119, 125–26; and positivism, 23, 28, 67–68, 80–81, 83; as professionals, 18, 25, 28; and Puritanism, 10, 44–45, 93–94, 144, 189n. 36; as reformers, 6–7, 20, 25–26, 97, 126–27, 138–39; as reformers of Yale College, 16–17, 50, 56–63, 65, 66, 102–3, 126; and religious modernism, 11; on the scholar, his role, 45–49, 101, 126, 140–41; scholarship of, 9, 12, 16, 38–39, 143; science, definition of, 67–68, 69, 72–73, 83; social thought, 118–25; social thought, idea of social change, 39–40, 48–49, 92–93, 101, 102, 141, 144–45; social thought, role of educated male elites in, 12–13, 39–40, 90, 99–100, 101, 125–27, 141, 146–47; social thought, role of women in, 13, 39, 101, 179n. 42; as transitional generation, 5, 11, 16–17, 45, 65–66, 104; as Whigs, 114–15, 116. *See also names of individual scholars*
New Haven Theology. *See* Taylor, Nathaniel William
New Humanists, 143–44
Newman, John Henry, 98–99

Niebuhr, Barthold Georg, 35, 46, 90, 130
Norton, Charles Eliot, 129, 135

Olmsted, Frederick Law, 172n. 11
Organicism, 3–4

Park, Edwards Amasa, 36
Parker, Theodore, 28, 33, 42, 63
Peirce, Benjamin, 74, 184–85n. 19
Phelps, William Lyon, 142–43
Philology, German, 35, 58. *See also* Hadley, James; Whitney, William Dwight
Pierson, George Wilson, 57, 183n. 38
Porter, Noah, 2, 26, 42, 77, 103; and Bushnell, 26, 32, 56–57, 176nn. 6, 7, 181n. 17; career of, 32–37, 40; on the college professor, 60–61; on collegiate reform, 182n. 32; as dictionary editor, 25; Fisher, and relationship with, 24, 173–74n. 22; German thought, its influence on, 36, 70, 131, 176n. 6, 183–84n. 5, 184n. 7; on German universities, 36–37, 177n. 17; on Greek history and literature, its value, 59–60, 96; historians' views of, 10, 85, 140–41, 194n. 13; on history, 87, 89; Holmes, friendship with, 100; *Human Intellect*, 37, 69–70, 71–72, 76, 85, 186n. 45; and idea of college, 15, 66; and idea of college as the home of higher learning, 15, 60–62; and idea of college as an institution of liberal culture, 51–54, 56–57; and idea of college as an institution of reform, 50–51, 140–41; and idea of college as a ritual process, 53–56; way of knowing explained in, 70–72; response to Matthew Arnold, 52; Parker, friendship with, 28, 63; on Positivism, 80–82; the scholar, definition of, 33–35, 39, 46–47; the scholar and his relationship to educated elite, 39–40, 51, 141; social and cultural criticism, 39–40, 116, 120, 123–25, 128–31, 136, 140–41; on social Darwinism,

79–80, 83; Woolsey, friendship with, 35
Porter, Noah, Sr., 14, 19, 33
Presbyterians, Old School. *See* Hodge, Charles; McCosh, James; Princeton University
Princeton University, 19, 27–28
Professionalism, 18
Progressivism, 45, 108–9, 144–45, 192–93n. 37; and idea of positive state, 116–17
Psychology. *See* Mill, John Stuart; Porter, Noah; Scottish philosophy; Trendelenburg, Adolf

Quarterly Christian Spectator, 33, 43–45

Ranke, Leopold von, 62, 90, 91, 92
Reading, in the nineteenth century, 128–30
Reform. *See* Antebellum reform
Republican thought, 113–14
Revivals, religious, 26; at colleges, 17, 19, 32, 57, 172n. 11, 181n. 17
Ross, Dorothy, 91, 194n. 13
Rubin, Joan Shelley, 142–43
Ruskin, John, 132, 133

Salisbury, Edward Elbridge, 2, 28, 35; and American Oriental Society, 24; Greek art, as a model, 96; scholarship, definition of, 38
Santayana, George, 9
Schaff, Philip, 45, 189n. 23
Scholarship: definitions of, 30–31, 33–35, 139, 143, 173n. 18; German, 35; shift to Progressive idea, 45–46, 144–45; at Yale, 31, 138. *See also* Porter, Noah; Sumner, William Graham
Science, changing definitions, 67–68, 84–85. *See also* New Haven scholars; Porter, Noah; Sumner, William Graham
Scottish philosophy, 4, 18, 32, 39, 56, 88, 146; enters college curriculum, 102–3; of Francis Wayland, 70
Scribner, Charles, 24, 38
Secularization, theory of, 7–9

Silliman, Benjamin, 20, 68, 73; and biblical inerrancy, 75
Smyth, Newman, 124
Social control, 114–15
Social Darwinism, 79–80, 193n. 37
Social Gospel, 124
Spencer, Herbert, 17, 23, 43, 53, 70, 81
Storrs, Richard S., 26
Sturtevant, Julian Monson, 63, 191n. 18
Sumner, William Graham, 9, 16, 64, 82, 173n. 21; and collegiate education, 65–66, 140; and New Haven science, 85–86; and Spencer controversy, 17; Woolsey to, 104, 111, 116–17, 190nn. 9, 10, 191nn. 22, 23, 30

Taylor, Nathaniel William, 1, 16, 31, 48, 174n. 22; and biblical inerrancy, 20, 68; Germany, attitude toward, 15, 35; and Scottish philosophy, 18, 32, 56; and sectarianism, 19, 27, 32, 44
Thacher, Thomas, 28
The Club, 22–24, 173nn. 20, 21
Thompson, Joseph Parrish, 26, 174n. 25
Ticknor, George, 129
Trendelenburg, Adolf, 28, 35, 38, 70, 73, 184n. 7
Truth, 3, 86, 104, 122; and scholarship, 16
Tyler, Bennet, 19, 31, 44

Unitarians, 18, 44. *See also* Harvard moralists
United States Exploring Expedition, 30, 73
Universities, late-nineteenth-century, 66, 183nn. 38, 39. *See* Historiography

Veblen, Thorstein, 104
Veysey, Laurence, 10, 138–39, 183n. 38

Walker, Williston, 16, 45

Webster's International Dictionary of the English Language. See Porter, Noah
Weir, John Ferguson, 23, 172n. 17; *The Gun Foundry*, 122
Whiggery, 5–6, 114, 116, 192n. 34
White, Andrew Dickson, 29, 51, 63, 140
White, Morton, 10, 192n. 37
Whitney, William Dwight, 2, 42, 138; career of, 25, 37–38, 41, 177n. 31; on conflict between science and religion, 81; and philology, 24–25, 35, 87; on the scholar, role of, 39, 47–48
Woolsey, Theodore Dwight, 42, 191n. 18; American history, criticism of, 109–10, 115–16; career of, 14–15, 25, 37–38, 47; on conflict between science and religion, 82–83; cultural and social criticism, 119, 120, 122, 125, 127–28, 145; on educated elites, 111–13; education, 15, 21, 35; and education as culture, 15, 58, 102; on history, 87, 89, 94; pessimism of, 82–83, 112–13; as political scientist, 102–5, 113; as political scientist, compared to Sumner, 104, 111, 190nn. 9, 10; political theory, criticism of, 105–6, 112; Porter, friendship with, 33; on the positive state, 106–9; science, definition of, 67

Yale College, 6, 9, 14, 19, 22, 23, 28–29, 144; curriculum at, 54–55, 102–3, 138, 140; faculty, 16, 41, 171–72n. 8; historiography of, 57–58, 63–66, 170n. 18; history at, 87–88; ideal of college life at, 55–56; reasons for reform, 19; reform, 1840–1890, 57–63; religion at, 26, 56, 138; revivals at, 32, 181n. 17; scholarship at, 1800–1830, 31; students, 64–65; "Young Yale" Movement, 63–64. *See also* New Haven scholars; Porter, Noah; Woolsey, Theodore Dwight
Yale Report of 1828, 16–17, 31
Yale Review, 43–45, 140